Cross-Cultural Competence

Why are cultural differences significant?
How can we prevent cultural clashes erupting into hostility?
How can understanding them contribute to business success?

Cross-cultural management is a crucial challenge for the successful development of international business, yet it is often badly understood and poorly implemented. Misunderstandings arise because culture affects both individuals and organizations, from our core values to our table manners. Yet attempts to understand, explain and interpret these differences have often been hidden by a welter of conflicting theories and paradigms, as well as biases and stereotypes.

This book aims to provide a much-needed guide to both the theory and practice of cross-cultural management. Using an innovative approach combining theory, tool-kits and applications, the book takes a fresh look at this complex topic. It is about recognizing cross-cultural differences, accounting for them in managerial communications and bridging them in a variety of negotiations, interactions and collaborative projects. At the end of the book, the author has developed an innovative approach to learning and teaching cultural sensitivity via the exploration of a number of classic film masterpieces.

As a crucial part of the global business environment and as an essential aspect of organizational understanding, this book will be welcomed by masters-level students of international business, HRM and organizational behaviour, as well as executives and consultants involved in cross-border negotiations and management.

Sławomir Magala is Professor of Cross-Cultural Management at Erasmus University Rotterdam.

Cross-Cultural Competence

Sławomir Magala

Routledge
Taylor & Francis Group

LONDON AND NEW YORK

First published 2005 by Routledge
2 Park Square, Milton Park, Abingdon, Oxon OX14 4RN

Simultaneously published in the USA and Canada
by Routledge
270 Madison Ave, New York, NY 10016

Routledge is an imprint of the Taylor & Francis Group

Transferred to Digital Printing 2006

© 2005 Sławomir Magala

Typeset in Sabon by Steven Gardiner Ltd, Cambridge

British Library Cataloguing in Publication Data
A catalogue record for this book is available from the British
Library

Library of Congress Cataloging in Publication Data
A catalog record for this book has been requested

ISBN 0-415-34965-6 (hbk)
ISBN 0-415-34966-4 (pbk)

Contents

Introduction
The shadow of the Tower of Babel

> The knowable world is incomplete if seen from any one point of view, incoherent if seen from all points of view at once, and empty if seen from nowhere in particular.
>
> (Richard A. Schweder)

We live in an age of measurement and incommensurability. We live in an age of measurement because the scientific approach to knowledge production has become dominant in bureaucracies running our societies. We live in an age of incommensurability because the house of science has many mansions and paradigms, and successful managers listen to many voices. Still, scientific knowledge enjoys a privileged status, in spite of a proliferation of paradigms, schools and visions of 'proper' and 'normal' science. In some of them theories and statements are competitively produced and compared, even though they are difficult to compare with one another. Still, openly or not, one measures, benchmarks, evaluates, compares, chooses, classifies, files away. Most of us can easily identify our own or other individuals' level of education, native language, intelligence and preferences, employment track and career potential, sometimes even social skills and aesthetic tastes. Some of us can identify and understand organizational cultures, climates and missions using one of many available typologies and applying ready-made organizational culture assessment instruments. We ask, for instance, what is more important: task or relations? We investigate what is more relevant: bureaucratic position or market potential? We try to determine if people are seen as personnel to fill free slots in a rigid scaffolding of an organization or as precious human resources to be treated as mature citizens, to be coached and developed, around whom organizational forms should be adapted, bent, changed, and improved. One begins to acknowledge the significance of emotional and social intelligence even in the most rigid of bureaucracies. Researchers, consultants, managers and professionals alike begin to uncover and exploit local and tacit knowledge, rituals, symbols, languages, and manners. One begins to appreciate cross-cultural differences between individuals and groups, and their influence upon personalities and organizations. Metaphors we live by and stories we are socialized with do matter. Differences between ways in which we have been socialized are perceived as a manifestation of cultural variety (diversity is perceived as a challenge and a chance, not a threat), which is increasingly treated as an opportunity for creative development rather than an obstacle and a threat to a co-operative team effort.

Culturally speaking, mankind had always been a joint venture of many subcultures (civilizations, nations, religions, classes, castes, generations, professions), from the Tower of Babel project to the epidemic growth of the world-wide web. The Tower of Babel project failed because of the ideological ambitions to reach a super-human level of perfection and meet unrealistic deadlines. Will the emergent multiple projects of a more just, though increasingly complex, global society follow suit? Can we shed some light on forthcoming problems, which had taken the builders of the Tower of Babel by surprise, and by so doing defuse them?

I think that we – the representatives of academic communities – can and should. Researchers doing so will heed Geert Hofstede's warning that surviving in a multicultural world depends on our ability to become aware of 'the constraints of our mental programs versus those of others' (Hofstede, 1991, 237).

Hofstede's voice is important because he has contributed the most robust theoretical framework for exploring and exploiting cross-cultural differences we have seen so far. He has done so by focusing firmly on national communities regulated by nation-states as the primary level of analysis. His focus has been justified by the significance of the nation-state for co-ordinating socialization in contemporary societies, especially the organized, educational part of it. The continuing relevance of his approach is an indirect tribute to the durability of the nation-state. It is still very much 'in the picture'. The nation-state remains the basic organizational form of contemporary societies – even in an age of globalization, regional integration and the electronically linked global village (although there are some reasons to suspect that it may be weaker in the 21st than in the 20th century).

But although the nation-state remains the basic platform and co-ordinator of socialization, relations between nation-states are not easily controlled, nor are differences easy to settle. Some networks have global reach and leave the state unable to cope (global pollution, international terrorism); some differences are so fundamental that agreement appears impossible. Attempts to manage discussions among nation-state representatives often resemble the confusion of the Tower of Babel project.

Last not least, the failure of the Tower of Babel builders was due to their over-ambitious ideology. They believed that given the power of technology and their superior managerial skills, the sky is not, and will not be, the limit.

They believed skilled application of objective techniques would suffice. They were stopped short by their biases, their natural languages, their ways of communicating with others, which they had taken for granted. Today, especially among researchers conducting critical management studies, there is a growing awareness of many biases in the exploration and exploitation of knowledge – especially scientific knowledge, which is often presented as objective and independent of ideological bias. Knowledge of cultures and organizations is no exception. Some of these biases blind us to relevant and important determinants of behaviour. Some make us turn a blind eye to salient aspects of organizational and national cultures. Some spread unexamined stereotypes that resist falsification. Some erect barriers to successful communication.

One of the most important biases built into managerial sciences is the ideology of 'managerialism'. It is based on an assumption that a top manager has a privileged view of what is going on among his or her subordinates. Researchers are perceived as the extension of top managers' eyes. They should provide management with the most valid description of what is going on in an organization. They should tailor recommendations to managerial needs and preferences. By doing so, they will help transform managers into impartial philosopher-kings. They will train consultants, who, in turn, will help managers run their organizational kingdoms. This technocratic ideology has provided a justification for a number of managerial fashions of the past years: Total Quality Management, Business Process Re-engineering, Empowerment, Transformational Leadership, Knowledge Management, Learning Organizations, the New Public Management, and large-scale privatization of health care and utilities are all cases in point. However, for the representatives of critical management studies, 'managerialism' is part of the problem rather than a solution:

> Managers compete with other groups in defining what is correct and good. . . . What pretends to be a technical, practically oriented knowledge interest is really often an ideological one; the attraction lies in appealing to fantasies of being in the elite, of being grandiose and omnipotent.
>
> (Alvesson, 2002, 172)

If we want to understand organizational behaviour, culture, conflict, development, and change, a view from the top is not always the best. Managerialism may prompt theoretical and organizational choices that lead researchers and managers away from relevant issues of their (and everybody else's) involvement in power struggles, embedding in economic institutions, socialization in cultural mental programmes, involvement in class and status inequalities, and ethical concerns. It may prompt the presenting a point of view of one group (for instance an organization's managerial elite) as an objective view from nowhere, thereby silencing views from 'manywheres'.[1]

What can be done to counter this pervasive ideology? One might say that managers should trade their utopia of total control for a more modest and democratic vision of corporate citizenship and piecemeal organizational engineering. They should heed the writing on the wall – or, rather, the fall of the Berlin Wall, which stood for one of the two most ambitious forms of political managerialism in the 20th century, namely the communist utopia of totalitarian control. Once the utopian designs of the Marxist revolutionaries (or rather of the communist party managerial cadres legitimizing their domination with revolutionary ideology) melted into thin air, managers of market companies in a global economy had to chase the shadow of the utopia of total control from their own organizational backyards and corporate boardrooms. They could not rely on an ideological comparison with their communist counterparts. As long as the Cold War lasted, and the world could be neatly divided into the first, second and third worlds, managers in the first, Western world, improved their ratings in the eyes of their employees and citizens by comparing themselves to party-controlled authoritarian technocrats in the second world. They could point out that under communism all managers are more authoritarian and the political system is a particularly authoritarian form of government by a single collective dictator – the communist party. As soon as the second world collapsed, this comparison became impossible. The end of the Cold War meant that managers of the western world lost easy access to politically comfortable benchmarking. They had to work harder to legitimize themselves.

There are indications that managers in the western world have already started adapting to the new situation and compare themselves not horizontally – across the Iron Curtain – but chronologically, across the time span from Henry Ford to Jack Welch, from Taylorism to learning organization. Western managers' earlier selves – their more authoritarian predecessors – replace managers from behind the Iron Curtain as ideological 'sparring partners'. Jack Welch speaks of 'unleashing people' (implying they had been leashed under the previous managerial 'regime') and hearing them out during specially organized 'workout sessions', where hierarchies disappear and creative ideas flow freely, improving company's competitive status and innovative image.

Most managers would agree that coaching individuals yields better results than subjecting them to strict controls, especially if the company's future is crucially dependent on its employees' creativity and commitment. However, few would be willing to ease their control within the dominant form of a business organization. Nevertheless, even if this coaching terminology remains only lip service to less authoritarian forms of management, at least they feel obliged to pay it in public. Reading their lips may thus be more interesting in more senses than one. Managers may constrain themselves when exercising power in their organizations. Some of them would, for instance, agree that cultural due diligence prior to corporate mergers and acquisitions could prevent future disasters and raise the very low percentage of those mergers and amalgamations that turn out to be a success. One or two might even consider reading a book on cross-cultural differences, or take a course on dealing with them, in order to develop skills necessary to build up their cross-cultural competence and increase their company's ratings with respect to, for instance, fairness, sustainability and other issues in an ethical code of corporate conduct. Last but not least, some managers would welcome the possibility to break free of the iron cage of managerialism and to educate their employees in creative community-building. The latter cannot be accomplished without developing cross-cultural competence – and behind the factory door too.

Chapter 1

The ends, means and meanings of culture

The language connection

1 Ends of cultural software

> What is a culture, if not a consensus?
>
> (Clifford Geertz)

What is a culture? The way we do things around here? Core values plus norms plus behaviour (about which there is some consensus) and artefacts? Subjective mental software copied from an objective tradition? Rituals that train us into socially approved habits? The web of meanings spun around us so that we can go on understanding and interpreting the world and ourselves? Practices, representations, languages, and customs? There are notoriously many, often incompatible definitions, but differences between them do not seem to bother us too much in our daily lives.

A general consensus could possibly develop around three basic meanings of the concept of culture. In the first, culture would be associated with 'cultivation' – originally of land, subsequently of mind and finally of a complex human civilization in general. In the second, culture would be a 'black box' of meanings, values, norms, and 'ways' (patterns of behaviour, artefacts) regularly demonstrated and applied by real individuals and their groups. In the third, culture would be the totality of sense-making practices pursued by individuals, groups and societies (the culture of the Renaissance in Italy, the cultural project of the Enlightenment in France, the neoliberal doctrine of management and governance in the US) and the totality of search engines individuals use to find them. In view of the many conflicting definitions, a more pragmatic approach usually prevails and we agree to live by a conventional, popular metaphor and a persuasive, convincing interpretation rather than by a precise definition. It is not uncommon to find social scientists settling for the following definition: 'culture is a way of summarizing the ways in which groups distinguish themselves from other groups' (Wallerstein, 2000, 265).

What is a culture for? For getting to 'yes' or for breeding dissent? For guiding our actions or for reflecting on what we had done? For helping us make sense of the environment and ourselves? To help us survive? With 'us' here being individuals, groups, organizations, companies, institutions, societies, or even civilizations? An evolutionary mode of thinking at the turn of the 20th and the 21st centuries linked culture to increasingly complex co-operation between individuals and to the increasingly uncertain survival of complex societies. Co-operation between increasingly different and distant individuals, organizations and societies, and the survival of increasingly complex societies came to be defined as problems, the solution of which required cultural engineering and re-engineering. This link became a tacit axiom of educated common sense. *Culture is tacitly assumed to be a survival kit carried as a backpack by members of our species going about their business.*

What is culture, then? What is inside this backpack? A bank of data, a bunch of methods and resources, some stores of knowledge, some toolkits of skills and preferences? Most scientists and scholars reflecting on culture agree that there is a 'core' of values, beliefs and norms, accessible through socialization, education and upbringing. Individuals can borrow ideas from one another as easily as they borrow books from a library. They profit from their implementation, as they profit from pooling resources and getting a credit from a bank to invest in their business venture. Not for nothing do we speak of data banks, knowledge assets or think tanks. Each of us can understand our environment, explain behaviour, deal with some problems and avoid others, survive. Each of us can do so much more quickly and efficiently because of access to the thoughts and feelings, explanations and interpretations of many other individuals in other places and from other times. Each of us, in turn, has a chance of contributing to human culture. We take loans from our cultural banks, but we pay them back, sometimes with interest. From the library of Alexandria to the world wide-web we gather knowledge, store it, access it, distribute it, register it; we provide feedback, contribute, preserve memories, perform rituals, cultivate traditions. Culturally speaking, we are all 'big spenders'.

No reader can claim that he or she has read all books in the great library of Alexandria. Usually, we do not really know what the 'whole' culture is like. One does not have to read all the books in a library to be able to spot and borrow relevant ones. Not everybody wants to explain the nature of the universe or apply the laws of motion and energy. Everybody, however, wants to explain the behaviour of ourselves and others. Everybody would like to know the most desirable ends and the most fitting means to reach them, first because everybody wants to find their way in his or her social world, and second because common sense provides insufficient resources for doing so. Surprises, hurdles, conflicts, and improvisations defy routines. Scenarios get modified, dialogues rewritten, timing reset, routes re-charted. Social scientists, experts, specialists have to be consulted. Our backpacks guarantee access to human culture, but we need guides to navigate huge knowledge domains that increase every day, and we need skilled coaches to learn how to apply cultural knowledge in situations we have never faced before.

A social scientist in general, and a representative of the organizational and managerial sciences in particular, wants to understand what people (managers, employees, leaders, functionaries, operatives) are doing, when they do what they set out to do. It seems simple but is not, because in order to arrive at an explanation and use it to design a plan of action, a business plan, we have to rely on experts. Experts usually rely on researchers, or conduct research themselves. Managers and their gurus often simply cut out common-sense explanations along with scientific ones from available sources and paste them without questioning their origins (unexamined common sense) or explaining the intellectual price tags (ambiguous research traditions, long-standing controversies among experts). Most researchers in the social sciences would, for instance, agree that a common-sense view of a man as a biological 'machine' with a spiritual 'ghost' inside is – roughly – correct. They usually assume that a man is made of material hardware with a mental programme (sometimes compared to 'software') inside, but they realize that this is an oversimplification of the 'real' composition of the universe of the human. Some of them realize that they are following Descartes in splitting human individuals into physiological clockworks or automata, on the one hand, and sophisticated ghosts (souls, personalities, minds, mental programmes, cultural software) on the other. Some say that automata can be studied by the natural and engineering sciences. They are, after all, mechanisms, homeostatic feedback systems. Ghosts (souls, personalities, minds, cultural software) should be studied by the social sciences – psychology, social psychology, sociology, cultural anthropology, economics, linguistics, sociolinguistics, history, in short, the behavioural, social and humanist disciplines (if we want to know and understand), and the organizational and managerial sciences (if we want to act and implement).

However, if we agree to look for ghosts in the machines, we have already turned a deaf ear to a whole alternative school of thought, which claims that this distinction is wrong. Reality is not neatly divided into mechanical bodies and spiritual minds. Bodies get spirited, minds matter, processes in both can have material consequences. Events exist and flow through space and time. Reality is composed of flows and processes, fluctuations follow capricious dynamic patterns, organizing is reversible and influences evolutionary change. Synapses connect into unrepeatable patterns of individual, flexible neural networks; organizations ally themselves, fall apart, break alliances and forge new ones. The world is not an empty stage filled with objects or bodies waiting to be copied by minds and registered by a scientific bureaucracy. It is a multidimensional stream of events twisting space and time as they flow by. Words and names do not simply reflect this flow, they can also influence it by focusing, urging, defining, co-creating realities. Human minds evolve along with their bodies, and viewing them separately and independently from their environments, both natural and social, distorts our understanding of both of them. Thus having set out to simplify our description of reality in order to explain it better, we end up misrepresenting it and offering inferior explanations. Distortions usually result from an attempt to squeeze dynamic reality into the rigid, bureaucratic categories of institutional science. The representatives of organizational sciences, for instance, usually assume that organizations are like Russian dolls. First, they have sub-organizations inside. Second, human individuals hide in these sub-parts of the organization. Third, within each individual, a mind with a mental programme can be found, and, finally, this mental programme can be separated from its carrier – an individual mind.

This common-sense vision of societies and organizations as Russian dolls and as ghosts in machines is contradicted by the results of research conducted at the level of each assumed Russian doll hiding in another. Societies are not passive containers for organizations. They unroll red carpets for some, facilitating their growth, and constraining others from flourishing or even emerging. Organizations are not mechanical storage facilities for individuals. They attract and develop some personality types, and reject and destroy the others. Individual minds are not impassive holders of symbolic culture. All individuals give their personal twist to the knowledge they acquire. Symbolic culture is not an immutable set of abstract entities independent of the rest of the environment. It is a dynamic, fluctuating 'cloud' of interrelated elements, which responds to changes in their environment. Individual minds do not grow and change independently of the bodies, cultures and organizations surrounding them. They co-evolve together. Nevertheless, this common-sense, middle-of-the-road, 'instinctive', mechanical 'Cartesianism' persists, because it meets a profound need. We would all like to feel certain that there is an objective world 'out there', different from the subjective world 'in here', and that the two are synchronized, that they work together. This is a tacit, commonly assumed, 'realist' philosophy of culture and society, automatically acceptable to researchers, managers and the broader public, disseminated through teaching and training programmes, designed and executed by large bureaucracies, sanctified by common sense. Is it safe to assume that since so many people think so, it must be true? Does safety reside in numbers? Is truth determined by polls?

Perhaps. But look who is polling whom. Polling a narrow club of experts rather than the broad public does not change the principle, only the scale. However, this safety has been paid for with insoluble contradictions. The complexity of a single human individual perplexes artists and scientists alike. One person's life-world of daily experience challenges even the most sophisticated research programmes. The intricacies of emotional bonds escape descriptive efforts and defeat explanatory schemes. The complexities of even the smallest organizations of interacting individuals challenge mechanistic and organic images (of companies and institutions, of networks and constellations) researchers work with. And complexities of evolving societies clashing or co-operating with one another challenge our attempts to understand and predict future developments. Moreover, complexities of the objects of study are matched by complexities of the methods that are being employed.

To understand individual and group behaviour, researchers can try to formulate abstract generalizations that explain broad classes of actions and predict possible outcomes of some situations. Predictions based on reliable and approved methodologies are important for employees of bureaucratic organizations. Their work requires legitimate and reliable knowledge. Reliable knowledge is professionally produced knowledge. It can be used legitimately, because it had been produced by professionals and approved by their community (by 'peers' defined within professional bureaucracies). It can be applied in planning, controlling, motivating, and guiding others according to formal criteria. The problem is that what passes for reliable and legitimate knowledge is often presented as 'objective', 'impartial', 'non-ideological', and 'value-free'. Scientists are not supposed to tell us where to go, only how to get there. Nevertheless, when they advise us how to get somewhere, they implicitly suggest that some ends can be reached and some cannot. If ends cannot be reached, then perhaps we should not waste time trying. A hint, a suggestion, an assumption, a stereotype – these are easily born. Most social scientists would agree that knowledge generated within social sciences is not, cannot be, value-free and 'objective'. Most of them, however, would also admit that scientific expertise looks much more convincing when presented as objective knowledge, when packaged as 'value-free', 'universally valid', produced without paradigmatic bias and ideological prejudice. One of the most popular ways of presenting it this way is to model it after natural sciences and to pretend that both natural and social sciences 'speak' the same language when describing and interpreting the world.

The temptation to imitate the natural sciences has always been very strong. Researchers wanted to discover the 'iron laws' regulating human behaviour – preferably to be isolated in a laboratory and then 'confirmed' in the course of empirical inquiry into human behaviour outside of it. They wanted to describe the 'mechanisms' of some aspect of behaviour. Managers wanted to hear instructions on how to make use of these mechanisms. Most of them were trained as engineers, not social scientists. They expected the expert advice to be couched in the same terms as instructions in mechanical engineering. Researchers, reading the expectations of managers and trying to imitate natural sciences, duly obliged. For instance, they studied decision-making in heterogeneous teams and generalized their results to explain decision-making in large organizations. They sought to explain the 'evolution' of organizational forms as if these were biological 'species' evolving due to the pressures of a changing environment. For instance, they sought to find out what organizational characteristics help small high-tech firms to survive, and see if these characteristics are present in the thousands of companies that actually do manage to survive. They asked what human resource policies were dominant in companies that survived, and what policies prevailed in companies that went bankrupt in the same area of business and in the same period. It was easy to assume that establishing organizations was like spawning a new generation of living organisms, say, a school of fish, and that closing them down was like the extinction of a natural species.

Most such attempts have been inconclusive and unsuccessful on their own terms. No grand theory of human or organizational behaviour, comparable to the theory of Newton or Darwin, or even Marx, Weber or Freud, has emerged so far. However, biology and theory of evolution did play a role in changing a common-sense approach to the social sciences. First, philosophers, politicians, managers, and sponsors of science sought to overcome the Cartesian dualism that separates a ghost (mind) from a machine (body). They have tried to get rid of the mind–matter, culture–nature dualistic problem. Some of them looked for a third world, one of objective culture, objective knowledge, where bodies and minds interact freely and dynamic fluctuations result in windows of opportunity for those who are able to seize them. They did so in order to demonstrate that there is no unbridgeable gap between two worlds of Descartes. Look, they said, we do not have to be imprisoned in a mind–body, ghost–machine, hardware–software stereotype. The third world of objective knowledge (populated, for instance, with scientific theories and works of art) can be accessed because human individuals have 'ghosts' (are able to reproduce pieces of objective knowledge in their consciousness) in their biological 'machines' (which are equipped with senses to access pieces of recorded objective knowledge). In other words, they have minds, and they can experience streams of consciousness linking their bodily impressions to intellectual operations in a seamless web. The third world of objective knowledge is thus open to the world of 'ghosts'.

On the other hand, once I write my theory down or e-mail it to my fellow scientists or colleagues in the media, it starts leading its own life. If I finish composing my symphony and give it to a conductor, this symphony, previously cradled and nursed only in my individual mind, becomes independent of my personal consciousness. Theories and symphonies are recorded, virtually preserved in some material medium (such as a printed book, musical score, digitally recorded compact disc). Moreover, they can acquire material reality. A mass of sounds (imagined in my mind once before and recorded as the notes of the score) can be produced by an orchestra, and so mark these sounds' presence in the first, material world. Likewise, if my scientific theory results in constructing a mobile phone or a nuclear power plant, the 'object' from the third world of objective knowledge will be embodied in a 'material' artefact, which belongs to the first world. It will also be embodied in the neural wiring of the experts who managed to learn the relevant theory and apply it in practice to produce the nuclear power plant. The third world of objective knowledge is thus firmly embedded (or at least potentially 'embeddable') in the world of 'machines' and in the world of 'ghosts'. It will survive temporary loss of either of the two. Even if I shut out my mind, stop thinking about this theory or stop listening to this symphony, they will continue to exist, will still be open to any other individual mind whose owner is able to read, listen, think, and experience. On the other hand, even if all nuclear power plants evaporate and there is no material object one might label in this way, the existence of a third world's blueprint for such a plant and the accessibility of this blueprint to learning individuals with functioning brains will allow us to reconstruct one fairly quickly.

This is how one of the most intriguing philosophers of science of the 20th century, Karl R. Popper, thought he had managed to avoid dilemmas of a split of reality into a ghost versus a machine. An open, democratic society honestly pursuing knowledge should build and maintain a bridge and a balance between 'ghosts' and 'machines', and learn how to manage traffic on such bridges. Citizens of this open society would speak the same universal language of united science, patterned after the natural sciences but sensitive to the humanities, and they would argue according to the logic of scientific discovery.

Popper's ideas reflect the widespread influence of an evolutionary mode of thinking about culture and society in the second half of the 20th century. Due to this influence, most of us came to see culture as an evolutionary 'bridge' between ghosts and machines. Culture arose as a result of the evolution of human brains and societies, and it has become mankind's most important evolutionary resource. It suffered many crises of growth, but did not crumble. It is still there and it still works. *Not the Tower of Babel, but a bridge of Babel. Culture is a bridge of Babel constructed by many different builders speaking different 'languages' – the languages of science, art, religion, morality, everyday life*. This cultural bridge is materially constructed, hence objectively preserved (recorded), and psychologically accessible, hence subjectively relevant. Within culture, there is an ongoing struggle between various building technologies, different designers, competing construction crews. Each of them claims that it provides the single most important component, which merits special attention because without it the whole bridge would collapse. The most successful promotional campaign is presently being waged by suppliers of 'scientific' elements of the bridge. They claim that scientists contribute much more than priests, managers or artists to the maintenance of this bridge of Babel. They also claim to be responsible for reshaping, developing and accessing culture in general, not just their own scientific lane.

There is some truth to their claims. Without archaeologists and conservationists we would have lost most of our records, buildings and other artefacts of symbolic culture, and without historians we would not have understood them. Without psychologists and sociologists we would be unable to continue understanding them. Scientists allow humans to manipulate both ghosts and machines much more effectively, efficiently and thoroughly than ever before. However, it is not their voices that we hear when noticing warning signs. It is not their voices we hear when we face sudden challenges, changes, transformations. We hear other, non-scientific voices, which warn us against collective seduction by an ideal of perfect knowledge and total control, presumably awaiting us round the next corner. Other cultural heroes try to persuade scientists and all users of culture that we should not remain imprisoned in metaphors we lived by for years, perhaps even centuries. Scientific communities are not seats of moral authority, and their seduction by the powers that be has often been recorded. The educated public has some access to 'the kitchen' of scientific communities, but this tends to be limited. Moreover, no matter how serious the warnings get, governments and managers listen to scientists rather than the educated public ('representatives of civil society', 'corporate citizens'), artists or moral authorities. Artists are seen as promoting their creations, moral and religious authorities as advertising their faith. Scientists are supposed to promote selfless knowledge and are thus considered more reliable. Are they always making responsible use of this favourable bias? There are reasons to suspect that at least in some cases the answer might be negative (cf. Mirowski, Sent, 2002).

Scientists have developed a number of techniques for building the trust of the general educated public. They often claim that their thinking is more rigorous and more accessible to an average member of society, for an 'everyman' (with a university diploma) than the thinking of artists or priests. One way of phrasing it is to say that scientists try to follow the logic of scientific discovery, accepted by all members of their research community and the authors of textbooks for schoolchildren. Scientists are also required to systematically check and legitimize their findings in an ongoing discussion, in which everybody tries to falsify his or her own hypotheses as honestly as possible. In this way, scientists claim that they have introduced a much more thorough total quality control of everything that is being produced in the evolving house of science. If this is so, then it is only just that they should be given preferential treatment when individuals and organizations look for knowledge, which will then increase their chances of survival. The best way to safeguard the survival of human societies, according to this educated common-sense view of social evolution, is to maintain an open (liberal) society.

An open society is the one in which nobody (including schools in science) has a monopoly on knowledge, nobody can claim that he or she can predict a future, which remains, well . . . open. An open society keeps future options open. An open society is the one that can resist political monopoly (demagogic dictatorship, fundamentalist ideological control, monopolistic media ownership) and technocratic bureaucracy (managerialism, technocracy, bureaucratic elites, 'nomenklatura'). Critics of politicians, state officials, scientific communities, and corporate officers should have, well . . . open access to mass media. An open society can safeguard the production of objective (i.e. scientific) knowledge and facilitate (i.e. manage) its continuous supply in the interest of the open-ended evolution of complex societies. Culture is about openness: transparency, open ends, open societies; it is about negotiating, re-inventing, re-engineering them and about keeping them open. This openness means that sometimes it will be logically and morally difficult to make – quite literally – ends meet. It also means that an open society is continually busy negotiating, renegotiating and re-engineering its values; otherwise it would be forced to become a 'carrier' of a single historical project, a preferred utopia. Popper thought that such utopias – be it Plato's, Hegel's or Marx's – are dangerous illusions and all too easily lead to terror. He preferred more cautious, piecemeal social engineering in his anti-utopian 'open society'.

2 Means – objective knowledge?

What is a cynic? A man who knows the price of everything, and the value of nothing.

(Oscar Wilde)

Culture is about society being able to initiate change and to continue changing in an open-ended way. But culture is also about a repertory of means for doing things – for instance, for staying the same ('this is the way we had always done things around here') or for changing ('this is the way things should be done around here'). We learn those repertories when acquiring knowledge, both explicit (when pursuing curricula) and tacit (when coached on a job). Acquiring knowledge we acquire 'knowledge assets' (objective, subjective and intersubjective). 'Objective' knowledge provides better means for coping with complex organizations in complex societies, because it is more abstract and can thus more easily be adapted to different concrete situations (note that 'objective' stands here for 'inter-subjective', i.e. agreed upon by many, or at least by relevant subjects). Therefore educational bureaucracies always choose to provide individuals with knowledgeable means, which are predominantly labelled 'objective', believing that these individuals can later cope with increasingly complex problems more easily than if they had been acquiring more 'local' and less 'abstract' knowledge. Large educational bureaucracies have to teach numerous students how to acquire and cultivate knowledge, how to know and acquire culture; in other words: how to accumulate means for dealing with future problems. Culture is then understood as a repertory of means (norms, rules, etc.).

In order to understand the origins of the contemporary educated, common-sense, liberal view of an open society and of its culture with core objective knowledge, we shall make a brief excursion into the now-forgotten philosophical debate of 1972. Few people noticed it at the time and a publication of one of the first international debates on this topic in 1970 (*Criticism and the Growth of Knowledge*) had been gathering dust on the shelves of the philosophy of science section of university libraries rather than stimulating debates about the place of science in an open society.

The term 'open society' had been introduced by Karl Popper in a pamphlet against political utopias from Plato to Marx, written in 1945, two years before the beginning of the Cold War between market democracies and communist totalitarianism. The term 'objective knowledge' had been introduced by the same author in a book on the evolutionary role of science in general (detect, avoid or prevent deadly threats to mankind's survival) and a critical philosophy of science in particular (expose individual and group pathology in scientific communities and try to remove it), written in 1972. The polemical context of the concepts of an open society (as opposed to a dictatorship) and objective knowledge (as opposed to a religious belief or a political ideology) may have been forgotten, but the concepts themselves have retained their significance for our understanding of the scientific community's fundamental self-image.

This view of objective knowledge (as the most important part of human culture ruled by inner logic and evolving in a continuous way) was attacked almost as soon as it had been formulated. An American historian of science, Thomas Kuhn, sought to distinguish some common thread in major scientific revolutions. If 'normal' science is a bureaucratic enterprise, rewarding conformity and discipline, punishing independence and rebelliousness, why should anything ever change? Why do researchers from time to time suddenly abandon their familiar principles and accept totally different ones? Why drop Ptolemy and accept Copernicus? Why leave Newton and join Einstein? Or why resist change? Why did researchers persist in loyalty to these now abandoned principles in the very long periods between such revolutions? In other words, why did they remain loyal in spite of mounting difficulties, anomalies, unexplained puzzles, ad hoc solutions? Should we find an answer to this, a complementary question raises its head: if researchers managed to remain loyal for so long, why all of a sudden such a radical turn-around? Why do they switch from one paradigmatic loyalty to another with such opportunistic zeal, trampling the logic of scientific discovery and methodological integrity in doing so? Why do these docile bureaucrats of research all of a sudden turn into a revolutionary crowd, stampeding past left-over loyalists and running towards a new paradigmatic leader?

Kuhn thought that the answer could only be local and temporary. Communities of researchers develop routines. Until some critical event triggers their abandoning of a routine, nobody questions it. Academic circles of researchers do not follow abstract principles of absolute rationality, nor do they subject their production of theories to a thorough critical assessment. Large communities of practice require loyalty to scientific research programmes and promote conformist career-makers, devoted disciples, disciplined employees. 'Normal science' is about making small steps, pushing forward, solving feasible problems, collecting points, which lead to individual promotion and a school's institutional domination. Normal science is produced by disciplined communities of researchers ruled by hierarchic bureaucracies of scientific managers. Communities turn a blind eye to contradictions and anomalies, until, some day, generations change, contradictions cannot be ignored and a scientific revolution blows up. The paradigm changes suddenly, a new scientific research programme quickly replaces the former one, and then, for all researchers, business as usual resumes. Continuity is an artificial construct promoted by a scientific community, guaranteed first by a tacit consensus and later by rewriting textbooks on the history, philosophy and methodology of science. In fact, the history of science is continuously rewritten in the light of new knowledge, which allows us to re-interpret and re-assess previous knowledge. Thus contemporary physicists claim that the superstring theory of matter allows us to understand relativity theory, quantum mechanics and later theories of weak forces and elementary particles as special cases of a more abstract theoretical explanation of matter and energy. Thus contemporary biologists claim that a revised interpretation of Darwin's theory of evolution (based on new palaeontological evidence and advances in biochemical 'genetic engineering') allows us to combine theories of genetic drift with theories of natural selection in a single theoretical framework that explains complexity and chance.

These developments make us suspect that one should not look for a universal logic of science (or for a formal logic of any scientific discovery) in order to explain the history of scientific knowledge. One should instead look for the dynamics of competition and co-operation between communities of researchers. One should look for signs of a new generation of researchers getting positions of influence in academic organizations and networks. Should they start getting Nobel prizes and large research funds, one must read these signs as an announcement that they are ready to drive the older generation out.

Neither Kuhn nor Popper won a Nobel prize. Had they done so, their debate would probably have had more impact, and more individuals and groups would have paid attention to their important arguments about the very nature of our culture and the limits to our cognitive ambitions. Nor did any other representative of social sciences ever get the Nobel prize, with the exception of economics (Sartre or Camus received Nobel prizes, but not for their philosophical oeuvre; rather, for their novels, essays and theatrical pieces). The economists, although rewarded, are very late arrivals on the award scene – the Nobel prize in economics was introduced as late as 1969.

This should not come as a surprise. There is an in-built bias against social sciences in the very organization of the international Nobel prize committee. There are no subcommittees on evaluating and rewarding outstanding scientific work in philosophy, sociology, psychology, or the managerial sciences. This bias may reflect a belief that only heavily quantitative economic theories can be rewarded on a par with theories produced in natural sciences. They seem to speak a language similar to the one spoken by physicists and engineers, or biologists and medical doctors. *Perhaps this fact explains why representatives of the social sciences are viewed as second-rate citizens in scientific communities and their theories are priced as products of inferior quality on cultural markets.* They are not even considered eligible for the highest price in the domain of scientific knowledge (i.e. for Nobel prizes established specifically for their academic domain: if a scholar in the humanities desires a Nobel prize, he has to follow Camus and Sartre and win it in literature). If they want to get a higher ranking, they have to move political activists, inspire writers and art critics, or appeal to the media and managers. No wonder they resent and question the hierarchy imposed on a province of scientific culture by the representatives of natural sciences, and try to understand and improve their inferior position in the house of science. So far, social scientists have not succeeded in changing the overall hierarchy, although they have made some progress and established some alternative institutions.

On the one hand, quantitative methods have been introduced and accepted as legitimate means of generating expertise for managers and politicians. Kenneth Arrow's *Social Choice and Individual Values* has been paradigmatic for this brand of social sciences, sponsored by RAND corporation and influential at the universities in the US:

> New rational decision technologies constitute a regime of knowledge production. This phrase is used to refer to how the formation of these tools and concepts led to a far-reaching and comprehensive system for defining appropriate beliefs and actions. Participation in the system was controlled by a new policy elite. These leading figures – including Thomas Schelling, Charles Hitch, Howard Raiffa, Henry Rowen, and Alain Enthoven – went from their humble origins as contractors for the US Air Force to controlling enormous budgets, influential departments of governments and universities, and key federal initiatives affecting all

Americans. It was their ability to redefine democratic decision-making to suit their agenda, using these analytic tools, that made such a breathtaking rise possible. Once this comprehensive regime came into place, it gained *de facto* legitimacy through ubiquity rather than proven merit.

(Amadae, 2003, 28)

On the other hand, qualitative studies, which question this rational choice paradigm in the social sciences in general and the organizational sciences in particular, are presently well established in academic communities, research programmes, scientific journals and networks of international communications, conferences, congresses, and workshops. Critical Management Studies are a case in point and so is the critique of managerialism voiced by, among others, Mats Alvesson, Stanley Dietz, Hugh Wilmott, Martin Parker, and David Boje:

Organizations produce press releases to be distributed and consumed harmoniously as common sense accounts that are designed to be taken for granted as narratives that do not mobilize resistance or bring any attention to ongoing power struggles over institutional sense-making. In short, hegemonic power operates behind the scenes in acts of socialization, in providing frames that make one's action appear harmonious and neutral.

(Boje, 2002, 79)

However, no matter how deep is the rift between those two schools of thinking on organizations and management, all social scientists still feel an urge to explain why they are being treated as second-rate professionals by academic institutions and political authorities. They have to come up with alibis for not having been elevated to the same ranks as their counterparts in natural sciences. Not having won a single Nobel prize so far,[1] researchers in social and organizational sciences usually come up with three such alibis in order to save face in society at large and to command some respect among corporate clients.

First, they claim that the very fact that the human world is heavily saturated with conscious games individuals and groups play makes it much more unpredictable than the world of stones and trees. Being much more complex and sophisticated, it is also much more difficult to 'grasp' (describe, explain, understand, predict). God does not play dice, Einstein reputedly said, meaning that once physicists discovered the laws of motion or energy, the predictability that these laws were the Creator's hoax, meant to ridicule scientific efforts, was very slight. In the social world, however, if people suddenly start believing some symbol or fiction to be real, this symbol or fiction will have real consequences. In a sense, culture may have enabled all of them to 'play dice'. What if they pretend to think that ideological fictions are truly real? Most citizens of the Soviet Union expressed their belief in the progressive and benevolent nature of Soviet society – but did not hesitate to admit they had been lying as soon as they saw a chance of doing so without being punished. In the context of the Stalinist terrorist state they learned how to increase their chances of survival by displaying flexibility in defining 'reality'. In the context of the post-Stalinist non-terrorist state Soviet citizens have learned that they will not be punished for expressing their 'authentic' views on reality (though they still seem to have retained the assumption that everything not explicitly allowed is thereby forbidden). A combination of a cultural product (ideological fiction) and a sociological mechanism (the totalitarian state) changed reality by twisting individual consciousnesses, and by producing reality-constituting, though purposefully untruthful individual statements. Individuals lied as a matter of course, because lies increased their chances of surviving repression. Outstanding individuals lied as a matter of course and indeed as a matter of pride, because lies increased their chances of making a career. Some regimes managed to elicit untrue, hypocritical statements from individuals who pretended they were speaking from their hearts. Were Germans honestly hailing and praising their leader at mass rallies, or just playing the conformist game to avoid totalitarian repression? Had they bought into a deal proposed by Hitler: you will not be allowed to question property in capitalist economy, nor will you be free to decide if I stay in power, but you can express your German soul in specially designed mass meetings provided you play your role of faithful Germanic tribesmen with conviction? If they were not honestly playing united workers or united tribesmen, how do we distinguish their behaviour from applause given by the US citizens to their democratically elected president? Have Soviet or Nazi or Maoist doctrines actually appealed to the 'captive minds' of ambitious intellectuals? Did anyone watching the 'Moscow trials' of former Bolshevik leaders – who readily confessed to the most absurd crimes – actually believe what he or she saw? Did the defendants themselves believe what they said when admitting they were Japanese spies or agents of international capital? If they only pretended, how do we distinguish them (or those like them) from honest actors in different organizational settings? For instance, from fundamentalist liberals praising tax reduction for the richest citizens? Have communist or Nazi policies succeeded in breeding generalized distrust in all ideological declarations in all other societies? Have they taught us to distrust social sciences, which all too easily fall prey to the ideological illusions of socialism, fundamentalism or managerialism? Were they exceptional in their criminal disregard of individual human rights – or can these rights be curbed equally easily under different ideological colours? Perhaps they were simply more extreme in employing the same control and persuasion techniques, which have often been found in liberal market democracies? After all, both Lenin and Stalin admired Taylor and Ford. It is quite clear that these problems and complexities go far beyond processes and phenomena studied by natural sciences. The god of nature may not play dice; the gods of human societies do.

The second alibi claims that the complexity of human behaviour is also brought about by the unpredictable influence of the values (which belong to culturally determined ends) and the emotions (which belong to culturally determined means for motivating individuals to action) they generate. It is far from certain if some values are or are not operative when behavioural choices are made, and it is far from certain what emotions will emerge when individuals take them into account. Machiavelli instructed managers to measure the fear they want to cultivate in the hearts of their subjects. According to his famous advice, fear was better than love for a power-holder, since fear made people passive. The ruler could then control them better. If you overdo it, however, he had warned, fear will change into hate, and hate mobilizes emotions, prompting hostile action and, triggering resistance against your power. When does one know that this, indeed, is happening? There is no golden rule that would allow a manager to detect early signals of fear turning into hate. Continuous supervision of employees, citizens or subjects (either discreet or open) is notoriously unreliable. Machiavelli is fondly mentioned not only by social scientists; 'cognitivists' also quote him with gusto as a patron saint of their individualistic approach to 'social intelligence' measured in individual careers. Moreover, paradoxes of emotional trade-offs in individuals and societies under investigation make predictions far more risky than in natural sciences. De Tocqueville noted that the French revolution did not happen during the period of the most widespread suffering and the heaviest hardships imposed on the population. Paradoxically, it was when things had started getting better, but just not quickly enough compared to the hopes these developments had sown among the masses, that people decided to challenge the authorities. Revolutions can thus happen when expectations about needs to be satisfied are rising more quickly than actual satisfaction of these very needs, and not necessarily when these needs are least satisfied, when any change should be much more desirable (as any outcome of a change looks much better than the present situation). When sociologists were describing US society in the mid Sixties, they concluded that a growth of a middle class of avid consumers had lowered the political involvement of citizens, and thus large-scale social movements were very unlikely. No sooner, however, had their books appeared in academic bookshops than the very members of the US middle class falsified their predictions. Instead of sitting in their suburban homes and watching TV, they went out into the streets and faced riot police to protest against the war in Vietnam.

The most famous of those predictions was made by Mancur Olson in *The Logic of Collective Action*, published in 1964 and falsified almost immediately by students in Berkeley. The latter started protesting against the administration's plans for turning a public park into a university parking lot, encouraged by emerging political leaders Mario Savio and Tom Hayden. The expertise and publicity they had gained in the 'Free Speech Movement' facilitated the rapid spread of student unrest, especially when an attractive and unifying issue was found in protest against the war in Vietnam. Soon millions of demonstrators took to streets, campuses and political conventions. Riot police and the National Guard had to be mobilized in order to restore order. The objective knowledge of experts turned out to be insufficient to understand the implications of a minor university bureaucrat's decision to turn a campus park into a parking lot. Neither was it sufficient to predict windows of opportunity for protest organizers created by a gradual escalation of the US involvement in Vietnam. Trivial triggers, dynamic clusters of processes, multiple causalities, huge political conse-quences – this level of complexity and chance certainly challenges all research communities, especially in view of the interconnectivity provided by the media. The latter co-define political reality, very much like individuals co-define social realities by defining, expressing and communicating it.

The rapid development of the mass media in the second half of the 20th century has been one of the most significant processes increasing the complexity of contemporary culture, through the rewiring of communi-cations and turning our private lives into publicly viewable 'cultural content'. As one of the former student activists had put it:

> Deeper currents of media operate not on patterned ideas but on feeling. . . . People attach to the media for their emotional texture, for the experience that takes place in the presence of the media, rewarded above all by that experience even as they expect confirmation that the world feels right. That is why the image of a burning flag or the spurious claim of a burning bra looms so large in popular reactions – because these images slip beneath the façade where our ideas live; they 'hit us where we live.
>
> (Gitlin, 2003, xvii)

Research communities are not the only ones challenged by the above complexity. So are professional managers in formal organizations. Their control of employees, members, clients, or stakeholders requires some insight into the causal links and potential triggers of individual and collective action. They want more than an access to a file with background data. In other words, they realize that a human individual and a group or a community do not passively reflect their sociological or economic, gender or generation backgrounds and do not simply respond to managerial or environmental stimuli. Individuals use the above characteristics as resources to be creatively and unexpectedly recombined in the light of values deemed worthy of preserving and under emotional pressure of unpredictable assess-ment of chances for success. If there is widespread hunger and repression, people may calculate the risks involved in standing up for their values and find them too high. When there is no hunger, only unequal distribution, and authorities start giving in, values unite people and make them feel safer. Appeal to these values can unexpectedly seduce people to start action, which is against their interests or even threatens their lives (if they take up arms against the government or face armed police at a rally). Such paradoxes make the life of social scientists and managers difficult: even the best sociologists fail to predict when a social movement will start, in spite of the perfect consumer seduction by hidden persuaders (as in student protests against Vietnam war in the US 1964–73), and when it will not. Even the best managers tend to fail when they need to recognize early signals of an accumulating crisis. Tracing past experiences does not suffice. Protests against the planned invasion of Iraq by US troops in 2003 did not have a follow-up once hostilities started and neither did violent protests during the anti-WTO demonstrations in Seattle, Washington or Genoa (even though there was relatively less repression than in the Vietnam war era and it has been much more limited to a few locations). The complexity of the reality to be mapped is matched by the complexity of the processes to be traced and predicted. This social need to predict and plan, and the managerial need to predict and control lead us to the third explanation given by social scientists for their inferior status compared to their counterparts in natural sciences.

In their third alibi, social scientists claim that they work in a much more competitive marketplace and power-place of academic doctrines, schools and paradigms than natural scientists do. Social scientists live in a period of a real proliferation of rival research paradigms, each of which wants to attract the ear of institutional power-holders and to expand within the scientific community. Different research languages make it as difficult to communicate within the house of social science as it used to be for the builders of the Tower of Babel. Thus what should have been a bridge as formidable in linking humans as the Tower of Babel was in dividing them turns out to be a tower bridge, full of smaller Towers of Babel. The bridge is being built by many quarrelling scientists and scholars, each with his or her blueprint of an ivory tower in mind. They claim that their domain (the study of individual and collective behaviour in organizational contexts) is torn by a methodological civil war between the representatives of the quantitative and qualitative research programmes. The representatives of the quantitative research programmes (who are sometimes labelled 'modernists' or 'neo-neo-positivists' by their adversaries) believe that some day social sciences will follow the natural ones and reach, to use the words of one of the founders of sociobiology, E. O. Wilson, a state of perfect 'consilience'. Words will match objects, theories reality, explanations offered by various academic disciplines will fit each other, etc. In other words, they will unify different disciplines – for instance brain science, human genetics, cognitive psychology, biological, social and cultural anthropology, organizational theory, sociology of culture and cross-cultural psychology, etc. Together, the representatives of all these disciplines will produce a uniform theory of human behaviour (ultimately unified under the banner of biology as a science of life and evolution).

Another variant of this uniform theory of human behaviour is provided by representatives of a small cognitive revolution in behavioural sciences, which occurred in the 1990s and at the turn of the 21st century, acquiring the label of 'connectionism' (introduced by Paul Churchland in his polemic with Feyerabend). According to this group of quantitative cognitive scientists, the social sciences are bound to change *after* the implications of cognitive sciences, especially 'connectionism' are duly recognized. These implications, according to Stephen Turner, clearly indicate that collective terms ('culture', 'tradition', 'organizational learning') are illegitimate imports from daily, common-sense parlance and have no place in a truly scientific vocabulary. They correspond to nothing: what actually exists can be reduced to 'connectionism', to processes in individual brains, which establish idio-syncratic connections between nervous cells through their synapses, thus creating the personal architecture of individual learning processes, in the course of which each individual emerges with an irreplaceable mind. Such a mind is

> the product of a distinctive and individual learning history. . . . This approach inverts the usual explanation of a tradition, for example, by not saying that its rituals are performed because people share a common framework, but by saying instead that rituals are behavioural tech-nologies that produce a certain uniformity of habits – a uniformity, however, which is literally superficial, a matter of external similarity, with internal or personal consequences that vary from individual to individual. For instance, prayer has effects on those who pray, but the effects vary from person to person.
>
> (Turner, 2002, 1, 13)

The followers of quantitative schools of social research are well represented in academic establishments and their publications are easy to find. For instance Paul R. Lawrence and Nitin Nohria, both of Harvard Business School, have recently published a book on a theory of human behaviour that explains it via a unified understanding of human nature. They advocate a reduction of scientific explanation of human behaviour to four basic drives (a drive to acquire, to bond, to learn, and to defend) and three basic levels (individual, organization and community).[2] They are, even if radically individualistic and looking for fundamental research in natural sciences (the biology of 'drives' or neurological study of learning processes in human brain), aware of the fact that throwing away the 'collective' terms (culture, tradition, shared inheritance) has to be compensated for – and thus less triumphantly they re-introduce terms like 'interlearning processes among individuals' (cf. Turner, 2002, 22), in spite of firm talk against any supra-individual level of culture, knowledge and learning a tradition:

> Something in the way of mental content – skills at interpreting, so to speak – is needed to convert what is explicit and shared, or collective, into personal mental content, lived experience and so on. . . . All intentional thinking, and this includes emotional responses as well as conscious problem solving, depends on the operation of mechanisms acquired by habituation. But it is a mistake to 'collectivize' them as 'shared tacit knowledge' or practice in the sense of a collective object possessed by members of a group. There is no way for such a hypothesized object to be acquired by the individuals in whom it is supposed to operate.
>
> (Turner, 2002, 3)

This quantitative approach has a distinctly 'individualistic' ring to it; according to methodological assumptions of quantitative, neo-positivist paradigms, researchers should focus on the individual level, because that is where the action is; it is an individual who learns, an individual who evaluates, an individual who makes choices, rational or not, and an individual who can be studied empirically (while collective entities such as societies and cultures are either aggregates of individual contributions or dangerous reifications). An empirical study of an individual is a study of what he or she has done with an individual black box, which – according to these cognitively motivated theories – includes not only linguistic, but also cognitive, emotional and cultural competence. Hence the concepts of cognitive, emotional, Machiavellian, and 'cultural' intelligence, all of which had been introduced in order to explain individual interactions. For instance, a recent study of cultural intelligence has as its subtitle 'individual interactions across culture' and presents cultural intelligence as an individual characteristic with cognitive, motivational and behavioural components:

> We treat CQ [i.e. cultural intelligence – SM] as individual difference and characteristics, much like a traditional work has treated cognitive intelligence. Each individual can be thought of as having his or her unique CQ, and this capability is based on unique experiences. CQ as a group level construct does not really make sense in the way we approach the construct, just as individual level definition of intelligence or personality does not apply to groups or teams without significant redefinition and adaptation.
>
> (Earley, Ang, 2003, 6)

The representatives of the qualitative research paradigms (they are often labelled 'post-modern' or 'critical' social and managerial scientists) question this approach on three counts.

First, they think that the vision of natural sciences, which are supposedly coming closer and closer to a unified theory of everything with every breath of every scientist, is far more fictitious than factual, and that recent advances in the sciences of complexity have dealt the final blow to the methodological validity of this utopian desire for uniformity.

Second, they think that methodological individualism makes it difficult to study the problems of political power struggles and inequalities between groups in societies and organizations and deliberately diverts attention from possibilities of a collective action and a reduction of unfairness in social and organizational processes. For instance, the concept of a stakeholder analysis conveniently obscures managerialist interests – as opposed to a concept of a 'class struggle', which mobilizes those who have been subjected to systematic unfairness in organized activities. The concept of an individual, incommensurable 'cultural intelligence' obscures the possibility of developing a shared vision ('collective ideology') and designing organizational processes to implement it.

Third, they are convinced that their methodological approach allows them to account for both the role of consciousness (by accepting reflexivity as a methodological principle) and the role of culture (by accepting a certain pragmatism in reconstructing individual's 'reality') in explaining human behaviour. They hope to offer a more sophisticated way to deal with a ghost in the machine and by doing so overcome reductionism (everything should have a material cause) and remove the mind–body, ghost–machine distinction. Meanwhile, the neo-neo-positivists are forced to reduce explanation to a single privileged factor (e.g. drives) and level (e.g. biological). No thank you, respond the qualitative researchers, we do not appreciate your hostile take-over of all scientific endeavours. Social sciences can and should be different from natural sciences. The human capacity, the collective ability to 'learn to learn', deserves something better than a reduction to one of many natural processes studied by natural sciences. *Unified science stands a lesser chance of spotting errors and correcting them than a divided one. Divided we stand, united we shall fail our stakeholders.*

As if to confirm their view, the very same Harvard Business School Press, which had published the above-mentioned study on four basic drives, had also printed Herminia Ibarra's *Working Identity. Unconventional Strategies for Reinventing Your Career* (Ibarra, 2004). The book is not based on a random selection of representative samples, but follows the logic of qualitative inquiry, described by qualitative researchers Barley Glaser and Anselm Strauss as theoretical sampling and a constant applying of the comparative method. The author conducted in-depth interviews and identified those individuals for whom changing a career has not been a contingent consequence of external circumstances. Rather, it has clearly been a result of a conscious choice made after a subjective feeling of having reached some fork in the road, had been registered, analysed and acted upon. Instead of reducing career choice to an underlying material and 'objective' determinants, for instance biological drives, Ibarra says that:

> our working identity is not a hidden treasure waiting to be discovered at the very core of our inner being. Rather, it is made up of many possibilities; some tangible and concrete, defined by the things we do, the company we keep, and the stories we tell about our work and lives; others existing only in the realm of future potential and private dreams. . . . Working identity is above all a practice; a never-ending process of putting ourselves through a set of knowable steps that creates and reveals our possible selves.
>
> (Ibarra, 2004, xi–xii)

Are qualitative researchers right? Is the concept and vision of 'consilience' a product of a neo-neo-positivist wishful thinking or is it really in sight? I think that it is the wishful thinking of some scientific establishments and some academic bureaucracies. In fact, *we are dealing not so much with consilience as with polycentrism, meaning that there are many different research communities pursuing many paradigms, which guide their respective knowledge production.* There are also many unexpected combinations, platforms, alliances, architectures, and networks of researchers, and not all of them claim adherence to reductionist programmes and a uniform vision of science. Representatives of the qualitative studies of the social and cultural domain claim that they are interdisciplinary, transdisciplinary or even counterdisciplinary. They express a preference for a multimethod approach and for the interpretive understanding (at the expense of causal explanation) of human experience. They also claim that researchers should become aware of their ethical, political and other biases acquired during socialization into particular communities. According to the qualitative scientists, researchers' responsibility does not stop at the sponsor's door. Scholars and scientists should be more responsive to the communities in which they live and work, pursuing 'civic' social studies and contacting fellow-professionals responsible for the implementation and exploitation of new knowledge products. This category includes all intellectuals and symbolic analysts; educationists, political scientists, clinical practitioners, communications and media specialists, cultural studies workers, managers, businessmen, diplomats, artists, other academics, etc. They also run and manage the business of culture – scientists are not the only ones in command. Nor are they monopolistic suppliers of knowledge and skills. *Scientific knowledge has many advantages, but not all of them.*

Diversity increases, and uniformity further decreases, with the proliferation of new paradigms growing out of the main critical traditions in social sciences: social constructivism, post-structuralism, critical theory, postmodernism. Researchers seem to agree on an incommensurate nature of 'disciplinary matrixes' competing against each other in social sciences. Some researchers actually refer to the Tower of Babel, when diagnosing the present situation in social sciences. A cultural anthropologist from Princeton, Clifford Geertz, writes: 'We are not apparently proceeding toward some appointed end, where it all comes together, Babel is undone, and Self lies down with a Society'.[3] His colleague, a cross-cultural psychologist from Harvard, Richard Shweder, adds that:

> The best option is to go ahead and see what each point of view (each genuine cultural tradition, school of thought, theoretical position) illuminates and what each hides, while keeping track of the plural (some might say, polytheistic) character of humanly knowable world.[4]

It has thus become clear that a researcher eager to understand individual and collective behaviour cannot disregard the cultural component of the world he or she is describing. In other words, what the neo-positivists, for instance connectivists, are postulating – a 'clean' and clinical neurological study of individual learning processes, producing context-free abstract knowledge – is a fiction. There will be no context-free knowledge, studying individuals will always happen in settings that will restrict and 'situate' knowledge thus obtained (and not necessarily 'transfer' it to another setting). A dream of a 'pure' knowledge, independent of the local ingredients and deviations from the 'iron rules' of human conduct or organizational hierarchy dies hard, but the concepts of 'local knowledge', 'tacit knowledge' and the 'knowledge-creating company' begin to gain currency in spite of attempts to radically eliminate 'collective object solutions' from cultural studies. Neither a political description of an institutional context nor a sociological analysis of organizational constraints can offer a privileged view of human behaviour in general. Neither a humanist interpretation of social background nor a symbolic analysis of cultural heritage can open a royal road to predictions about human plans. Neither psychological analysis of individual personalities nor a biological theory of motivational anchors can offer the last resort, the ultimate foundation, on which the best and the brightest theoretical knowledge about what we do when we set out to do what we want to do could be built. Representatives of all these different methodological schools have to accept a certain form of a cognitive democracy under which they can argue their superiority, but they cannot impose it.

Luckily, we are not looking for the best and the brightest. *Finding a civilized way and a language to disagree about the best and the brightest also contributes to the growth of objective knowledge. In fact, in an open society it is the best way to cultivate cultural and cross-cultural competence.* We usually want to answer the question about cultural competence in general (for instance What is it? What is the best way of recycling it? Upgrading it? Can we compare it to software in our heads? What can we do with it? Can we exchange it?), and organizational cultures in particular (What do they mean? How do they change? How do they fit with larger cultural environments? How are they learned? Is enhanced learning a token of a successful organizational culture?).

I would like to consider cross-cultural competence as a backpack or a toolkit all learning individuals assemble, if they have to deal with different cultural softwares in one place (for instance in a multicultural workplace) and at once. They learn because they have to move among different cultures and subcultures (it happens more often than we realize, and we realize more often than we admit). Let us see if we can acquire cross-cultural competence and if we can do so in the same way as we acquire other types of competence, for instance, when we learn to understand and speak foreign languages. Maybe by asking how we learn it we shall gain insight into what it means as means.

3 Meanings: learning cultural codes as languages

> We must learn the culture just as we must learn its language, and we must learn it in the same way; by learning how to participate in meaningful practices.
>
> (John Hooker)[5]

Individuals and societies do not cross the cultural bridge for free. There is a toll booth. No matter whether they want to reflect on ends or to acquire means, they have to learn about meanings and ways of making sense. They have to learn how to cross the bridge, how to use it. Learning is often compared to breaking a code of linguistic and behavioural conduct. That is an oversimplification, because learning the first natural language is actually a complex process, which we do not fully understand. Learning a language is necessary for starting to think and for developing cultural competence, but it is not sufficient. One has to communicate increasingly complex messages to others and successfully respond to theirs. One has to function in a society, enter meaningful interactions and form significant relationships. Moreover, the expression 'breaking a code' smells of a spy's candid camera (stealing a code invented by an enemy) and of a scientist's laboratory (stealing a code hidden among nature's sensory appearances). It evokes an aggressive image of a cognitive superman shoving obstacles out of the way, cracking the shell of conduct and spooning the hidden treasure of meaning out for general use. Moreover, the concept of a code itself is not very clear.

In biochemistry one speaks of a genetic code, which has to be cracked in order to allow scientists to design genetic engineering or re-engineering programmes. In this genetic metaphor, a code would be some hidden 'core' sequence of elements (of chromosomes, for instance), determining the meaning and form of protein molecules, which, in turn, would produce organisms, which, in turn, would then demonstrate some verbal and behavioural conduct (let us mercifully gloss over a number of serious simplifications in this view of 'breaking' the genetic 'code of life'). The search for an equivalent of 'chromosome sequence' in human language played an important role in the first cognitive revolution in social sciences, which took place in the Sixties, under the influence of the linguists (especially de Saussure) and phoneticians making use of computers to detect hidden 'core binary oppositions' within each natural language's 'deep structure'.[6] Language is not the only example of a code; researchers in semiotics had tried to demonstrate that there were many other codes: traffic signals, card games, aesthetic rules, table manners, class taste, dress codes, etc. Ethnographers and cultural anthropologists also tried to 'break' the codes of customs and rituals: Levi-Strauss hoped for a reconstruction of a universal 'key' to cultural classifications and taboos (speaking of the universal distinctions between 'the raw' and 'the cooked'). Codes made a career as meanings agreed upon and attached to some symbols. What one usually means is that acts of verbal and behavioural conduct are performances on a social stage, and they will not succeed if they are not understood (i.e. if no one has a clue as to how their meaning has been 'coded'). Therefore individuals playing on social stages follow certain rules, blueprints, scripts, instructions, scenarios, schemas, and plans, prompted by various codes. These codes, often conceptualized as symbolic structures, are, in turn, related to social structures, and change along with them. One does not break any code once and for all: breaking it means opening a long series of interpretations and re-interpretations. In fact, in view of the formidable complexity of cultural competence, learning is more often than not a joint venture with many local partners, and an exercise in patience, humility and negotiated interpretation of meaning. Sharing mental models does not stop at a single agreement; learning (including learning to learn) is, indeed, a permanent, lifelong activity.

Learning a language, learning how to dance or mastering table manners are all examples of more narrowly defined tasks than breaking the code of a different culture. In becoming a fluent speaker of a foreign language, one masters only a verbal channel of social interaction and intercultural communication. It is very important, highly significant, but it is not the only one, especially in highly contextualized, collectivist cultures. Breaking the code of culture means being able to recognize the context, to interpret ambiguities. In learning how to dance, one breaks the code of behaviour that is limited to a dance floor. Breaking the code of culture means being able to dance in the streets, board rooms, everywhere. Mastering table manners allows one to perform faultlessly only in a limited range of situations: formal dinners, elegant receptions, consuming meals together with others. Breaking a code of culture means being able to perform faultlessly and gracefully in an office, at a party and in a classroom. To put it in a nutshell: having 'broken' the code of a given culture, one should be able to generate creative statements and perform acceptable acts in social situations one has never faced before.

'Breaking' the codes of other cultures (or rather, reconstructing their 'inner logic') is a much more complex task than mastering one of the channels of communication, even one as sophisticated and basic as a natural language. In spite of having excellent table manners, one may find oneself in a situation, when cross-cultural competence advises to drop these manners, for instance, to avoid irritating one's partners with a snobbish display of an upper-class upbringing. The code of social tact is elevated above the code of table manners. One has to compare and shuffle these codes at all times in order to come up with an understanding of some behaviours or in order to choose how to behave under given circumstances. There are many codes woven together, and most of them have to be 'cracked' simultaneously if we are to make sense of what people do and what they mean. A formidable task – but accomplished often enough to secure increasing co-operation among increasingly distant cultural communities.

The fact that breaking the code of a hidden language of interpersonal interaction happens so often could be seen as empirical evidence that intensified interaction between culturally distant individuals and groups can lead to a successful bi-cultural or cross-cultural competence. This evidence is not intuitively obvious, since our social communication is heavily influenced by the dramatic requirements of the media. The media tend to select cases of a clash of cultures, because they are more picturesque, while glossing over much more numerous cases of successful cross-cultural communication. Cassandra-like warnings that a mega-clash of civilizations is nigh sell better than a report that foreigners are warmly accepted and adapt themselves successfully. Cassandra-like warnings that hedonism, consumption and exploitation of nature will inevitably result in the break-down of the western civilization sell better than a report on improvement in the ethical conduct of an organization, an introduction of sustainability audits or facilitating of dialogues in the workplace. 'Dark age ahead' (cf. Jacobs, 2004) attracts more attention than a more balanced list of those 'pillars' of our society that show signs of fatigue, decay or need for maintenance (e.g. higher education, self-regulation of the learned professions).

Cultural misunderstandings are more 'dramatic' – tragic or comic – and thus attract more attention than business as usual. Struggles, quarrels, angry demonstrations, open hostilities always get more coverage at the expense of cases of successful cross-cultural dialogue and competence. Misunderstanding, friction, conflict, hostilities offer more exciting images and sharper contrasts than do stories about successful co-operation and overcoming of differences. Terrorists make exciting news and attract more viewers than committed citizens patiently cultivating a just community against overwhelming odds. A clash of civilization attracts more attention to Islamic fundamentalists than an emergence of a modern TV station in Arabic as part of the modernization efforts in the Arab world. Threat of a Hispanic *reconquista* of the southern states of the US sells better than a story of successful integration of bilingual immigrants in these states' economies.

Nevertheless, modern mass media notwithstanding, successful cross-cultural co-operation is on the increase. The conflict between Greenpeace and Shell over the Brent Spar oil platform in the North Sea lasted a few months, while the co-operative platform they established afterwards continued working for years and finds many imitators to the present day. Both parties learned: Greenpeace, that it does not pay to mix too much ideology in a public presentation of a scientific research report on potential environmental impact; Shell, that it does not pay to ignore NGOs and public opinion, to make deals only with political elites and to view each country as an independent operational theatre. The general public learned that large corporations can be subjected to critical scrutiny in the media in spite of commercial clout in advertising. Individuals in both organizations learned, first by clashing with a totally foreign culture, and then slowly by establishing dialogue and learning more about the foreign culture.

In the beginning, however, there was a cultural shock. Shell appeared as an embodiment of the ideology of managerialism, Greenpeace as a symbol of an informal, grass-roots, alternative 'nest' of social movements and protest actions. A 'corporate bureaucrat' faced an 'alternative hippy'. Only when media attention petered out and the oil platform ended up, uneventfully, in a Norwegian fjord, did both parties begin to reflect on their own organizational cultures, slowly becoming aware that organizational culture not only guides them, but blinds them as well. *They stopped taking their own organizational cultures for granted.*

Their experience has been the lot of millions of expatriates, exiles, tourists, and immigrants. Let us imagine this situation, which has become a commonplace for the upper and middle classes of all contemporary societies, and for all classes of the most affluent ones (i.e. for all those who travel, be it only to cheap summer resorts). One comes to a foreign country, strange city, unknown organization. Communication skills have to be honed, the ability to succeed in a different environment developed. One does not speak the language, does not understand local customs, written and unwritten rules, or religious taboos. Tolerance for ambiguity, empathy, flexibility, and open-mindedness become indispensable. One makes a *faux pas*. Learning and tolerance gain importance. Unsuspected meanings are attributed to our behaviour. Mental models of our rudeness emerge. Sinister motives are hinted at. We realize that something went wrong but are at a loss as to our actual offence. It is a painful experience. Everybody around seems to be following some grammar of motives, some hidden code, some stage instructions, some invisible blueprint for performing in encounters with others. One begins to think about this code. It must be learned. Otherwise, the pain of *faux pas*, of misunderstanding and of cultural shock cannot be avoided. Slowly but surely, by trial, error, instruction and imitation, one learns how to avoid *faux pas*, then how to behave and speak so that the others accept it. One learns to learn about contexts and interpretation, to do the balancing act:

> The list [of cross-cultural competencies – SM] covers knowledge (for example, cultural knowledge), skills (for example, communication skills), abilities (for example, ability to succeed in multiple and diverse environments), as well as dispositional traits (for example, empathy and open-mindedness). Second, there is a common assumption of 'the more of these, the better'. But some practitioners hold the view that in operating across cultures, the valuable skills are in balancing and reconciling competencies, not in having extremely large amounts of one or the other. It is clear that operating internationally, for instance, that flexibility is good – but if all one does is to be flexible, how does one know where to draw a line, for example where ethical standards differ across cultures? It seems, therefore, that it would be more useful that training in cultural intelligence should produce individuals who understand when it is culturally appropriate in that culture to be flexible, and when not to be.
>
> (Earley, Ang, 2003, 264)

If one arrives in a different cultural environment with children, adults learn from them. Expatriates' children develop a dual cultural identity: they become fluent in the culture of their school peers and the language of a host country. They are also fluent in the culture of their parents and speak their mother tongue. In both cultures they can expertly use non-verbal communication forms: kinesics (gestures, touch, facial expressions), chronemics (time), proxemics (personal and social space), etc.

What has happened? How did they arrive at a competence that allows them to move freely in a foreign culture, interact with others, take hints at all levels, express themselves? How did children manage to nurse a little Tower of Babel within their conscious minds and unconscious personalities, easily switching between various languages and cultures? How did the activists of Greenpeace and corporate officials of Shell manage to nurse understanding of one another? How do they recognize hints, which allow them to determine to which culture they should quickly switch, which codes they should follow?

In educated common-sense explanations we answer this question by saying that a successfully integrated individual has internalized the norms of conduct, i.e. managed to break the code of norms and knows which ones to apply in a given context, so that his or her behaviour is acceptable to native speakers and 'doers' of a host culture. Children do it tacitly and spontaneously. Expatriate managers have to follow formal courses and ask for expert advice.[7] However, both children and adults are perfectly able to learn cultural codes and to master different grammars of motives – different, that is, from the ones they have been born into. When asked how they accomplish it, they often compare their knowledge and skills in moving around in a different culture to fluency in a foreign language. This should not come as a surprise, because learning cultural codes has often been compared by teachers, instructors, journalists and commentators to learning a language.

This 'linguistic turn' in explaining and understanding cultures indeed did not come as a surprise. Successful deciphering of ancient inscriptions by archaeologists, reconstruction of lost languages by linguistic historians, cracking of enemy coding patterns by counter-intelligence scientists, all such cases of successful breaking of an unknown code spoke to the imagination. Moreover, formal studies of languages, especially of phonetics, have been greatly facilitated by the increasing use of computers. Advances in linguistics led to a popular belief that in order to explain linguistic competence, one should break the code of the black box of every individual's linguistic competence. The influential concept of 'generative grammar', devised by Noam Chomsky, was an attempt to demonstrate that one can construct such a box, which then could serve as a formal model of everybody's linguistic or cultural competence. This black box generating grammatically correct sentences merits attention not only because of its author's theoretical works on structure of human languages. Chomsky had also revived the philosophical concept of 'innate ideas'. These are the ideas we are born with, not nurtured into; ideas that resemble templates we activate as we start experiencing our environment. Along with many other linguists, researchers interested in semiotics and 'structuralists', he had contributed to the shift in the Sixties from 'behaviourism' to 'mentalism' in the social sciences. Behaviourists assumed that ways of attributing meanings to gestures and objects are mostly learned in direct individual experience, so we have to observe individuals and describe their experiences. Mentalists assumed that we are, at least partly, born with some device for generating meanings, so we also have to interpret and 'reconstruct'. From the perspective of the next, 21st century, one might say that this structuralist–mentalist turn, that soon filtered through the academic world, was the first attempt at a cognitive revolution. It had been linked to the research carried out by Chomsky on structural linguistics, transformational grammar and the Cartesian 'idea' of innate ideas. Chomsky went on to a public discussion with Jean Piaget on the acquisition of linguistic skill by children, but moved from the research community in mid-career in order to devote much of his efforts to political and social criticism of the US political establishment and its domestic and international policies (one of his best known books was *Manufacturing Consent. The Political Economy of the Mass Media*, Chomsky, Herman, 1988, and many others followed).

According to the 'behaviourists', the best way to study language is to observe verbal and physical behaviour, to compare notes and to make generalizations. Looking for founding fathers in philosophy, behaviourists claim that Locke was right. Children are born with the clean slate of a newly-formed mind – a 'tabula rasa' – on which information provided by our senses is recorded as a child grows. Because the senses write on this clean slate, one should study what passes through the senses and stimulates them, noting responses. This means studying an individual's growing experience in order to explain the origins of thoughts and deeds. However, according to 'mentalism', children are born with innate ideas, i.e. with a universal 'core' of any natural language they might get in touch with. They do not wait passively to register whatever the senses might bring in. This is why every child is perfectly capable of adjusting and tuning this 'core' to the variety of human language spoken in its nearest environment. One should not focus on studying concrete experiences, the subsequent 'notes' jotted on the *tabula rasa* of the mind. One should focus on the slate itself, because it is by no means 'clean': it contains a black box and we should be interested in how this box works in all possible contexts. The best way to study universal 'cores' present in every natural language is to reconstruct the deep structure present in every native speaker's competence, i.e. the essentials of a universal grammar. Every individual mind has this 'core', this inborn black box of potential linguistic competence, the holder of a 'universal grammar' that is always ready to be triggered into fluency in any native language. This is why we are able to learn a language at all, to learn foreign languages and to preserve this ability to learn for most of our lives. Not surprisingly, one of Chomsky's books was entitled *Cartesian Linguistics*. There is a ghost in a machine, but it is not a mind trapped inside a body. It is a black box of linguistic and cultural competence located in our mind/brain. Our mind switches this black box on and tunes it in, depending on the situation registered by our senses, but interpreted in this black box of our linguistic competence. A child develops its linguistic competence and ability to generate more complex and relevant sentences with every new situation and new utterance. At the same time, the child also hones its ability to think in increasingly abstract terms and to evaluate according to increasingly universal ethical norms. This is how humans learn to make sense of the world and to attribute increasingly sophisticated meanings to their words and acts.

Let us note that with this concept of linguistic competence developed with the help of an inborn 'black box', human evolution acquires a discreet sense of direction. Thinking can proceed in increasingly abstract concepts (and it does, according to Piaget, who studied the development of abstract thinking in children). Evaluating can be done with increasingly universal criteria (and it is, according to Kohlberg, who studied the stages of moral growth). We are born with black boxes, but black boxes can be improved and developed (and they are, leading us towards Popper's increasingly 'objective knowledge'). We are born with the black box of core cognitive competence, but in human societies we learn to cultivate it in ways that allows us to make the most out of this cognitive competence. We are born within concrete environments but we can simulate, envision and design virtual ones. We side with our kin and care about in-groups, but we are able to write the universal declaration of human rights and thus overcome the limitations and restrictions of an in-group. This is our evolutionary definition: *Homo sapiens*, a cognitively fluent, learning, thinking, passionate, fair, knowledge-able, generalizing animal with universalistic ambitions and a fair chance of historical improvement by overcoming local constraints. This is what we could say about the evolution of human societies – so far: from a sequence of Towers of Babel towards a bridge of Babel.

We also experience emotions (somewhat lower and cruder evolutionary devices), which motivate us; we enter relations (somewhat more complex social networks and structures), which turn us into team players and collaborative agents – the mentalists concede that much. However, they also claim that at the core of our species identity there is a cognitive competence, of which the linguistic one is the best illustration. To be true to our human nature and destiny, claim the mentalists who engineered a second, more modest cognitive revolution in the social sciences of the 1990s, we should focus on cognition. First comes cognition, then moral sentiments and social relations. True, in the course of the evolution of human species, moral sentiments, cloaked in mythology and religion, came first, but we have managed to notice what pays in the long evolutionary run and thus elevated cognition above moral sentiments. We have managed to do so because scientific and scholarly communities succeeded in collecting, describing and systematically analysing patterns of 'distribution of shared individual cognitions and representations', so that we stand a chance 'to understand the social factors, bundles of which we often call culture, that cause certain patterns of agreement and disagreement' (Ross, 2004, 7–8).[8]

It is important to understand that all our definitions of culture are heavily influenced by these patterns of agreement and disagreement, which press scientific communities' points of view into educated minds, no matter which particular research community and which paradigm happens to be dominant at the time.

It is also important to understand that all these cognitive definitions of culture are limited. First, they assume that emotions and relations are secondary, while cognitive self-definition and identity are primary. This is not necessarily true, because our moral sentiments and experienced relationships can influence our cognitive strategies and thus play a much more fundamental and leading role in determining our cognitive choices. Second, they assume that these cognitive definitions are orderly placed within our minds and allow us to build a single dominant identity. This is not necessarily true because single individuals can hold multiple or overlapping identities, experience passionate allegiances, invent elective affinities, all of them in a state of flux, some of them triggered by unexpected circumstances and events. But what does it mean if we accept these simplifications anyway?

It means, among other things, that we have decided to support a single ruling metaphor of a conscious individual agent making independent cognitive choices and thus embodying the world's highest achievable rationality.[9] We have tacitly rejected other available metaphors we might live by. A model of a rational subject, a calculating, rational *Homo economicus*, has been selected at the expense of a *Homo sociologicus* or *Homo sentiens*, in spite of the fact that in order to understand ends, means and meanings of culture and action we require access to all three conceptualizations of a human agent. Perceived as *Homo economicus*, a man or woman calculates and makes choices according to the principles of instrumental rationality (matching means to ends). Perceived as *Homo sociologicus* he or she follows social norms reflecting his or her embeddedness in groups and communities (matching ends–means mixes to one another). Perceived as *Homo sentiens*, he or she expresses his or her emotional identity and moral concerns (matching ends to other ends, experiencing their implementation). While most social scientists focus on *Homo economicus*, others, for instance sociologists, try to bring *Homo sociologicus* to academic attention. Still others, for instance researchers of cross-cultural differences and representatives of cultural studies are slowly beginning to assist visual artists, novelists, or film directors as students of *Homo sentiens*.[10] Who knows, maybe as their work advances, the toolkits of cross-cultural competence will become more sophisticated, user-friendly, and individually and locally customized? We shall return to this question in the concluding remarks to this chapter.

Their efforts, however, have only just begun to have an impact on the social sciences in general and the managerial sciences in particular. Mainstream research and popular literature in managerial studies still focuses on a rational agent, *Homo economicus*. This *Homo economicus* is a walking mind that calculates rational choices, though in a slightly bounded – limited

– way. This focus means that we agree to suspend disbelief and criticism. A simplified view of *Homo sapiens* as a thinking, learning, knowledgeable social animal, producing culture under the scientific management of academic communities and democratically controlled government bureaucracies (and granted some right to satisfy emotional and culturally defined needs on the side), is incomplete.

However, it is also very helpful (especially for pragmatic managers) just because of its simplicity. It is also very desirable because of its ideological compatibility with 'managerialism' (it is easier to sell to the top managers than more – potentially – subversive or simply egalitarian views). Simplicity helps in managerial planning. It helps to see culture as a wrapping around neatly communicated knowledge, a flavour added to core knowledge, an idiom in which more basic truths (calculated decisions) have been expressed. It helps to see culture as a bridge to collective managerial control of nature, society and individual. This is why a simplified view of the calculations of individual and of culture (that merely adds local flavour to global rationality or helps rational managers create a corporate *esprit de corps*) is tacitly assumed by most educators and educated people. It provides a scientifically legitimated cornerstone of the 'educated common sense'. This is what culture means to us. We talk about 'educated' and 'common' sense because in developed societies almost all citizens have gained access to education, which means that a significant part of their learning is socially designed, planned, organized, managed, stratified, and controlled.

One of the recent strategies for dealing with these matters without offending the ruling rational choice theoreticians (of *Homo economicus*) is the attempt to proliferate various sub-concepts of the concept of intelligence. *Emotional* intelligence has been invented in order to supply a non-cognitive kind, and produced at least one bestseller. Again, *cultural* intelligence has been introduced in order to help:

> figure out the appropriate rules and implications for behaviour in a new cultural context. Cognizing and knowledge operate at a meta-level of organizing and this is the key to cultural adjustment and enactment. . . . High CQ [cultural intelligence – SM] people are able to come into a radically unfamiliar social environment and figure out how to learn appropriate cues to attend in order to figure out what is actually happening within a culture. . . . It means looking at a new cultural setting afresh without imposing a number of existing ideas about what things must mean or how one needs to operate to proceed.
>
> (Earley, Ang, 2003, 18)

Learning in general, and learning cultural codes in particular, usually takes place in large bureaucratic institutions disseminating scientifically produced knowledge. Knowledge approved by producers (scientists) and disseminators (politicians) alike is disseminated in a standardized context of educational institutions. The extraordinarily explosive growth of educational institutions, which administer and manage organized learning to almost all individuals in almost all phases of their lives, is one of the least-studied and least-understood evolutionary inventions of human societies. It has profoundly changed the way we examine and explain or interpret what we are doing, the way we attribute meanings to our actions. Teaching based on a vision of *Homo economicus*, calculating man, is bound to neglect social relations and emotional bonds, to provide a one-sided cultural competence. It is also bound to inhibit criticism of educational institutions, thus protecting their managerial elites at the expense of everybody else. This has already happened. For instance, the democratic reforms of educational institutions, that had been achieved by the student protesters of the 1960s were largely neutralized in the 1990s. Managerial efficiency replaced academic democracy. No wonder we are barely aware of the processes triggered within student populations during their interactions within educational institutions. If relations and emotions are secondary and cognitive training comes first, asking about power struggles or emotional climates appears irrelevant.

Needless to say, it is not. Ends, means and meanings of culture are coloured by the cognitive, relational and emotional experiences of students and teachers alike. What happens to the knowledge teachers disseminate and students acquire? How do they frame and reframe it in a curriculum? How does their framing influence the meanings of knowledge? After all, knowledge students acquire in educational institutions is subsequently customized, applied, adapted, twisted, re-interpreted, re-negotiated, changed, and used in many different contexts. Do students realize how much the form and content of their courses depend on obscure power struggles within academic communities? Do they realize the amount of reprocessing, recycling and repackaging of knowledge involved in curricular decisions? Do they understand the production of knowledge they acquire? Are they aware of the twists and turns it had to pass through before entering their memories? Do they realize that knowledge is only one of the ingredients in individually acquired cultural competence? It is a collectively developed, social, organizational, and individual resource inventory, which is socially maintained and recorded. However, neither recording nor maintenance of this domain of our competence is uncontroversial. Theories should have price tags, packaging, consumer warnings, bulleted one-liners, update certificates, methodologies, ingredients listed on the package, applications, trade-off descriptions, etc. What cultural knowledge, then, becomes the core competence of educated individuals? What, quite literally, does it mean? How meaningful is it for the evolution, survival and change of individuals, groups and organizations? In sum, what is cultural and cross-cultural competence and how does it work in contemporary organizations?

4 Ends, means and meanings of culture: a language connection

Metaphors connected to language and to language-learning are often used in cultural studies and in theoretical explanations of cross-cultural competence. They have been given a new lease of life due to the development of formal and structural linguistics, supported by computer technology. Computers and bureaucracies drove the linguistic turn in cultural studies, prompting a search for linguistic universals.[11] Science was supposed to deliver 'black boxes' of cultural, linguistic, technological, and any other competence necessary to run complex organizations and technologies. In order to run them successfully, we have developed complex professional bureaucracies. Most of us grow up and spend our working lives in bureaucracies. Bureaucratic organizations favour culture's cognitive component and prefer the theoretical products of scientific communities. Bureaucratic choices are best legitimized by rational explanations that claim objective status. Hence the influence of scientific calculations on ends, means and meanings of contemporary culture in a society dominated by large bureaucratic organizations. However, talking scientific language, bureaucracies have to accept the mutability of scientific knowledge, due both to the changes in ruling orthodoxies and to the rearrangement of the 'regimes' for knowledge production (different mixes of corporate laboratories, university academic departments, political regulations, economic incentives and military projects). Each new recipe for producing scientific knowledge and each new phase in the development of these recipes requires, for instance, another kind of dominating producer: a corporate laboratory, an elite research university or a global network of research projects financed by a globally operating branch of industry (biochemical, pharmaceutical, etc.).[12] Another language has to be constructed for education. The history of science has to be rewritten and the view of progress re-adjusted. Another set of textbooks for students, another set of mental models for their teachers, another set of philosophies of science for research communities and for the educated public have to be developed. Finally, another alignment of the main institutional actors mentioned above has to be completed.

Evolutionary changes (the gradual shift from physics to biology as the most prestigious discipline) and revolutionary breakthroughs (qualitative research methods growing at the interfaces between science and consulting, teaching and management) are difficult to explain. Having accepted the superiority of scientifically produced knowledge, members of bureaucratic organizations must also suffer the consequences of hidden injuries from long-standing philosophical (the mind–body duality), methodological (quantitative–qualitative research) or paradigmatic (behaviourist–mentalist) divisions, or accept diversification of knowledge producing institutions and their historically changeable configurations.

This is not the end of the mutability of scientifically produced knowledge. It has to be applied. We apply it in order to attain our individual and collective ends. The ends of human actions, either within these organizations or outside of them, are determined according to the core values of our cultural software, but choices are triggered by local circumstances. The means of human actions are selected from inventories and toolkits listed in our cultural software as norms and rules, but preferences vary and are contingent. Behaviour and artefacts result from individual choices and matches between values and norms, but these matches are envisaged in the light of cultural interpretations.

Cultural software in our minds develops at all times: when we access objective knowledge, when we subjectively interpret it and when we inter-subjectively apply it.

Objective knowledge is the core component of culture in complex and open societies. It is produced, recorded, maintained, and disseminated by bureaucratic organizations. These organizations work via routines, but are open to periodical re-engineering. The culture they produce helps complex societies survive and reflect on their evolution. Culture may, as we have seen, be compared to a bridge of Babel. Like the Tower of Babel, it is built by individuals speaking different languages and quarrelling about their merits. Unlike the Tower of Babel, however, this bridge ultimately brings people together, in spite of their differences. This bridging becomes possible when individuals develop cross-cultural competence, the ability to understand and overcome differences in cultural software. Because the scientific community contributes most to culture's core component, its focus on breaking cognitive codes has resulted in relative neglect of relational (for instance, political) and emotional (partly unconscious) ones in managerial knowledge (though not in managerial practice). However, cultural competence requires the ability to break the codes of all three at once and to compare them. Social context and emotional climate shape us and are shaped by our actions as much as our thoughts. The ability to play three games – breaking the cognitive, relational and emotional codes and comparing them – all at once, can be called a cross-cultural competence. It is not easily acquired. Among many popular myths in the managerial sciences, the one expressed by McNamara, who said that running the Department of Defense is no different from managing the Ford Motor Company or the Catholic Church (i.e. all can be led with the same managerial expertise) – dies hardest. Nevertheless, it does die. Linguists and sociolinguists are trying to develop a theory of *cultural scripts* (a theory of culture-dependent, learned expectations), which has been taken over by organizational scientists and economists analysing the concept of social capital, organizational learning and 'trust'.[13] Sociologists and social psychologists, cultural anthropologists and political scientists are trying to develop theories of interaction rituals accounting for code-seeking programmes and 'the cultural turn' (cf. Collins, 2004). One additional advantage of developing cross-cultural competence is that it allows us to see more clearly how complex and internally differentiated organizational cultures are, and to how many uses can they be put by an organization's members:

> Organizational cultures are best understood not as unitary wholes or as stable sets of subcultures, but as mixtures of cultural manifestations of different levels and kinds. Even in seemingly homogeneous and stable organizations such as universities, cultural configurations are multiple, complex and shifting. People are connected to different degrees with organization, sub-organization unit, profession, gender, class, ethnic group, nation, etc., cultures overlap in an organizational setting and are rarely manifested in pure form. Sometimes these variations and dynamics are created by changing external circumstances of organizations and in particular how these are constructed within an organization. Sometimes internal processes trigger reactions and social groupings bringing forward a particular cultural configuration, not earlier salient.
>
> (Alvesson, 2002, 190–1)

Nothing illustrates cross-cultural competence of professional bureaucracy better than an action undertaken in the face of organizational change imposed from the outside and sabotaged from the inside by competent professionals. Let us turn to a case of such an action. Incidentally, the concerted action of this professional bureaucracy as a whole clearly indicates that reducing cross-cultural competence to individualist concepts, for instance cultural intelligence, leaves us at a loss as far as explanation of concerted, collective action based on shared values goes.

5 Professional bureaucracy in action: the case of the BBC [with Martin Harris and Victoria Wegg-Prosser]

The British Broadcasting Corporation (BBC) is a very large and complex organization in British society. Its Home Service produces cultural content and runs the medium through which this content is disseminated. It is a large professional bureaucracy of 21,000 employees. Externally, the BBC is known to most of the world's TV viewers as a supplier of high-quality programmes in the language of choice of international co-operation. Sheltered by political, economic and legal protection for many years, its professional bureaucracy developed a strong corporate culture and considerable self-confidence. The BBC differs from commercial TV stations because it preserved some degree of autonomy from market pressures (it is not as dependent on advertising revenue as are commercial TV channels). On the other hand, it did not become a multimedia extension of the executive branch. It is not a propaganda machine of government institutions. The BBC preserved relative autonomy from political parties and to a certain extent from government pressures (at least compared to the other TV companies in Europe and in the US). In short, the BBC has become one of the world's largest media establishments ('cultural bureaucracies') run by a managerial elite ('cultural bureaucrats'), whose members see their distinctive cultural (and cross-cultural, mediating) competence as a resource in resisting the pressures of the market and of the state, and in representing the impartial fourth estate ('the light of reason', 'public opinion').

Pressure from state and market was steadily mounting in the late 1980s and early 1990s. Technologically speaking, the flexibility and ubiquity of new information and communication technologies and digital multimedia required a major investment in telecommunications and digital technologies in order to stay on-line as well as on the TV screen and in the aether. This led to pressure on the BBC to modernize in order to retain a competitive edge in future. Politically speaking, the ideology of managerialism and of curbing excessive spending on the part of public institutions by subjecting them to the financial discipline of commercial companies has become part of the neo-liberal ideological offensive of conservative governments. The state has not only given up its monopoly on the media market. Control of the media has purposefully been undermined by the emergence of new private companies with global (Murdoch) or national (Berlusconi) reach, which had been encouraged by liberal governments. Public bureaucracies have also lost ground through the introduction of conservative, neo-liberal deregulation. For instance, the UK Conservative government had already encouraged independent producers' access to the BBC by granting them rights to a 25 per cent share of BBC programme orders as early as 1986. In the mid 1990s, the BBC underwent a complex and highly ambiguous process of restructuring, which was designed by its top managers to facilitate the conversion to digital broadcasting and to become a more profitable player on the media market.

Marketization and *digitalization* were official targets. They were considered necessary for restructuring this large and complex public institution led by a strong cultural bureaucracy. The latter was supposed to lead an organizational change with the following key expected outcomes: increased accountability, reduced bureaucracy, ongoing internal (over)capacity reduction, competitive use of external resources and subcontractors, programme budgeting in 'full cash costs'. The whole project was expressed in the fashionable language of business process re-engineering and organizational rejuvenation or renewal.

However, in spite of external, primarily political pressure to change, the actual implementation of change was handed over to the very cultural bureaucracy that was supposed to be the object of change. The same individuals who had been sheltered from competition for so long had now to become cash-conscious, self-critical (self-reducing) and subjected to increased market discipline. In other words, leading the change process that should have resulted in weakening the bureaucracy's power was the very same cultural bureaucracy whose excessive power triggered the whole change project in the first place. No wonder members of the BBC's bureaucracy were busy defending its (their) power rather than abandoning it. 'Officials' were expected to design their own eventual phasing out, and the removal of those who failed to turn into 'managers'. They were supposed to implement the Producer Choice Project and by doing so to wither away as a professional elite.

The Producer Choice Project was the name given to a trading system based on an internal market within the BBC in 1991–4. It was imposed on the BBC by the Director General, John Birt, as a business process re-engineering project in the first two years of his directorship (1993–6). It was instituted in order to create a more flexible organization, which would be capable of managing its resources in a much more efficient manner. Before its introduction, creators of a broadcast programme did not have to choose producers and producers could not choose between subcontractors; allocating orders to technical crews on the BBC's payroll was a matter of a bureaucratic choice, not a commercially motivated decision. According to the managerialist ideology of the Conservative government of the period, the introduction of a disaggregated, networked, loosely connected organizational form would help in finding out what the costs of production services were and in driving them down (by avoiding over-resourcing). Producer Choice was designed to enable the BBC to adapt to an emergent, changing environment. On the outside this involved mainly multimedia digital technologies and competition among content providers. On the inside the aim was to reduce bureaucratic inefficiencies by enhancing managerial focus on commercial transparency. Subcontractors' costs could be compared, while costs of the technical crews on the BBC's payroll remained hidden within the larger bureaucratic structure. Separating broadcasting from production and letting the internal market work was supposed to send a signal to the government: that the BBC was indeed changing, streamlining its operations, producing more with less resources and at lower cost and generally speaking, successfully implementing the Producer Choice project.

However, the invisible hand of the authentic market, which, according to the liberal doctrine of the Conservative government should have guided market-oriented changes within the organizational structure of the BBC, turned out to be the quite visible, very bureaucratic and rationalist hand of the managerial planner. The paradox was obvious: while the project was based on a *liberal belief* in the invisible hand of the market, its top–down imposition by political authorities meant that it was bound to be *bureaucratically implemented*. Top managers in the BBC could thus create a *quasi-market* for parts of their organization, but they never decentralized vital decision-making and never gave up the assumption that internal markets designed and implemented in this way were in fact inferior – less efficient – to the former bureaucratic mechanisms they were supposed to replace. Their staff (ca. 21,000 employees in five 'directorates' – News and Current Affairs, Television, Radio, Regions, Resources) shared this belief. Their combined, culturally embedded and institutionally versatile resistance profoundly undermined the project's original goals (though data produced for bureaucratic reports superficially conformed to the targets set in the change agenda).

Actual participation of employees in the restructuring programme was thus somewhat different from that envisaged by top managers and external consultants. The restructuring projects had been adopted and paid lip service to, but the goals and interests of top and middle managers, their cultural values and situated practices were too deeply embedded within the BBC not to influence the outcome of the transformation.

First, they were supposed to provide raw data for the accounting audit conducted by external consultants in order to benchmark the output efficiency – but by exercising discretion, they maintained a certain degree of control over the input to consultants' calculations. Second, they were supposed to re-group into business units, which had to trade with the other business units and break even or face bankruptcy – but by negotiating informal terms of trade between heads of new business units, they could preserve former bureaucratic solidarity in internal pricing and billing practices. Third, by mixing full cash cost analysis with the more elusive over-heads in transfer pricing policies, BBC managers managed to protect some services from 'market forces' (in spite of the rhetoric of full cash costs). Fourth, pressure to reduce staff and to become a smaller, less bureaucratic organization were resisted. As a result, the BBC remained Europe's largest single broadcaster and managed to retain 75 per cent of its production core intact. Negotiating by contract and marketization were resisted. Measurement of contractual relations turned out to be difficult, while free choice of producers could not be exercised because the BBC had limited 'cash' resources during the implementation phase and made use of cross-subsidies from its publicly funded activities. Generally speaking, experts conceded that: 'the BBC continued to operate as a well-run bureaucracy, adjusting itself, as it has always done, to prevailing enterprise orthodoxies' (Anthony Smith, President of Magdalen College, a former TV producer, and close to BBC affairs, in 1995).

Bureaucratic elites within the corporation turned out to have played the game of both embracing the change project and mediating the complex process of restructuring in a way that protected their positions and safeguarded the influence and stability of the very bureaucratic structures the change project was supposed to undermine. Cultural resistance to negotiating by contract, marketization, disaggregated production networks, and a top–down utopian view of technocratic organizational transformation proved to be too strong for the Producer Choice project. One of the ironies of the BBC case is the evident paradox that bureaucracies (cultural, academic, military, political) do play a central role in formal and informal network formation, in a variety of 'knowledge intensive' settings (hence the term 'cultural bureaucracy'). Their ability to function under different ideological regimes does not mean that members of these bureaucracies are willing to sacrifice their positions in formal organizational structures and to promote loosely structured, disaggregated, networked business units exploiting purely commercial advantages on an open market (even if they formally agree to do so by embracing the ideology of change). In fact, they can be the most successful enemies of a transition from bureaucracies to networks, defending the spirit of managerialism (anchored in power and control) against the letter of its liberal ideology (anchored in unleashing creativity and safeguarding competition). Members of a cultural bureaucracy of the BBC accepted the ends of the project, matched them with means designed to fail in those aspects that were relevant to them, and conducted meaningful resistance to a top–down change programme while formally embracing, supporting and implementing it.

This is the story of the Producer Choice Project. They exploited the language connection by accepting the idiom of a neo-liberal market-oriented re-engineering, but subverted it via their skills in exploiting ambiguities and contingencies. There are reasons to suspect that they have not been exceptionally unique in these activities. Professional bureaucracies can follow the ideology of unleashing creativity and increasing market discipline, both apparently at the expense of a solid professional bureaucracy, while at the same time preserving vital hierarchies within the re-engineered networks. The old saying that contemporary organizations are networks floating on hierarchies acquires a new meaning in the case of one of Europe's largest cultural bureaucracies subjected to ideological transformations from the 'outside' (digitalization) and from 'above' (marketization) but capable of retaining control 'inside' (bureaucratization).

Successful resistance of the managerial elite of the BBC to the marketization and digitalization campaign offers an interesting clue for social scientists and politicians who want to understand the dynamics of post-communist societies in central and eastern Europe, as well as the two separate cases of Russia and China. In all three cases – the central European countries of Poland, the Czech Republic, Hungary, Slovakia, Bulgaria, and Romania, and the states formed out of former Yugoslavia, Albania, Ukraine, Moldavia, and Byelorussia and the three Baltic states, Lithuania, Latvia and Estonia, together with Russia and China, the former political power elite (top politicians, their younger protégés and the young generation of the secret service functionaries forming the invisible 'core' of the *nomenklatura*) managed to adopt the language of liberal democracy and the market economy, while at the same time preserving group privileges and securing a dominant position in economic, political and media activities. Interestingly, what we get is a system in which political and economic elites overlap due to the fact that political privilege becomes indispensable 'capital' that has to be invested in a new cycle of accumulation of capital and power in a professional bureaucracy.

Chapter 2

Clashing civilizations
The global connection

Attempts at governance, including global governance, are a natural result of increasing interdependence. They also help to create the conditions for further development of the networks of interdependence that are commonly referred to as globalization.

(Robert O. Keohane)[1]

I Cross-cultural aspects of globalization

Having discussed the meaning of culture as a language in which we express ourselves and through which we become aware of our ends, means and meanings, let us now examine culture as a 'navigator' of our actions. Culture can be viewed as practical, useful 'software', which helps generate blueprints for individual and collective action and which patterns our interactions. Individuals can modify blueprints they want to implement and adapt them to circumstances, but there are limits to their improvisations and innovations. We share some blueprints, we negotiate some, and we reject some. Broad and intensive contacts between individuals with different cultural software in their heads (and, consequently, different attitudes, habits, expectations, and patterns of action) can lead to co-operation, i.e. to successful planning and undertaking of actions together, but they can also impede co-operation and lead to its breakdown. Millions of successfully completed interactions inside and between complex societies demonstrate daily an overall 'compatibility' of our cultural softwares and an equally ubiquitous 'flexibility' in adjusting it to our changing needs. By enabling us to plan, predict and co-ordinate these frequent, complex and inter-dependent activities and interactions, our cultural software demonstrates its flexibility and our creativity in making use of it. The individuals co-operating rarely have the time and opportunity to analyse cross-cultural differences in depth. More often than not they use stereotypes to quickly label strangers, predict their expectations, prevent or limit conflicts, and bridge potentially damaging differences. Culture then functions as an inventory of simplified social labels ('logos'), which we pin on individuals and groups – the ones we recognize as somehow 'different', as 'the Others':

> To understand what stereotypes are it is useful to consider three prin-
> ciples which guide work on the social psychology of stereotyping . . .:
> (a) stereotypes are aids to explanation, (b) stereotypes are energy-saving
> devices, and (c) stereotypes are shared group beliefs. The first of these
> implies that stereotypes should form so as to help the perceiver to make
> sense of a situation, the second implies that stereotypes should form to
> reduce effort on the part of the perceiver, and the third implies that
> stereotypes should be formed in line with the accepted views or norms
> of social groups that the perceiver belongs to.
>
> (McGarthy *et al.*, 2002, 2)

Differences are perceived at different levels. Encountering a Muslim man or woman I know that he or she would celebrate Friday as we Christians celebrate Sunday as a holy day, and Ramadan instead of Christmas and Easter. I can reasonably expect that all of his or her roads lead to Mecca rather than Rome. On the other hand, I should be ready to adjust my stereo-type or even reject it altogether, if an educated professional and apparently 'Westernized' woman voluntarily begins to cover her head not because of a pressure from her religiously motivated family, but in order to compete against male professionals and feel safe in spite of being excluded by 'old boy' professional networks (which happens in Cairo). Likewise, I should suspend my labelling and stereotyping if, quite to the contrary, an apparently devoted, religious woman starts demonstrating Western clothing and uses head cover as a playful gadget rather than a religious symbol (which happens in Teheran, where well-educated women are challenging religious control of social life), or if journalists on an independent Arab TV station (Al-Jazzira) use religious imagery to convey their criticism of local political authoritarianism.

If an Arab woman tells me, for instance, that women covering their heads in public is an old prejudice, increasingly difficult to maintain and irrelevant in a modernizing society, I can conclude that she does not believe that *sharia* interpreted by conservative clerics should be the legal basis of civil society. If she concedes that one can pray once a week instead of five times a day, her cultural software may have been shaped more by studying in the US and working as a professional in Cairo or Teheran than by the religious background of her ethnic group. The fact that she had been born in an Islamic society may not be salient to her, nor, perhaps, to her family or company or both, and thus it may fail to shape her identity at all or shape it by her negative, critical attitude towards it. On the other hand, when facing the negative stereotyping of the Arabs in Western media and the paternalistic attitude of her Western partners, she may start to cultivate her Arab and even religious identity as means of safeguarding her pride and autonomy confronted by an external threat posed by Western arrogance.

Globalization opened us up to many more encounters with many more different kinds of cultural software, and since it continues to give rise to many more new stereotypes, we should consider their appearance and their relatively rapid change a symptom of our coping with these differences. Successful co-ordination and integration of complex activities allows for flexible adjustment of stereotypes and eventually for their replacement with a more differentiated, subtler view of different 'Others'. Stereotypes are useful for quick recognition; differentiated, regularly upgraded and 'customized', they are useful for long-term co-operation. Cultural 'software' integrates ('We, the people of . . .) and differentiates ('. . . shall never be slaves'). We identify with it or others do it for us. Using gender, age, ethnicity, religion, class, caste, or profession we go on 'branding' individuals and their groups, teams, companies, institutions, communities, and societies. The more distant and different 'brands' confront each other in fast-growing networks, the more crucial cross-cultural competence becomes. The more complex our societies become and the more global networking accelerates and intensifies, the more we need to know how to deal with differences. After the fall of the communist systems and the end of the Cold War, after the explosive growth of the internet and both legal and illegal international organizations, most social scientists concluded that transnational and transcontinental networking really accelerated. This is how the ideology of 'globalization' was born, almost simultaneously giving rise to 'antiglobalist' initiatives. Both the ideology of globalization and the antiglobalist movements assumed that globalization was a Western invention and that it had been endorsed by the newest 'empire' – the US. As soon as this opposition crystallized in violent clashes between the police protecting world conferences of globalizing agencies and a broad coalition of 'antiglobalists', the concept of globalization was deconstructed, stretched in time, criticized on both sides of the barricades. Part of this criticism has been linked to the very approach of globalization and to the relative importance of its economic, political and cultural aspects. The struggle to define the most relevant scientific disciplines capable of co-ordinating research on processes labelled in this way (i.e. as 'globalization') continues and increasingly critical voices are now being heard:

> We need an architecture for area studies that are based on process geographies and see significant areas of human organization as precipitates of various kinds of action, interaction, and motion – trade, travel, pilgrimage, warfare, proselytization, colonization, exile, and the like.
>
> (Appadurai, 2001, 8)

We should note that this plea for 'area studies' is an interesting reflection of a new methodological and political awareness of 'blind spots' generated by the growth of mainstream institutional science (which often simply identified globalization with Westernization, and Westernization with 'Americanization' as the only way for societies to follow after the end of history had officially been announced by a former adviser to the US president). Critical approaches to globalization, especially to the neo-liberal political project of the post-communist world order, have given rise to an attempt to re-engineer the research community in order to enable social scientists to focus on unequal distribution of human rights and organizational responsibilities. Moreover, this re-engineering might facilitate a more systematic study of global inequalities, which remain conveniently marginal and under-investigated within 'normal' science, i.e. within the established regime of knowledge production, with its tacit claim to universality. Nevertheless, some critical scientific communities question these claims.[2] Some social scientists have cautiously noted, for instance, that most of the growth associated with globalization in the economic sense has been limited to North America, Europe and parts of South-East Asia, i.e. to the areas where multinational companies design, finance, trade, and sell, and where most of the educated and affluent users of the internet live. Globalization thus has close affinities with the modernization (and colonization) of 'the rest' (of the world) by 'the West' (understood as Western Europe and the US). The market economy and parliamentary democracy in the particular historical mix resulting from the history of Europe and the US are tacitly or explicitly promoted as the best 'soil' for cultivating democratic social institutions and securing the economic welfare of society's members. *The ideal of globalization – of filling the world with safe markets and sound democracies* – has often been presented as an objective, almost 'natural' process, which can – at least in principle – be adopted by everybody everywhere. It had been considered so natural, in fact, that it prompted some ideologues (such as Francis Fukuyama, who reversed his view after the second war in Iraq, however) to proclaim 'the end of history' understood as a blind search for such a mix of markets and democracies. Needless to say, it is not, and has never been, a 'natural' process. Its course, scope and timing result from choices made by individuals, organizations and societies. In other words, the course of globalization does not depend on a hidden 'intelligent scenario' coupled with visible and invisible 'hands'. It depends on a huge number of choices and decisions, which together shape an unpredictable course of collective history, which does not appear to have ended. Choices, in turn, are influenced by cultural 'software', which, compatible or not, do not appear to be becoming 'blended' into a single 'universal' and 'cosmopolitan' matrix.

A liberal blueprint for globalization in Western eyes is only one of many blueprints generated against the background of 'Western' (not to mention 'non-Western' and 'cosmopolitan') cultural software. Not all cultural software makes us equally critical in judging whether the invisible hand of a market has to be guided by a visible policy of a democratically ruled society. Not all business recipes are written in the West. Cross-cultural studies cannot be based on an assumption that a single kind of cultural 'software' and an institutional cluster developed on a single continent should be granted the unique and privileged status of 'universal applicability'. Although such universal applicability is often tacitly assumed in the wake of the so-called Enlightenment project, which still provides the most fundamental legitimacy to institutionalized science in Western societies, in practice it is often compromised and belief in it is often tacitly suspended (though not totally abandoned: the dream of a universal and uniform theory of everything dies hard).

International networking of state, corporate, NGO, social, cultural, and individual activities has certainly been going on for a long time, long before the capitalist world system or parliamentary democracies came into being. However, the making of the modern nation-state, the evolution of parliament as the legislative power and the global expansion of capitalist economies, have intensified in the past 500 years, and the transformations of the last 50 years have accelerated the ongoing processes of change in all walks of social life. Culture was no exception: socialization into social, political and economic roles has been institutionalized, formalized, standardized, and bureaucratized. Powerful educational (ministries of education and their net-works of schools of all levels) and media (BBC, Time-Warner) bureaucracies have been constructed to upgrade and disseminate cultural software. Most of them have been managed or controlled by nation-states. States are still by far the most important interface between global markets and local political constituencies. States form international governance bodies: the United Nations, the World Trade Organization, the International Monetary Fund, the G6, 7, 8, 10 or 20 – and they attempt to control multinational corporations. Corporations form alliances, link suppliers, bond partners, and build cross-national infrastructures in order to invent and invest, produce and sell. However, even multinational, apparently 'footloose' corporations are still linked to nation-states as their countries of origin, and their resources can be subjected to state controls. Corporations have to obey the laws enforced by state bureaucracies worldwide – the courts (including the International Court of Justice), the police (including Interpol), the tax offices, the armies (including their alliances, such as NATO). Top managers of Enron had to appear in court financed by the US taxpayers, whereas public officials of the US government did not have to appear before corporate boards of directors. Corporations are thus far less powerful than nation-states, and their power is far less legitimate. Their CEOs are not elected in free elections and their strategic plans are not discussed in public nor voted on in parliaments. They can lobby much more successfully than single individuals, and thus can exercise control over some politicians or parties, but they can also be subjected to state control, albeit less easily and less directly than individuals. Not everything that is good for GE, Haliburton or Microsoft is good for the US, and the decision whether it is so or not is not up to the corporations. Governance is not just another name given to the dictatorship of powerful multinational corporations behind the official political stage; it is a trial-and-error process of piecemeal social engineering negotiated between national governments, business corporations and organizations of civil society (e.g. international non-governmental organizations), most of which emerge within the 'globalization from below' and manifest the role of cultural 'software' in mobilizing for political action:

> Emerging global civil society can be defined as the sphere of cross-border relations and collective activities outside the international reach of states and markets. This concept identifies a sphere of international relationships among heterogeneous actors who share civil values and concern for global issues, communication and meanings, advocacy actions, and self-organization experiments. . . . According to Richard Falk, who has introduced this concept, *globalization from below* has the potential to 'conceptualize widely shared world order values: minimizing violence, maximizing economic well-being, realizing social and political justice, and upholding environmental quality'.
>
> (Pianta, 2003, 237)

The 'widely shared world order values' mentioned above are values, which belong to cultural software of individuals who have become aware of their identity while networking to oppose the globalization from above. In a sense, we can say that these critical globalists from below are taking a 'free ride' on global communication networks imposed by globalization from above. Socialist agitators of the late 19th and early 20th centuries took a 'free ride' on urban concentrations of the working class in large industrial centres, which facilitated the distribution of subversive leaflets and the formation of oppositional parties. Alternative globalists follow this pattern, though in their case there is less thrust towards the formation of an alternative bureaucracy, either as a political party or an international organization with stable layers of professional officials, than was the case with their 19th-century predecessors. One of the reasons for that is that the present-day alternative countercultural software is much less rigid than that of their socialist forerunners. Confronted with many more different kinds of software due to the world-wide web and internet communications, they are much more suspicious of action blueprints and refuse to implement a single utopian ideology. Implementing a single ideology (Marxism) coupled with a single organizational form (a revolutionary party) was what their 19th-century predecessors did. Contemporary globalists from below have become much more reluctant to accept any set of institutional and organizational solutions as superior to all others and endowed with universal applicability. The overall result is that decisions with respect to organizational forms and the institutionalization of social movements become less predictable and more easily reversible in the context of dense cross-cultural communication exchanges, media struggles and political confrontations.

What has also changed in the second half of the 20th century is overall social mobility, both within nation-states (upward and downward social mobility of social, ethnic and professional groups) and internationally (horizontal mobility of professionals, tourists and immigrants). We travel more often and more quickly, mass immigration waves are triggered more frequently than ever before (air travel and mass tourism became accessible to lower classes, networks of illegal immigration routes have become professionalized). At present, even at the individual level (and indeed even among groups with lower income, status and education) we have learned to deal with trans-national mobility and global networking. It should be added that only a relatively small proportion of this newly won expertise and competence is being studied, recorded and used to facilitate future contact. One of the reasons for this relatively low retrieval rate of potentially valuable individual experiences is the partitioning of different groups of relevant individuals between distinct bureaucracies. Illegal immigrants are 'processed' by police, expatriate managers by their corporations, missionaries by churches, diplomats by governments, journalists by media companies, soldiers by the military, mobile professionals by academic and consulting agencies. There is little, if any, exchange of expertise between these agencies, and little, if any, attempt on the part of researchers to notice analogies and affinities between the mixes of knowledge and skills required by such professionals employed by the different bureaucracies.

Increased mobility can be inherent in routine professional activities, as in travelling to academic conferences or undertaking a pilgrimage to a holy site, or in communicating with other members of international fan clubs. We can participate in real and virtual communities of practice. We can also function in global governance structures of supranational co-operation networks. Increased mobility can also be part of the more intimate sphere of lifestyle, enabling us to exercise some discretion, as in visiting foreign tourist holiday destinations. It can be part of our professional activities, as in linking up with others in international voluntary associations (it is at our professional discretion whether to join, split, or form an alternative). None of these networking and border-crossing activities happens in a vacuum. Cultural software, the blueprints they generate and the actual interactions prompted by both are all registered, analysed, guessed at, confirmed or falsified, stereotyped and de-stereotyped, on a daily basis. Modern multimedia allow us to examine our reflections at all times. We are, quite literally, constantly looking at our own reflections as we work for the state powers, corporate profits or for personal pleasures. We are, to use a familiar metaphor, continuously being 'framed' (cf. Gitlin, 2003). Some of our 'looks' in these frames reveal transparent biographies or organizations, some reveal bias inherent in the frame. Some of the reflections we see resemble those in distorting mirrors, some belong to the past, others are guesses about the future. All of them, however, become accessible through modern multimedia networking, which facilitates communication patterns, which, in turn, can become subversive from the point of view of established authorities and experts, thus further increasing the pool of potential 'building blocks' of political doctrines, social ideologies, organizational subcultures, and alternative movements:

> The Web tends to eliminate a number of the characteristic defining points of the knowledge hegemony. It is quite easy to set up an official-looking knowledge base on the World Wide Web. . . . The rules essential to maintaining the distinction between the expert paradigm and the rest of the world can no longer be enforced.
>
> (Walsh, 2003, 368)[3]

French literary critics in the 19th century thought that novels were 'mirrors' walking down the road and enabling society to look at its own reflection. This was the role they assigned to printed literary works of art in an early industrial society. Apart from literature and printed press, the multimedia of the 21st century ensure that instant mirrors are globally available (satellites) and individually portable (mobile phones). The continuous presence of modern multimedia creates a virtual open stage, a boardwalk, an agora, a virtual space for a giant global village. Audiences from all over the world stay tuned and expect that their attention will be attracted to a succession of 'infotainment' bites – pieces of information mixed with pure entertainment in a seamless web of cultural content broadcast via many channels at all times. No wonder that dramatic effects increase the chances that the attention of numerous audiences will, indeed, be attracted. Rules of attraction have also changed. If Walsh is right in claiming that contemporary multimedia tend to subvert authority, then one should pay attention to new ways in which choices are being patterned when hierarchy disappears. If hierarchy holds, choices are facilitated by a ready-made frame of reference. If no such frame is available, rules of attracting attention change and become more egalitarian. Let us assume we are to choose which novel to read. If cultural bureaucracies distribute literary awards and rank writers, an individual choice is facilitated. Novels can be divided into those written by Nobel prize winners (top category), those composed by skilled and acknowledged writers (mid-category, *appellation controleé*), and those produced by anonymous craftsmen following genre recipes (the 'cheapest' category: thrillers, romances, science-fiction, fantasy).

One 'shops' in a different category of respect granted to writers by cultural bureaucracies (critics, reviewers, educators, publishers, media people, etc.), keeping in mind that rankings are being continuously revised and upgraded. Different categories of cultural products (say, novels) require different methodologies of attracting attention and appeal in a variety of ways to different target groups.

There is a certain irony in the fact that when cheap novels first appeared as a regular supplement to daily newspapers and had not yet matured into a major literary genre, they were considered a 'vulgar' attack on the idea of the sublime and beautiful in artistic communication. Not so web communications. The appearance of new 'framing' media (which had not yet been corporatized as were the 'older' ones) had been immediately recognized and acknowledged as a legitimate broadening of the means of communication and expression, as a means of more egalitarian 'framing'. In the absence of a hierarchy, what directs our choices and decisions about accessing knowledge products? There are reasons to believe that it may be a successful search for attention, which replaced more sophisticated and elitist forms of disseminating cultural products. It is not enough to compose an important message; one has to express it in terms that will attract attention. Hence the catastrophic tone of the ecological reports on pollution or finite resources, forthcoming social explosions or the deterioration of international relations. This explains also some of the Cassandra-like undertones of recent globalization debates. The Cassandric tones can be explained by the new political economy of attention[4] in contemporary multimedia. As Gitlin puts it:

> People attach to the media for their emotional texture, for the experience that takes place in the presence of the media, rewarded above all by that experience even as they expect confirmation that the world feels right. That is why the image of a burning flag or the spurious claim of burning bras looms so large in popular reactions – because these images slip beneath the façade where our ideas live, they 'hit us where we live'.
>
> (Gitlin, 2003, xvii)

Authors of academically respectable theories, which 'hit us' where the patterns of thinking are shaped, providers of cultural 'content', including theoretical interpretations of cross-cultural encounters, duly respond. Two prognoses, two types of predictions, that emerge from these cross-cultural debates merit particular attention from the cross-cultural point of view. First, the concept of the inevitable clash of values that cannot be reconciled, as in Samuel Huntington's 'clash' of Islamic and Christian civilizations (external conquest) or a Hispanic 'threat' to the 'American Dream' (internal subversion). A similar critique has been voiced by Benjamin Barber. Second, the critique of the inevitable loss of quality (and the growing irrelevance of core values) in secular, market-driven modernization, as in George Ritzer's 'globalization of nothing'. Rapid development of standardized, global networks for selling commodities and services is supposed to deprive individuals of *couleur locale* and of a *genius loci*, replacing their authentic experience of time, place and unique individuals with a prefabricated quasi-experience of standardized shopping malls, fast food restaurants, the 24/7 economy, and employees (or answering machines) enacting scripted roles instead of engaging in real exchange. A similar critique is regularly voiced against the excessive focus of individual and social life on market transactions, as in *The Loss of Happiness in Market Democracies* (Lane, 2000).

None of these warnings is new. Historically speaking, the doomsday scenarios predicting large-scale conflict with a powerful, aggressive civilization have always been present in European culture, especially with China in the role of a potentially explosive global danger. The warnings about decline of 'the West' (with Spengler's *Untergang des Abendlandes* figuring as prominently as Huxley's *Brave New World* and Orwell's *1984* in this series of dystopian prophecies of gloom) and the moral decay of Western Europe had been sounded in company with gloomy predictions that a huge wave of invaders will sweep over the European plains and bring about a new, authoritarian political order that displaces decadent democracies. Warnings of a 'yellow peril' are now sounded not with respect to an oriental threat of military conquest or revolutionary subversion of Western societies, but with respect to the rate of economic growth of the People's Republic of China (warnings of Japanese domination of world financial networks are a variation on the same theme). The only difference between the catastrophist writers of the early 20th century and Huntington is that he replaced the Chinese threat with an Islamic one, focusing on militant fundamentalism.

2　Two Cassandras of globalization: Huntington and Ritzer

> What is good for a global organization, its shareholders, employees and the government in its role as tax collector, is not necessarily positive for the third parties.
>
> (Eichhorn, 2003, 34)

Both Huntington and Ritzer sound a warning. The former warns of the forthcoming 'clash of civilizations' (which are bound to clash if their followers take values and organizations seriously), while the latter warns of the excessive rationalization of the whole of social life patterned as a consequence of the 'McDonaldization' of fast food, fast credit and fast consumption (which would mean a meltdown of core values and the convergence of all civilizations on a global consumer culture).

Ritzer criticizes global expansion of a 'McDonaldized' prefabricated 'experience economy' as a perverse effect of an extreme utilitarian rationalization of market-oriented activities. Standardization of products and services and their global distribution results in a proliferation of locations and agencies that offer the same 'experience' for the mass consumer (be it experience of an easy credit, a cheap hamburger, a giant shopping mall, a prefabricated theme park, a standardized educational path, a simplified health clinic, or pre-scripted call centre advice). Local flavour and feeling of place and community ('something' – a unique, free, randomly shaped, and open-ended interaction between strangers) are lost. So is the unique mix of knowledge, skills and experience of professionals, who become de-skilled in running McDonaldized service centres. What gets standardized and disseminated is the opposite of 'something', i.e. 'nothing' (an empty script, a standard product, both repeated endlessly and enacted indiscriminately):

> Four types of nothing are dealt with here: 'non-places, non-things, non-people and non-services. Thus, people around the world are spending more time in *non-places* (the shopping mall, the Las Vegas casino) and with *non-things* (Old Navy T-shirts, Dolce and Gabbana dresses), *non-people* (the counter-people at Burger King, telemarketers) and *non-services* (those provided by ATMs, Amazon.com).
>
> (Ritzer, 2004, xi)

Note that those two critics sound warnings that are based on a very similar assumption about our culture, namely that something will radically, qualitatively change our core values. They agree that core values will change; they differ with respect to the direction of change. Huntington thinks that we shall stand by our values and so will the others – until somebody gets killed. Ritzer thinks we shall not stand by our values, since they will become irrelevant. Either a radical incompatibility of cultural software will result in a violent clash (Huntington) or a radical incompatibility of software will become irrelevant, because standardized locations and scripted encounters will make distinct core values melt down and converge (Ritzer). Further rationalization of market-oriented activities will result, according to Ritzer, in gradual subversion of the desirable (genuine, individual, local, regional, authentic) lifestyle, further limiting meaningful interactions with others. In other words, the Huntingtonian critics claim that people will rather die for their cultural software in dramatic wars than modify and adjust the stereotypes about 'Others' (and globalization means that they will be exposed to the Others more often than in the past). By contrast, Ritzerian critics claim that all cultural software will be equally dramatically cleared of important and precious values for the purely pragmatic reasons of managerial efficiency (and globalization means that this process will leave no safe continents for any future pilgrim fathers to escape to). Huntington thus claims that stereotypes produced by our cultural bias will eventually destroy us. If we hold them dear – because they are salient to our identity – they will become dangerous. Ritzer claims that stereotypes produced by our cultural bias will eventually become irrelevant. If we dilute them in an indifferent 'content mix' of mediated standard experiences for everyone, every time, everywhere (a meal at McDonald's or a night in Las Vegas), they will become a random 'flavour' of standardized consumption, not guiding principles for our behaviour. They will evaporate – disappear into the thin air. They may – at best – add artificial local 'flavour' to a McDonaldized economy, mass tourism, themed parks and 'malled' (as in shopping mall) society (full of franchises, superstores, discounters, cybermalls, cruise ships, casino hotels, and home-shopping television networks). However, values reduced to the status of 'flavours' cannot guide individuals and societies trying to resist powerful forces of global pressure to increase the scale, scope and penetration of any aspect of social life by the markets – which Ritzer calls 'grobalization' (i.e. globalization of economic growth, a drive to increase the economies of scale and expand the volume of products and services):

> Commodities and the media are the key forces and areas of cultural change and they are seen as largely determining the self and groups throughout the grobalized areas of the world.
>
> (Ritzer, 2004, 77)

Let us now take a closer look at globalization and examine the critical claims of both authors in the light of cross-cultural competence in dealing with differences, which – if we are to believe their claims – will either kill us (because we shall deny the right of the Others to their otherness) or disappear altogether (because we shall all become standardized consumers of global supply chains and there will be no otherness to speak of), leaving us with a nostalgic feeling that everything solid has melted into thin air.

Globalization itself, as well as 'antiglobalist' or 'alterglobalist' movements, is a highly ambiguous mix of processes, whose ebb and flow has been reflected in multimedia and the analyses of academic professionals in a very limited and highly politicized way. It was primarily perceived as an economic networking of multinational corporations accompanied by nation-states acting as facilitators and constructing infrastructures. This networking, linked to the privatization drive, emerged as one of the ways of securing global flows of capital, commodities, information, and labour. Multinational corporations were supposed to expand globally, while national governments construct and maintain the international infrastructure for their activities. Multinational corporations were like fast cars on a globalization highway, while national governments were supposed to collect some tolls, repair all damage and generally speaking behave as a night watchman (a figure from early liberal ideologies of capitalism). This approach, which reduced the concept of globalization to the expansion of a market economy all over the whole world, has been criticized both in practice and in theory. In practice, it has been criticized by a broad variety of social movements, whose appearance on the world stage was marked by violent clashes with the riot police in Seattle (WTO conference of December 1999) and at the sites of subsequent conferences or in the course of questioning specific policies (e.g. the pricing of medicines for poor African societies by large multinational pharmaceutical companies, or the conditions the World Bank and International Monetary Fund imposed on credit-receiving governments). Another practical critique has been supplied by nation-states, whose global activities and initiatives demonstrate the return of the state to the centre of the world's stage (such as renewed interest in the United Nations in times of international crisis and regional integration in the EU along nation-state, regional and continental lines).

In theory, globalization has been criticized by historians (Braudel, Wallerstein), sociologists (Robertson, Appadurai), ethnographers (Burawoy, Harvey), political scientists (Held, Castells), philosophers (Negri, Said), and economists (Myrdal, Stieglitz). Most social scientists agree that globalization cannot be identified with the simple extension of Western modernizing influences to the whole world. Along with the development of global brands and global infrastructure for moving commodities, services, capital, and ideas, there has been a parallel growth in the variety of local responses and a parallel increase in local awareness of global influences (leading to *glocal* responses, and a degree of *creolization* of cultural forms, e.g. Latino pop music, Japanese cartoons and comic strips). Local communities and transnational networks both started inventing ways of dealing with the globalizing tendencies and influences. Selective emulation, adaptation and elaboration of global trends resulted in a proliferation of local tastes, hybrid creations and cross-cultural compromises. One might say that spontaneous growth of cross-cultural competence followed the accelerated expansion of the capitalist markets after the end of the Cold War.

Most sociologists, economists and political scientists would agree that globalization as a process accelerated again after the fall of communism and consisted of a growing 'interconnectedness of the world as a whole and the concomitant increase in reflexive, global consciousness' (Robertson, 2003, 461).

Robertson stresses the fact that not only does interconnectedness grow, but also our awareness of this interconnectedness and our critical reflection, thereby generating new knowledge, which in turn opens new possibilities for even more complex and sophisticated interactions in the future. Awareness of global interconnectedness can give rise to a stronger personal experience of local identity. Cassandras present heavily biased points of view, but even they view local identity as worthwhile and desirable (although Huntington locates his in an imaginary and conservative WASP ideal, and Ritzer in the Romantic cult of an authentic experience).

Cassandras are bound to exaggerate. Eating a hamburger at McDonald's does not automatically turn a responsible citizen into a mindless consumer. Criticism of the legal system in a different civilization does not turn one into a fundamentalist terrorist. Thinking and acting globally can reinforce thinking and acting locally. Robertson coined the term 'glocalization' to describe this process of an increased awareness of local distinctiveness and of adapting, so to speak, global brand values to local taste values. Reflexive global consciousness is being shaped by, among others, local citizens who undertake initiatives to defend their identity or construct it anew, and by critical intellectuals who sound warnings about dangers ahead (and thus increase the awareness of identities, which might have been dormant or less salient before). Traces of this glocalization can be found in the ongoing debate about whether one should follow the well-known slogan 'think globally, act locally'. Even Ritzer, his Cassandra-like warnings notwithstanding, admits that there is no 'historic necessity', nor necessarily a causal link between the advances of globalization (grobalization) and 'nothing-ness' of shopping malls, McDonald's restaurants and taped call-centre answering machines. Their relationship, which explains the relative ease with which a standardized way of servicing customers spreads on a global scale, resembles an 'elective affinity' rather than a causal bond. And elective affinities are – well, 'elected', not 'natural'. If they can be elected, they can also fail to be elected in future, or be exploited in pursuit of 'subversive', alternative ends.

A similar opinion with respect to the 'hypercentral' role played by the English language in the European Union has been expressed by a Dutch sociologist, de Swaan. He follows his French colleague, Bourdieu, in urging Europeans to grasp the advantage of the growing popularity of English as the most favoured language for international communications, but suggests that the Europeans should give it a continental, European twist, comparable to that given it by Indians when producing their variety of this language. Along with the English of the inhabitants of England, Scotland, India, or the US, there would emerge (in Bourdieu's famous phrase) a 'de-anglicised' English of the non-British members of the EU. De Swaan notices that although the dissemination of English increases the cultural domination of 'power relations that prevail in the global constellation, where English is the hypercentral language' it also increases the chances to articulate (and disseminate) an opposition to it:

> As the language of global communication, English also allows dissident voices to make themselves heard all over the world. If English is the language of the powers that be, it is also the language of empowerment.
> (de Swaan, 2001, 192–3)

If we do choose to 'think globally, act locally', we suggest all responsible citizens should start thinking about, for instance, an ozone layer for the whole planet and they should start lobbying with their local politicians for relevant environmental legislation. Thus can we contribute to making global ideology of sustainable development, which will bear on our local situation. Alternatively, we may follow Hofstede's suggestion, and reverse the slogan so as to suggest 'think locally, act globally'. What we then mean is that if one grasps the *couleur locale* of one's situation, one is best equipped to come up with adequate solutions (better, at any rate, than a world organizational expert flown in from one of the metropolises). If so, then maybe one's original solution may become useful for the others – hence becoming a global acting script. Still other authors advocate a programme for a systematic 'localization' as a response to globalizing processes, suggesting the new 'protect the local, globally' – version of the above slogan (Hines, 2003, 397).

Warning against the forthcoming clash of values identified with Christian as opposed to Islamic civilization focuses not on an environmental threat but a political one. Predictions of a bloody clash of religiously motivated fundamentalist armies are the best-known cases in point. Similar alarm over a clash of values has also been expressed, in a somewhat different form, as a warning against the continuing incompatibility of a religious fundamentalism (which presumably allows for a Holy War to settle differences and does not accept any compromise on values) and an extremely rationalized world of efficient and profitable organizations (which pushes for a McDonald's restaurant everywhere and renegotiates values until they become irrelevant for the smooth functioning of the market). The 'logo' of a *jihad*, or holy war, has been applied by Benjamin Barber to fundamentalist religious communities, thus negatively stereotyping some of them (e.g. an Islamic one, which is supposed to breed terrorism and humiliate women), though not the others (e.g. Jewish, Mormon, Amish). Likewise, the logo of a 'McWorld' has been applied to the 'Western world', in particular to the global expansion of multinational corporations originating in the US, thus negatively stereotyping some, though not all of them; for instance, McDonald's gets a worse press than Disney, and Nike than Microsoft.

What makes modern equivalents of the ancient prophet of doom, Cassandra, think that fundamental values of some clusters of societies (historically linked and disseminated by religious doctrines) can never be adjusted? What makes them believe that the stereotype of a *jihad* against non-Islamic infidels can never be revised and reconciled with peaceful proselytizing and a stable pattern of co-operation with non-Muslim communities, states and civilizations? What makes them believe that immutable stereotypes are thus bound to lead communities to a violent clash, to a bloody conflict, to a bitter, unrelenting struggle?

First of all there is a tacit assumption that identifying with certain cultural values closes the possibility of taking a less-committed, less-partial view of oneself, thus excluding the possibility of compromise and leading to armed conflict as the only method of dealing with the differences. This rejects tacitly but definitely the possibility of developing a cross-cultural competence (in spite of empirical evidence to the contrary: millions of Muslims live and work in Western societies and a majority of countries with Muslim populations participate in global exchanges). According to this view, civilizations close our minds. Once a fundamentalist, always a fundamentalist. Once a fundamentalist believer believes – and encounters someone who believes something else – both have to fight it out and whoever wins will be able to impose his or her values on a defeated enemy. *Tertium non datur*: there is no alternative. Compromise and rational or pragmatic procedures for arguing differences and seeking an outcome acceptable to both parties are not an option (in spite of a series of international institutional inventions that demonstrate the contrary, e.g. the Iran–US Claims Tribunal in The Hague).

Second, there is an explicit geopolitical assumption that only a strong 'core' state can shape policies and command the respect of the entire region, which would allow it to articulate the interests of 'the Muslims' in the international arena. Lack of a state, a strong state, is an original sin and forces the Islamic populations into the arms of terrorists with the force of predestination. Hence a negative conclusion is drawn from the empirical evidence that the Islamic world failed to produce a core local state with the status of a regional superpower and the ability to cluster other Arab states around its policies in a global arena (the fact that it has not always been so and that Christian communities had no core state for most of their recorded history either is simply glossed over). Unable to identify with a strong state commanding international respect, some

> Muslim groups such as Palestinians, Bosnians, Kashmiris, Chechens, Akbar Ahmed alleges, are like 'Red Indians, depressed groups, shorn of dignity, trapped on reservations converted from their ancestral lands'.
> (Huntington, 1998, 264)

Third, there is an empirical observation that generational and gender conflicts accelerate if social and political institutions are unable to respond to the new aspirations of educated women (Iran, Afghanistan) or baby-boom generations (Huntington's demographic 'bulge' or explosion). Young Muslims choose violent protest or terrorism because they see themselves as a 'no future' generation ruled by corrupt and absolute rulers at home and humiliated by richer nations abroad. Having thus characterized Islamic civilization, Huntington places it alongside the world's other civilizations – Western, African, Sinic, Hindu, Japanese, Latin American, and Orthodox.

He strongly advocates a new world order based on a global agreement signed by the representatives of each.

It is clear that this division of the world's nation-states into 'civilizational blocks' has been prompted by predominantly religious considerations – and that religions have been chosen because they promote 'sacred values', for which individuals are – presumably – willing to fight. Let us also note that the author assumes internal cohesion in each 'block' – even though his very own civilization, the Christian one, is internally divided into at least three dominant church organizations, the Eastern Orthodox, the Western Catholic and the North-Western Protestant, and the same holds true with respect to the other civilizations, most notably Islam.

Huntington's warning against the clash of civilizations is thus based on the following reasoning: at the core of cultural 'software' are the basic values, which have been expressed in religious doctrines and translated into political norms. Norms cannot be enforced by relatively weak and non-democratic states in the Islamic world, and therefore young baby-boom Muslims are socialized directly by religious fundamentalists, without the compromise-based influence of the political organization of a modern state and without a mediating influence, which a free public opinion would exercise in democratic societies.

What can be done? Clearly, Huntington's advice is designed for Western ears only. He does not comment on democratic social movements in the Arab world, on emergent democratization and feminization in Iranian politics, nor does he express his support for an excellent TV station, Al-Jazzira, which is becoming an Arabic BBC cultivating an independent public opinion. He has nothing to say and nothing to offer to his Muslim counterparts, the academic and media intellectuals who shape Arab public opinion in Cairo or Jakarta. Neither does he have practical suggestions for the Western politicians, apart from a vague call for unity. The US leaders and the EU leaders should unite under a single banner of 'Western' civilization. Having done so, they should take care to identify their equivalents in other civilizations. Then, the leaders of the Western civilization should presumably negotiate directly with the leaders of the Islamic civilization, to work out a compromise that could then be imposed on their subjects. That would allow explosive young Muslims to worship a slightly different hierarchy of values but at the same time it would authorize them to co-operate with 'infidels' without potentially dangerous conflicts. The same negotiation process should be repeated with the representatives of the other civilizations – thus in effect simplifying the United Nations Organization into the UCO or United Civilizations Organization, with eight full members and a residual category of 'others'. It is hard to see any reason for any nation-state to follow Huntington's advice and surrender political sovereignty to an appointed custodian of religiously defined values – to a core state of a respective 'civilizational' cluster of states. If this is the remedy Huntington proposes to defuse conflict and prevent the clash of civilizations, then the cure is worse than the malady. A re-engineering of the international community leading to the emergence of strongly religious, fundamentalist states dominating weaker states with populations sharing the same faith is an attempt to return to the situation Europe experienced in the Thirty Years War, before the treaty of Münster. If this is nation-building, then Huntington ends up designing nations along the lines of the revolutionary Black movement of the 1970s, 'the Nation of Islam', and generalizing their sectarian ideas onto the whole world.

The problem, apart from the difficulties of imposing a utopia with a civilizational focus on nation-states, is that this 'value connection' overstates the unity of both the 'West' and of the 'Rest', particularly of 'Islamic civilization'. Who is the ultimate custodian of the Western values? The Catholic Pope? A network of Protestant communities? The president of the US or the EU? An acknowledged philosopher specializing in ethical values at a respectable university (Derrida, Habermas, Taylor, Rorty)? The winner of 'the most moral person of the year' award? A Nobel Prize for Peace Laureate? Similar doubts can be expressed with respect to the representatives of the Muslim communities. No matter whom we choose on whichever side, we are bound to wheel and deal and ultimately to compromise both on rules or regulations and on values. This is how Protestants and Catholics found a *modus vivendi* in Europe (but not without prolonged wars and power struggles) and how the Popes gave up the Holy Inquisition and co-founded the World Council of Churches, a kind of a religious UN (but not before burning at stakes and crusades had been tried). This is how we reconcile our Christian identity with decreased participation in Sunday church services and with shopping on Sundays and religious holidays. Even if representative delegates of the most important civilizations were found and agreed to negotiate, the results of their discussions would probably be less than satisfying (and it would be hard to predict whether their recommendations would be followed).

Attempts at founding a United Religions Organization have already been made in the past, though interestingly enough not in the Western world. A great Mogul emperor of India, Akbar, is said to have once invited the religious sages, leaders of the Hindus, Muslims, Christians, and Jews, to his palace in Fatipur Sikri and asked them to work out a theological compromise. They were supposed to come up with a kind of a religious Esperanto, which would be acceptable to all religious groups among the emperor's subjects. There are no records indicating whether they ever came close to delivering any report to the ruler, nor that he followed their advice in managing the different religious groups under his rule. Nevertheless, one may see his project as an early – unsuccessful – attempt at the cross-cultural management of religious differences within a single political entity (empire).

It is difficult not to find irony in the fact that the author of the advice expressed in a book entitled *The Clash of Civilizations and the Remaking of the World Order* had acted against his own instructions and lashed out against one of the most devoted and religious Christian communities in the world. In an article published in *Foreign Policy* ten years later, he argues that 'the Hispanic Challenge' (represented mainly by legal and illegal immigration from Mexico) requires a unified political response of the White, Anglo-Saxon, Protestant, English-speaking elite of the US. The new Hispanic immigrants, who often grow up in virtual ghettos where Spanish not English is spoken, were summoned to accept the fundamentalist creed that was a product of fundamentalist Protestant settlers, 'the Founding Fathers':

> Key elements of that culture include the English language; Christianity; religious commitment; English concepts of the rule of law, including the responsibility of rulers and the rights of individuals; and dissenting Protestant values of individualism, the work ethic, and the belief that humans have the ability and the duty to create a heaven on earth.
>
> (Huntington, 2004, 11)[5]

There is no possibility of a negotiation in the above credo, nor room for a compromise. Spanish is ruled out as a language, Catholicism as a religion, Italian city-states as pioneers of a market economy, Polish or French constitutions as alternative foundations for democratic states, etc. The author is apparently unaware that were it not for a Catholic Spaniard, Bartolomeo de las Casas, universal rights of man would have taken longer to emerge, and were it not for a Catholic monk, Paccioli, capitalist book-keeping would have taken longer to mature. He does not realize that without Genoa and Venice there would have been no Amsterdam and Antwerp, and that without Amsterdam and Antwerp there would have been no New Amsterdam. His ideological vision is pure and simple. Should Mexicans refuse to become white, English speaking Anglo-Saxon Protestants, they will not be accepted as fellow-citizens: 'Mexican Americans will share in that dream and in that society only if they dream in English' (ibid.).

This does not make for a very convincing argument, but it certainly is a very convincing example of a negative national stereotype. It illustrates a profoundly fundamentalist conviction about the superiority of one's own cultural values as a product of one's own unique culture. John Milton had been equally blunt when he stated that God reveals Himself, as His manner is, first to his Englishman. However, he did so 400 years ago, when religious wars belonged to a repertory of legitimate and universally acknowledged means for dealing with different values, and the right of a ruler to impose his religion on subjects was taken for granted (*'cuius regio – eius religio'*).

It is very hard to understand why a white, English-speaking, Anglo-Saxon Protestant from the US social and political elite is exhorted to negotiate with the leaders of the Islamic civilization (which implies a recognition of their 'difference'), while at the same time it is being urged to ruthlessly subject the Spanish-speaking, Catholic, Mexican and other Hispanic citizens of the US to a linguistic and religious conversion and to the forced acceptance of the supreme cultural 'software' of the ruling class (which implies that this 'difference' will not be recognized and respected). Is the latter 'software', in Huntington's extremely exclusivist formulation, compatible with democracy, even the one constructed by WASPs? Is it compatible with an increasingly cosmopolitan project of globalization, in which

> the ideologies of modernization anchored in national projects are being displaced by transnational ideology of the market – that is, by neo-liberalism as an emergent civilizational project. In each case examined . . . the question of rights (rights of the people, of men, of the citizen, or of human beings) erupts as, and still remains, a hindrance to cosmo-politan projects. . . . Critical cosmopolitanism today faces at least two critical issues; human rights and global citizenship to be defined across the colonial difference.
>
> (Mignolo, 2002, 161)

Clearly, Huntington does not think that compromising Western values would contribute to a general promotion of the latest version of Western modernization and globalization projects. It is quite possible that he is critical of the neoliberal globalization project and looks for a remedy in case of its failure, trying to find it in a return to 'the local' understood as an earlier cultural ideology of the US – a version of the 'American dream' and of 'American destiny' as the world's only superpower and 'political representative' of 'the West' in world politics.

If Huntington warns that civilizations may clash when defending their values against other equally strong but totally different identities, Ritzer warns us against the disappearance of values during a gradual meltdown of all identities into a standard 'content' of conspicuous and ubiquitous globalized consumption. Huntington warns that there may be no compromise; Ritzer warns that everything may become too compromised, if consumers can be persuaded to become 'judgemental dopes': 'Truly rational choices require some real alternatives, not endless copies of the same or similar things' (Ritzer, 2004, 215).

Huntington's warnings against external and internal 'clashes of civiliz-ations' were based on an assumption that 'real' alternatives exist. Ritzer warns against the absence of real alternatives (there will be no clashes of civilizations because there will be nothing to clash about as all of us will line up in front of the same McDonald's counters). In his negative utopia of a consumer civilization, culture becomes a flexible and endlessly recycled set of ready-made software packages switched on and off and consumed in some virtual reality game. Everything, including stereotypes, will be recycled, changed and re-applied somewhere else. Tomorrow's multimedia will spread stereotypes all over the world. We will enact them in endlessly repeated, ritualized, scripted encounters.

However, by the same token, the blow-ups in the media will also expose stereotypes – more than ever – to critical examination and re-examination, engineering and re-engineering. As Ritzer himself rightly observes, expansion of fast food gave birth to the slow food movement and fusion of slow cuisines. Far from being judgemental dopes, consumers are not content with arriving at a judgement. They want to express it, share it and build up collective action on it (as the gradual progress of Ralph Nader from a marginal consumer protection activist to the centre stage of US politics clearly indicates). We are continually recycling and rejuvenating our stereotypes, and trying to compensate for negative consequences of using them.

Traces of our creative processing of stereotypes are found everywhere in cultural products of all classes and levels of sophistication. If all Western philosophy can be described as 'footnotes to Plato', quite a number of our cultural identities can be seen as footnotes to footnotes to some older stereotypes. In fact, even those of us who like relying on stereotypes and enjoy feeling superior to a stereotyped 'Other' are quite pragmatic and ready to adapt, revise and adjust – but not necessarily end up with 'nothing' at all. Values may have the aura of sanctity, but upholding all values of individuals from all cultures all the time is impossible. So they may lose the aura, but still perform an important role in guiding our behaviour. The light of reason replaced divine revelation as the guiding principle for producing knowledge under the ideology of enlightenment – but human societies at large and scientific communities in particular accepted this value without a sacred aura and did not pessimistically conclude that values have lost all meaning such that a new principle had to be adopted, namely 'anything goes'.[6]

Business as usual does not mean that we disregard the standardized content of 'fast food' or 'fast science'; we make local adjustments, we compromise and we renegotiate, we replace former, apparently solid hierarchies with provisional ones. These can work without being legitimized as 'eternally valid'. Political parties and sporting clubs take on the negative names hurled at them by angry opponents and re-design them as their positive 'logo' ('Tories', 'Sansculottes', 'Red Socks'). In spite of the prophets of doom, global co-operation increases rather than decreases and so do attempts to construct the infrastructure for global governance. Therefore one should view another prophecy about the future death of a 'global culture'[7] with a pinch of salt. Loss of aura – especially of the 'sacred', religiously sanctioned kind, does not mean loss of orientation (though it may mean that some bureaucracies – for instance, churches or states – lost some control over the implementation of values). Is the threat perceived as a slow 'fading' ('withering away') of values from cultural software – and hence of their motivating power, their raw energy, which is difficult to tame but may be even more difficult to recover when gone – a real one? What will remain of cultural software if values are removed, secularized, modified, and selectively reinserted? What will happen, if instead of core values, there is a yawning vacuum in the centre of our culture? If it becomes 'pasteurized', well-rounded, pragmatic, universally applicable, and efficient, but unable to help us decide what to do?[8]

What will remain will most probably not be the cultural software of 'one size fits all' type; bowdlerized, neutralized, streamlined, McDonaldized, Disneylanded, clean, meaningless, and manageable, which Ritzer has been warning us against. From the point of view of values, a future 'culture' could became more easily conveyable, 'communicable' and disseminated software (which does not mean that it would lose all its power to differentiate those who would accept it). This software could support any individuals employed in any efficient but faceless McDonaldized companies seeking growth and expansion at any price (and compensating lack of values, though with additional 'authentic, local, community-embedded' flavours or preservation of *couleur local* in company architecture). However, by the same token it could also facilitate international networking of the representatives of a new social movement. When Jack Welch claims that he believes in all company values expressed in a corporate culture of a General Electric designed for '10–15 years', we are, indeed, very close to a negative utopia of a corporate culture coded as portable software and disseminated throughout the corporation by managerial design and will. However, at the same time there is increasing awareness that the way in which actual, really existing social and organizational cultures grow, and the same Jack Welch stresses his devotion to the 'workout sessions' with high- and low-level employees of his company brainstorming about 'finding a better way everyday' and trying to overcome the negative influence of hierarchic organization upon their creative thinking. Empirical studies of corporate cultures confirm the hypothesis about organizational subcultures and their emergence 'from below'. Even in Ritzer's fast food restaurants some customers in some countries manage to slow down and socialize the process of consumption. Does it resemble a top–down imposing of a corporate culture by managerial design? Does not even McDonald's change under the influence of consumers, who force local variations of food (teriyaki sauce in Japan, vegetable 'greenburger' in the Netherlands, lambburger in India, beer in Germany), location (carefully reconstructed historical buildings preserving the 'atmosphere' of old railway stations as in Budapest or of a medieval cellar as in Cracow), or rhythm of consumption (Asian youngsters who hang around having a coke or a coffee instead of leaving immediately after a meal), etc. Does not even McDonald's change under the influence of social movements, lobbying for sick children, reducing fat in their burgers, organizing more conscientious waste processing, trying to introduce more employee-friendly, less trade-union hostile policies? Does not, then, even McDonald's compromise, or, rather, become compromised, hybridized, creolized, subjected to a subversive, creative re-engineering from below?

The way out of the maze of Cassandric prophecies is through the acceptance of a daily reality of cross-cultural compromises. The way out of doomsday scenarios is through respect for multiculturalism of societies, whose members cope with the processes of globalization. Can resistance of consumers, believers, citizens, professionals, or participants in a social movement succeed in gaining the respect of those who are in charge of the globally disseminated new means of consumption? Can this resistance succeed in gaining respect for those who are conceptualized as a mass of 'targeted consumers' and segmented according to their purchasing power? Some sociologists (Ritzer, 2004; Wallerstein, 1999, 2004) and philosophers (Said, 2004; Taylor, 2004) think that this would require a new critical, normative focus, and imply that some form of cultural mobilization of resources would be necessary. As Ritzer puts it:

> Fast-food restaurants and credit cards are not only of economic signifi-cance. They are certainly influencing the world's mode of discourse, but I also think, in contrast to Robertson, that they are creating normative constraints on the way people eat and consume. . . . Credit cards and fast-food restaurants are changing, at least to some degree, people's definition of self.
>
> (Ritzer, 1999, 90–91)[9]

What Ritzer implies is a major accelerated change of cultural values. Contrary to the assumption tacitly accepted in most theories of culture in sociology, social psychology and cultural anthropology, patterns of cultures (values, norms, beliefs) appear to be changing more quickly than used to be the case before the middle of the 20th century. Ritzer is not alone in claiming that a number of social processes have been increasing their influence on human cultural 'software', and that these processes have been influencing even those core values that were assumed to remain relatively stable at least in terms of decades, if not centuries. If this increased mutability is indeed the case, how can we account for this shift, especially if it turns out to be continuous, accelerated and permanent? If theoretical and empirical studies of tourists, sojourners, immigrants, students, business people, and refugees provide ample examples of cultural shock as a daily experience and cultural adaptation as a routine task in large urban centres? How can we develop instruments to account for this rapid cultural change? How can we report on a change of cultural values to newly emerging professional communities of social psychologists, sociologists, cultural anthropologists, intercultural trainers, therapists, social workers, urban planners, HRM managers, and a variety of consultants (cf. Ward, Bochner, Furnham, 2001)? How can we, in other words, account for the influence of multicultural locations upon cultural software and for the influence of new, culturally modified software upon interactions, locations, organizational and behavioural patterns? Is the concept of multiculturalism an attempt to deal with this newly accelerated rate of emergence (or of perception, or of both) of culturally manipulated software?

Let us take a new look at the concept of multiculturalism and at Hofstede's theory of national cultures, whose typology is based on characteristics following four (or five) basic dimensions. Are we justified in following the assumption of stability in national cultural software in the individual and collective mind? Suppose that we turn out to be unjustified in holding the view that core cultural values are relatively stable – have discovered that these values and their configurations are indeed changing. What should we do in order to continue profiting from the robust theoretical framework introduced by Geert Hofstede? It is not only a question of academic preference for a well-established theoretical framework. It is also a question of finding a way to navigate individual and collective enterprises in a world that is rapidly changing and claiming more space, attention and resources for

> the burgeoning populations of India, China, Indonesia, Pakistan, Bangladesh, Brazil, Mexico, and Nigeria. Their needs, requirements, tastes, and appetites will transform not only the world economy but also the way the world works and lives.
>
> (Lewis, 2003, 270)

3 Cross-cultural compromises and multiculturalism

> The world at large and the social worlds of most societies in it are affected by global (as distinct from nationalizing) forces that can be called 'multicultural' in the sense that peoples of different and often incommensurable cultural affinities live in sufficiently real – or, at least televisual – proximity to each other as to be well aware of each other, and their differences – often to the point of open civil, or, even armed, conflict.
>
> (Lemert, 2003, 298)

The concept of a multicultural society is relatively new and was originally employed by urban planners, social workers and professional politicians concerned with the ghetto-like developments in major cities of Western

Europe and the US. Processes of economic reconstruction and growth after WWII increased the numbers of immigrants into western Europe, while the US, which has always been a country of immigrants, also had to deal with increased levels of both legal and illegal immigrants, especially in the aftermath of local armed conflicts in the Cold War. Gradual development of electronic mass media and the emergence of satellite links and the World Wide Web confirmed the prediction of Marshall McLuhan about the coming of a 'global village', whose inhabitants share gossip and news in real time. Originally, the concept of a multicultural society had an ideological ring: it was supposed to reflect a growing concern of the left and liberal city planners, politicians and social workers about recognition of immigrants and their children by the rest of society and their successful integration in spite of persisting income and educational inequalities. In other words, it was introduced to defuse the original distrust and hostility, and to prevent a virtual civil war. Danger of social unrest and clashes between foreign immigrants (competing in the job market with the poorer sectors of the indigenous population) and various groups of the host societies, often along racial or religious lines, has loomed large in social and political imagination. Some of these immigrants lost their jobs when the oil crisis of 1973–4 ended the long period of economic growth, while their children never found any jobs whatsoever. Children of *Gastarbeiter* had to work harder within the Western European educational system (to make up for the lower educational level and linguistic skills of their families), received an inferior education (compared to their local counterparts, who had easier access to the welfare state), and were negatively stereotyped, which further reduced their chances of landing jobs. They formed visible clusters – of Turks in Germany, Moroccans in the Netherlands, Algerians in France, or Pakistanis in Great Britain. Their street gangs, incidents of conflict with neighbours or schoolmates and teachers, their criminal networks and their exploits have been particularly often depicted in the media, which created and sustained negative stereotypes about such groups.

The term 'multicultural' society has thus been a theoretical reflection of a politically motivated recognition of a cultural difference between members of the new underclass in Europe's inner cities and citizens of European nation-states 'included' in the ranks of citizens and covered by state welfare programmes. The term 'multicultural' has also been an ideological label designed to appeal to public authorities and citizens at large, exhorting them to respect these differences and to mobilize for fairness in housing, job hunting, educational chances, and political representation.

It was used, for instance, in the early 1980s by the Red–Green coalition in Frankfurt am Main's city hall, where the 'Reds' (social democrats), the 'Greens' and former student rebels in their ranks – Joschka Fischer or Daniel Cohn-Bendit – tried to cope with social inequalities and rubbed shoulders with young social scientists pursuing 'critical theory' around Habermas (cf. Honneth, 1996) or with ambitious young politicians looking for a viable model of cultural policies. The representatives of 'critical theory', whose founding fathers focused on dangers of ethnocentricism, were looking for a theoretical concept that could increase tolerance for 'strangers' in host societies and found it in the idea of 'identity' (which bears many similarities to Hofstede's 'software of the mind'). According to their concept, identity is first shaped by individuals within their own culture (the 'frame of reference'), and subsequently is acknowledged and recognized in other cultures ('respected'), or not. The representatives of the newest generation of 'the Frankfurt School' in social sciences were aware of the multicultural context in which identities of members of complex societies emerge – and of the dangerous position of those who remain unrecognized, negatively stereotyped, excluded from membership in social networks, and ultimately 'scapegoated' and rejected.

In reconstructing the context, in which the term 'multicultural' was introduced into the political and theoretical debates, one cannot fail to notice that it had relatively little to do with the nation-state's nationalist ideologies of an 'imagined community' (cf. Anderson, 1983) connected by a single language, territory and history, sometimes also religion. It had been introduced in order to deal with the subculturally constructed identities of the second generation of *Gastarbeiters* in crime-plagued urban ghettos. They could not be the 'we's' of their parents' cultures of origin (because their parents have already adopted to the host country's culture) and they found that the shaping of 'me's' in generational subcultures of inner cities does not always result in acceptance and embedding in the local community (the Dutch use the term *inburgering*, which can be translated, literally, as 'citizenating', 'turning into a citizen').[10]

Dimensions and consequences of culturally constructed identities look different when viewed from the perspective of politicians dealing with discriminated minorities in the hearts of European cities rather than from modern industrial and office complexes built by multinational corporations in protected suburban locations all over the world. Does this shift in the point of view require theoretical adjustment of our concepts? With the concepts of multiculturalism and cultural identity we begin to view cultural 'software' from a politician's position, marked by fear of a civil war, rather than from a CEO's position, marked by managerial desire to meet targets (e.g. increase profitability to satisfy shareholders). Does this shift of focus prompt theoretical revisions, does it require a new, more critical glance at Hofstedian theoretical framework, which had originally been designed to guide organizational, managerial interventions?

Hofstede's popular version of Culture's Consequences *(1980), namely* Cultures and Organizations *(1991), has two subtitles: 'Software of the Mind' and 'Intercultural Cooperation and its Importance for Survival' (Hofstede, 1991). The first subtitle reveals Hofstede's original 'embedding' in the problems of a multicultural workforce in a globally operating, multi-national corporation. The second subtitle demonstrates his awareness of and sensitivity to the problems faced by politicians concerned about social stability in the face of persistent inequalities and conflicts.* Hofstede is very much aware of the moral responsibilities of a business manager, an organizational leader, a public office holder. Both subtitles are significant, since they signal two major influences exerted by the world's most famous Dutch engineer and social psychologist on the entire field of organizational sciences, managerial consulting and multicultural politics.

The first subtitle stresses Hofstede's fundamental assumption that all 'identities', which individuals design, assemble and employ in their various activities, are composed of elements acquired during their socialization (because this is how the cultural software of an individual emerges). What makes one tick ticked already in patterns of cultural heritage transmitted as acculturation proceeded. This assumption is followed by another, which assigns a privileged status to the 'national' hue of individual cultural identities. Since the above-mentioned socialization is to a large extent conducted by smaller and larger institutions and organizations co-ordinated by nation-states (the dominant form of organization in the past two centuries), these components of individual identities are tinted (although not necessarily tainted). Bureaucracies of nation-states maintain and manage cultural heritage, prefabricating the building blocks of individual identities and thus exerting a dominant influence upon the individual creation of cultural software and 'identities'.

Differences between the two components of individual identity from different national cultures are not 'visible' (as are differences in language or folk dances), but have to be investigated and reconstructed. They can be plotted in a model of national culture, with four (later five) dimensions. These dimensions are relevant for shaping individual's interactions and for the choice of organizational forms. They have consequences for a preferred design of organizations within a given nation-state and for the performance of individuals socialized within national culture. If, for instance, individuals have been socialized in a low power–distance culture characteristic for a given nation-state, they are likely to believe that superiors and subordinates should consider each other as existentially equal. They are supposed to treat these organizational hierarchies, which assign them unequal roles, as useful fictions, which can and should be changed. They expect that the asymmetry of power and influence will be addressed, for instance by their managers. These managers should consult their subordinates before making decisions that will influence everybody. If, to the contrary, an individual has been socialized in a large power–distance culture, forms of management that require subordinates to be consulted will not work, since employees will expect to be told what to do by their superiors, who are supposed to 'know better' and deserve to be obeyed by subordinates.

Hofstede quotes approvingly a similar conclusion drawn from a comparative study of a French multinational in France, in the US and in the Netherlands. The author of this study, Philippe d'Iribarne, attributes a much more vivid emotional experience of hierarchical differences in France (as compared to the US or the Netherlands) to a difference in national tradition. In France, this tradition follows a 'logic of honour', which regulates the relations between essentially unequal social strata or classes across all kinds of interactions. In the other two countries, this national tradition follows a 'logic of contract', which regulates the relations between essentially equal partners in specified exchanges (cf. d'Iribarne, 1989). What matters is that in following the logic of honour, we take inequalities between interacting parties for granted, while in following the logic of contract we assume their equality.

Hofstede then introduces the next four dimensions (individualism/collectivism, femininity/masculinity, uncertainty avoidance/unavoidance, and long-term/short-term orientation) and operationalizes them in a questionnaire, which allows researchers to survey attitudes and finally to plot the results of these surveys on graphs. National cultures plotted on a graph according to their position on the five dimensions cluster around certain points in five-dimensional space. Different positions of national cultures allow researchers and managers to predict expectations, which individuals brought up in various national cultures will have with respect to the style of management, idea of fairness or organization of work and assignment of responsibilities, etc. Hofstede's results, and the results of numerous surveys that replicated his own studies, make it possible – at least theoretically – to generate hypotheses about the consequences of any given national culture's positioning in the five-dimensional space for the success or failure of organizational forms, managerial styles and policies of human resources departments in organizations. This cautious proviso – 'at least theoretically' – arises from the fact that we are not dealing with a direct causal bond. Another variable intervenes between 'national cultural software' and 'organizational HRM policies', namely individual internalization of values and beliefs, and partly individual, partly social choice of norms to follow in actual behaviour.

The theoretical construct of Hofstede, a model of national culture as a collective programming ('software') of an individual mind, was developed theoretically by postulating a connecting variable between the position of a national culture in Hofstede's theoretical five-dimensional space and a 'visible' cluster of organizational designs. This variable must be 'distilled' from individual behaviours and statements on the one hand, and linked to an 'invisible' core of postulated, reconstructed values and beliefs on the other. Thus what we are explaining are different organizational designs (e.g. more or less rigid hierarchies) and different organizational behaviour (e.g. as measured by the average efficiency, productivity, innovativeness, etc.) of individuals with different cultural software in their heads. What are we explaining different organizational designs and individual behaviours with? With values and beliefs in clusters and rankings tinted by national socializ-ation, which we managed to capture and compare thanks to the theoretical concept of 'dimensions' of a national or organizational culture. The five-dimensional space of dimensions of national or organizational culture is a scientific 'net'. This net allows us to catch some, though not all levels of culture (but at least those levels that are relevant and salient for individual identities and organizational behaviour). Hofstede warns against, for instance, using his value survey questions in order to discriminate between influences of subcultures focused on gender, generation, social class, and organization (Hofstede, 2001, 464).

The positioning of national cultures seen as species of fish caught in our net is not random. Since the positions of national cultures along some dimensions are correlated, we can draw a multi-dimensional 'map' of nationally shaped cultural software. The position of fish in the net provides a starting point for understanding 'what makes the fish tick'. By finding out what the core values and beliefs in a given national culture are, we are able to predict the 'culture's consequences', i.e. organizational forms, which will best 'fit' individuals with this particular cultural software in their heads, or expected types of individual behaviour that will fit some organizational forms better than the others. The sequence can be reversed: by gathering data on dominant organizational forms and dominant types of behaviour in a given country or organization, we can reconstruct values and beliefs (which are more difficult to investigate than behaviour and artefacts). In a famous and succinct definition, which together with a robust set of empirically confirmed predictions made it possible for a new sub-discipline of organizational sciences (namely the science of cross-cultural or inter-cultural management) to emerge and establish itself in academic environment, Hofstede summed up the role of cultural dimensions as follows:

> The main cultural differences among nations lie in values. Systematic differences exist . . . with regard to values about power and inequality, with regard to relationships between the individual and the group, with regard to the social roles expected from men and women, with respect to ways of dealing with the uncertainties in life, and with respect to whether one is mainly preoccupied with the future or with the past and present.
> (Hofstede, 1991, 236)[11]

Note that this assumption – 'the main cultural differences among nations lie in values' – can be maintained only within a relatively stable and relatively 'synchronized' nation-state system of sovereign states, which allow their respective civil societies to search for the most successful organizational forms in family socialization, political governance and business activities.

It is thus clearly an assumption that, at the time it was first made, did not hold for the central-eastern half of Europe, namely the one behind the so-called 'Iron Curtain'. Within the state socialist system of the Warsaw Pact countries, no amount of differences in national cultures could influence the organizational choices in political governance (socialist nation-states were in fact single-party dictatorships subjected to direct control from Moscow). Neither were there differences in business corporations; all economic planning was performed by top state bureaucracies, which managed all enterprises as the property of the state. The Poles, Czechs, Hungarians, Russians, Bulgarians, or Lithuanians did not cease to have national cultures, but these cultures were artificially and violently prevented from influencing the organizational forms in political and economic activities. Thus Hofstede's assumption was invalid outside the European Economic Community. We shall return to this restriction on Hofstedian theoretical framework in the next chapter.

The second subtitle of 'Cultures and Organizations' stresses the necessity for individuals with different cultural software to co-operate and to facilitate the survival of increasingly complex and networked societies (nation-states) and organizations. Instead of remaining prisoners of our identities, we should be able to see them as flexible and mutable, thus contributing to social and cultural evolution by our self-reflexive input. We should reflect on our own identities, compare them to the identities of the others, try to defuse predictable conflicts and dampen shocks – ultimately working out a common design for more desirable organizations and for less lethal identities suitable for tolerant and co-operative individuals. The second subtitle thus refers to the potential application of theoretical knowledge about the link between core values of national and organizational cultures and individual and collective constructs (among them the 'identities' people are referring to when answering the questions in the researcher's questionnaire).

Hofstede notes that acceptance of his framework for recognizing and dealing with cross-cultural differences is heavily biased towards the 'universalist', 'individualist', 'Western' values as exemplified, for instance, in the Universal Declaration of Human Rights. This declaration of human rights, in fact an artificial, internationally negotiated construct, was imposed by the coalition of the strongest nation-states on the rest of the world in the wake of WWII. Its acceptance by the intergovernmental and other international organizations followed. Nevertheless, most researchers would agree with Hofstede that this biased, but aware of its own bias, historically embedded but tolerant, 'open' view offers a good starting point for further negotiations: 'Increasing the respect for human rights is a worthwhile goal for a multicultural world' (ibid., 245).

Criticism of Hofstede's theoretical framework, which has become more frequent in the past decade, has been increasingly focused on the following characteristics of his approach:

(a) In-built Western bias

This pro-Western bias manifests itself not only in constructing a general four-dimensional model with dimensions that can be discerned from the Western European point of view but not necessarily from the others, for instance from a Chinese one. It has also been validated by selecting exclusively Western researchers (either from Western Europe or from the US), who gathered and processed empirical data. If any local culture contained dimensions that were salient for individual identities but 'invisible' to those unacquainted with the natives' 'tacit knowledge' and thus 'unplottable' in the four-dimensional (later five-dimensional) cultural space 'made in the West', they went unnoticed or were labelled as aspects of these assumed four dimensions, not independent dimensions in their own right. They may have been disregarded (e.g. high context vs. low context or shame vs. guilt typologies), thus continuing the colonial tradition of imposing a single model of culture and rationality on all cultural communities. This bias comes so naturally to a Western researcher who takes it for granted that scientific knowledge is simply produced in the high-tech labs of the West that most of us ignore the fact that 'more marginal regions in the world are not simply producers of data for the theory mills of the North' (Appadurai, 2001, 5).

Identities are always an indigenous product and should be studied by researchers familiar with local cultural software (Roberts, Boyacigiller, 1984) – just as climbing unknown mountains is safer with native guides to accompany the expedition than without them. A multicultural world requires self-reflective examination of cultural bias at all times and moving beyond 'sophisticated stereotyping' (Osland, Bird, 2000). One way of doing it would be to network enough experts in local cultures in research platforms and projects to make sure that no relevant and salient characteristics of cultural software or individual identities go unnoticed. Hofstede notes this problem, but directs his critical warning to those replicating his studies and more generally, to those who use his dimensional model of culture as a paradigm:

> The IBM-based questionnaire is not necessarily the best instrument for detecting the essence of cultural differences in other populations. Researchers studying national and ethnic culture differences . . . may borrow some of the IBM questions, but they should primarily develop their own survey instruments aimed at the particular populations studied and based on empathy with the respondent's situation. Sample in-depth interviewing and participant observation are ways of acquiring such empathy.
>
> (Hofstede, 2001, 465)

However, even if researchers heed his warnings, they will still leave some crucial parts of their bias unexamined. Both Western and non-Western researchers tacitly assume that economic development through the establishment of a market economy and political democratization through the construction of parliamentary representation are universal criteria for measuring progress. Lawrence Harrison's 'The Cultural Values and Human Progress' project at Harvard is a case in point:

> We define culture in purely subjective terms as the values, attitudes, beliefs, orientations, and underlying assumptions prevalent among people in society. This book explores how culture in this subjective sense affects the extent to which and the ways in which societies achieve or fail to achieve progress in economic development and political democratization.
>
> (Harrison, Huntington, 2000, xv)[12]

Criticism of tacit 'Eurocentrism' should thus not be limited to those who scrutinize Hofstede. It should be expressed not only with respect to the five-dimensional model of culture. It should be applied *en bloc* to most representatives of Western social sciences and to most models offered by them. In the case of Hofstede's theoretical framework, an argument about 'pro-Western bias' should be directed both at the methodological bias (conceptual categories have been obtained by empirical generalizations from Western European socio-historical research, disregarding non-European sources),[13] and at the ideological bias, namely the universalist claims of the ideology of modernization. This universalist bias also has a distinctly Eurocentric ring to it. It is legitimized via the 'unfinished Enlightenment project' and expressed in a European vernacular. The latter imposes the Western 'mix' of 'market plus parliament' as the only truly universal and legitimate goal for all human societies, east, west, north, and south.

The first, methodological, thrust of criticism we shall deal with below. The second has often been quoted by African, Asian and Latin American authors, who claim that genuine economic, political and social development in Africa can only be engineered if the hidden injuries of colonial rule – lasting well beyond the formal political dependence – are duly noted, properly acknowledged and jointly removed. However, they are not being noted – hence, for instance, 'deracialization' and 'detribalization' as major strategies of accelerating modernization of African societies remain 'invisible' and 'unthinkable':

> What would democratization entail in the African context? It would have entailed the deracialization of civil power and the detribalization of customary power, as starting points of an overall democratization that would transcend the legacy of a bifurcated power. A consistent

democratization would have required dismantling and reorganizing the local state, the array of Native Authorities organized around the principle of fusion of power, fortified by an administratively driven customary justice and nourished through extra-economic coercion.

(Mamdani, 1996, 25)

The same argument has been expressed very elegantly by a contemporary Western philosopher concerned with identity, multiculturalism and recognition:

We finally get over seeing modernity as a single process of which Europe is a paradigm, and . . . understand the European model as the first, certainly, as the object of some creative imitation, naturally, but as, at the end of the day, one model among many, a province of the multiform world we hope (a little against the hope) will emerge in order and peace.

(Taylor, 2004, 196)

While this criticism of tacit biases in the Western research culture and its record in justifying political and economic inequalities is certainly justified, Hofstede should not be singled out as its only target. On the contrary, it may be claimed that he has contributed to increased sensitivity to the differences and has honed our intellectual instruments for searching them, recognizing their nature and subjecting them to non-hostile uses. His refusal to bow to academic hierarchies (which prevented him from developing a 'school' embedded in a university system) demonstrates that he has been committed to overcoming the most painful inequalities in our organizational inter-actions not only in thought but also in deed.[14] Incidentally, it has also meant that in spite of a tremendous *intellectual* impact upon global research and teaching communities, he has remained academically marginalized in his own country. A research institute he co-founded (the Institute for Research on Intercultural Cooperation – IRIC – at the Tilburg University) had just gone bankrupt as this was being written, and no clearly identifiable Hofstedian school has emerged as a result of an *institutional* impact upon academic institutions.

(b) In-built static and conservative nature of the dimensional model

The model presupposes relative stability of core values and beliefs in national culture, making it impossible to trace and report changes brought about by the development of countercultural values and beliefs around sub-national identities (age, gender, race, profession, organization), and by the advancing supra-state processes of regional and global integration due to political, economic and cultural (mass media and multi-media related) processes. Therborn's 'audio-visual Americanization' and the increased popularity of English as a second language among European high school students are cases in point (Therborn, 1995), as are studies demonstrating that respondents identify with age or gender communities rather than with the national ones (cf. Gooderham, Nordhaug, 2002). The latter authors also claim that they have found many instances of convergence of European national positions on Hofstedian dimensions when replicating his research in the late 1990s:

> The notion of a largely convergent Europe is given more impetus when one looks at the findings for the Uncertainty Avoidance and Individualism dimensions. France differs significantly from the mean country Finland in terms of Uncertainty Avoidance. Beyond that there are no significant differences. Clearly this is a very different Europe from that which Hofstede mapped.
>
> (Gooderham, Nordhaug, 2002)

Integration and institutional harmonization on regional and global scales and a rapid development of communication technologies might, according to these critics, have brought about accelerated cultural convergence, not necessarily along national lines.[15] Identities are being constructed in changing circumstances, and with broader frames of reference due to the integration processes, national frames either do not hold or only hold for a shorter period of time and in a more limited range of contexts. *What matters is that growing interconnectivity across former social barriers undermines a stable pattern of socialization (family, school, workplace), which might suggest that the dominant position of the national culture is undermined.* Socializing functions are 'taken over' by a number of new agencies and networks, platforms and associations, for instance, by the web:

> If we see the Internet user as a social being, the outcome of Internet use is affiliation, with money coming from membership fees rather than content. . . . web tools are developed to create social connections rather than links to information.[16]

The main change in contemporary processes of 'identizing', as compared to the mid 20th century, is the slow erosion of a stable pattern of socialization and linear career pathing. Our culturally determined software is not 'produced' in four major places – at the socializing assembly lines of family, school, workplace, and the political sphere (as Hofstede assumed in *Cultures and Organizations*). There are a number of processes that undermine the smooth transition through these phases of identity formation and disrupt the mutual reinforcement of identities under the protective shield of the nation-state and its specialized bureaucracies.

For instance, families change, shrink and limit interactions between family members (especially if parents are immigrants with little command of the local language, while children acquire education in the host country and become aware of their parents' limited cultural resources, which further limits family socialization). Family members pursue their different trajectories, with children leaving their parents at an early age or remaining in the same household but virtually never interacting in a meaningful way with other family members, for instance parents (though they maintain meaningful relations with members of their peer groups and full connectivity via e-mail, mobile phones and regular meetings). Popularity of the 'Walkman' or of personal, mobile phones illustrates the separation of these trajectories, even if children stay in the same household, even if they are physically sharing the same space. Their communication lines do not require contacting other family members nor do they involve co-operating with others to make communications possible. Technology contributes to the evolution (and weakening) of family interactions. The Walkman, an invention designed to protect the others from audio environment of a single listener, became an instrument of the individualized consumption of cultural content at the family level, further isolating family members from one another as each family member was free to separate himself or herself from the rest of the family in listening to a different radio station or compact disc.

Another example of the weakening of control exerted by the nation-state over the socialization and acculturation of individuals is the growing presence of multicultural labour within a single organization (an individual socialized into his or her organizational roles cannot take the cultural software of his or her fellow employees for granted) and the appearance of multinational organizations with strong corporate culture and distinct HRM policies (an individual socialized into the organizational culture of a multinational does not necessarily acquire values of this multinational's country of origin) and general convergence of organizational cultures as a result of increasing co-operation and competition on a global scale. The emergence of organizational culture by design and the proliferation of corporate universities indicate a new variant among privatization processes, namely the privatization of educational activities, which in turn increase the influence of an organization on individual cognitive development – at the expense of the nation-state, whose bureaucracy has to step back and deregulate some areas of education (thus an MA or MSc degree is still the monopoly of state-owned or state-recognized universities, but an MBA is not). All this means that we cannot take for granted that cultural software is shaped within an individual mind in clearly defined contexts, under the standardizing and supervising control of nation-states. If not, then the influence of national culture may indeed be declining, and the influence of innovation-seeking multinational professional and other communities may be increasing (leading, in turn, to the relative growth of non-national identities and thus suggesting the need to modify the Hofstedian theoretical frame of reference).

(c) In-built methodological bias

This is linked to the choice of an attitude-survey questionnaire as the basic source of data, which can be questioned on a number of levels, including its suitability for culture study and the reliability of the respondents (cf. Tayeb, 1996), the influence of occupational, professional or organizational culture (McSweeney, 2002) and the 'zipping' up of sub-dimensions (Boski, 2003). For instance, when investigating the Uncertainty Avoidance dimension and comparing the results of House's 'Globe' project studies with the results of studies that replicate the Hofstedian approach, we find that it is either the Greeks who emerge as the least uncertainty-avoiding nation (Hofstede) or the Swiss (House). I tend to subscribe to the view, first expressed by Pawel Boski, that if the Hofstedian dimension is methodologically 'unzipped', we discover the clustering together of different themes, perspectives and levels of reality or desirability.

Let us begin with three *themes*: the degree of closure of the individual mind (is one open to new ideas and the challenge of progress, or does one prefer to stick to the tried and tested, more 'conservative' ideas?); the individual 'escape from freedom' (is one avoiding situations that call for initiative and creativity or does one actively seek and pursue them as windows of opportunity?); and the internalization of organizational culture (does it contain many detailed checklists and rules that structure my action, or is it more flexible and open in characterizing the objectives, which allows me to take liberties?). Which theme should we focus on?

Second, we have to distinguish two *perspectives*: whether respondents try to avoid uncertainty with respect to goals and leave means less strictly structured, or the other way round (they see to it that means are always transparent and available, leaving them free to tackle all potential goals). This explains the diametrically opposed classification of Greeks and Swiss in the Hofstedian and Housian studies (cf. House, 2004). The Swiss and the Greeks are placed either very high or very low on the uncertainty avoidance scale (differently in each of the studies). Apparently, bureaucratic over-regulation allows individuals to focus on goals and take the organized set of means for granted (as with the Swiss), while administrative chaos forces them to fix the goals and concentrate on accessing and using the means, which have to be extracted from an inefficient bureaucracy (as with the Greeks).

Another variant of the same criticism is provided by those researchers who question Hofstede's assignment of a position along the Individualism–Collectivism dimension to a particular link to willingness to either compete or collaborate:

Contrary to commonly shared beliefs, certain aspects of collectivism are positively related to entrepreneurship, and some individualistic tendencies help intensifying cooperation. Also, values, more than the norms, seem to mostly affect behaviors.

(Ferrara, Roberson, 2004)

Finally, in investigating values and beliefs via attitude surveys, researchers have problems distinguishing between *reality* and *desirability* (values actually referred to and operationalized by respondents into norms or counter-norms in real life situations, as distinct from values they see fit to declare but not necessarily to follow, especially in some specific circumstances; hence they do not translate into norms, which can be defined more flexibly depending on the particular context). Identities are played with and values promoted and demoted in individual and collective identities, with norms treated much less reverently than values by most individuals.[17]

Hofstede dealt with some of the criticism levelled against him in both the latest edition of his fundamental study *Culture's Consequences* (Hofstede, 2001) and in articles concerned with refutation of counterarguments (cf. Hofstede, 2002). *In spite of the increasing criticism of his theoretical framework, it is still the most widely acknowledged, accepted, improved upon, and used approach to studying, classifying and managing cross-cultural differences in sciences of organization as practised in schools of business.* These share all the biases Hofstede has been charged with. Some of these biases are gradually coming under critical fire – not only in Hofstede's writings – and are now being questioned as a result of a self-reflective critique of critical representatives of academic communities. In other words, the representatives of the academic communities are ready to re-engineer their (our) identities, responding to what is perceived as a too narrow, local, exclusive, and evolutionarily 'obsolete' identity. In doing so they also notice that they are not alone in contemporary society, that re-identizing has become a common occurrence among increasingly broad groups in the population. How does this re-engineering or re-inventing of an identity proceed?

First, it is acknowledged that these 'biased' theoretical concepts have emerged within the Western cultural tradition as a result of the managerial revolution of the past century and thus reflect the 'managerialist' bias criticized by representatives of critical management studies. Second, these biased theoretical concepts have emerged in the period of the global domination of the Western European nation-state (perceived as a privileged form of governance) and thus reflect the relative dominance of national culture as the nation-state's ideological legitimation. This domination is being increasingly criticized by critics of global world systems and of neocolonialism. Third, they have focused on nation-states and business enterprises as the main actors in globalized markets and thus reflect the bias towards the post WWII Cold War world order as the most natural governance infrastructure. This tendency to see frozen state alliances (as in the Cold War) and business corporations as the only counterparts of nation-states is criticized by anti-globalists. There is thus a close fit between the Hofstedian approach to cultural identities and the research, teaching and consulting context of business schools with academic standing, all of which developed in the 'Western' world. *National and organizational identities still form the core frame of our personalities, sense-making and identizing, but we experiment with other identities (personal in life-styles and professional in career pathing) in changing configurations and in varying proportions.* A relatively local group of fans share the fortunes of their football clubs all the time, but as all other citizens of a nation-state they join real and virtual ranks of 'nationally identified crowds' for the period of international championships, be it only once in five years or only at the time of the major televised games.

In spite of the continuing, if undermined, core position of national and professional identities, it is also becoming clear that the Hofstedian framework has to be reviewed and critically developed in order to deal with the honing of identities (cf. Magala, 2004) that is resulting in extreme subjectivities at the individual level and a cultural evolution of identities (age, gender, professions) at the collective one. 'Unzipping' the theoretical concepts of the various dimensions and tracing context-bound changes in the ranking of values should contribute to a better understanding of individual and organizational identizing. The self-critical 'unzipping' of Hofstedian dimensions, interestingly enough, is mostly undertaken by researchers who identify with his framework (Boski, Ferrara) and by the representatives of the older academic disciplines involved in the analyses of business management (Ritzer, Mirowski). Hence critical economists, who study their science as an 'outcome of an interactive network of cognitively challenged agents' and ask 'what will happen to the university once research and teaching are spun off as separate privatized self-contained endeavors?' (Mirowski, Sent, 2002, 58). Hence critical sociologists, who study the 'McDonaldization of science' and 'the globalization of nothing' (Ritzer, 2004). Hence critical studies in recent history and philosophy of science, whose authors trace the influence of political ideologies and institutional governance structures in shaping contemporary science during the Cold War (Fuller, 2002, Amadae, 2003).

In all these areas, as in cross-cultural management studies, there is a growing awareness that socializing into personal identities has been individualized and 'privatized' among new, different agencies, which an individual encounters during his or her increasingly more complex and non-linear 'career pathing'. Every organizational form gets re-engineered, re-invented, re-juvenated, re-structured, re-designed – far too quickly for an individual to adjust himself or herself to it, let alone become socialized into it. These changed conditions of individual socialization are probably responsible for the relative decline of the national culture's influence upon individual 'identizing', which is not as standardized and does not accompany a standardized 'career pathing'. It is especially difficult to compare with linear upward mobility within a single corporation that offers life-time employment, as used to be the case in the 1950s and 1960s, i.e. in the first quarter of a century of the post-WWII and the Cold War period. The student unrest of 1968, which emerged on both sides of the Iron Curtain and outside of it in the Third World (Mexico City, Yugoslavia), put an end to this period of a relatively stable socialization, while the oil crisis of 1973–4 and the development of digital and satellite-linked global communications accelerated a further change in socialization processes, leading to the replacement of 'Organization Man' (who climbed the ladder of the corporate hierarchy) with 'Spider Woman' (who built his or her career out of projects, assignments and endeavours, which did not necessarily add up to upward mobility within a single corporation's hierarchy) and to a new process of self-identizing, less dependent on concrete organizational and institutional frameworks than ever before:

> It is important that we remake our understanding of ourselves whenever the old definitions seem to be failing. Climbing the organizational hierarchy is no longer like climbing stairs in a stable structure. The stairs have become rope ladders, with managers clinging desperately for balance. Organization Man is changing into Spider Woman.
>
> (Johansen, Swigart, 1994, 8)

4 Shifting cultural identities: the global connection

Thank God I am an atheist.

(Louis Buñuel)

The global connection inherent in cross-cultural competence in management is, after the linguistic connection, the second most important factor defining our ability to co-operate across cultural and other borders in an increasingly interconnected and globally transparent world. This global connection is objectively present (global networks of trade exchange and communicative connections will not cease to exist if a single individual withdraws from them) and is inter-subjectively engaged with. Procedures in international disputes are slowly but surely being regulated on the basis of multilateral agreements; professional communities are learning to accommodate regional differences. Individual cultural intelligence (praised as a privileged locus of learning processes in individualist methodologies) certainly helps us cope with differences, but it is *cross-cultural competence* (a collective phenomenon emerging out of inter-subjective processes and interactions) that is needed – if, that is, we want to understand the symbols, interpret communications and successfully undertake joint ventures with individuals, whose cultural software differs from our own. Cross-cultural competence is necessary if we want to understand generational shifts in cultural identities due to changing circumstances of socializing and acculturation.

Cross-cultural competence – social, shared and transmittable (and not a figment of our imagination, not a shadow of a collective illusion in our monadic minds, as methodological individualists would like us to believe) – is needed to navigate our personal and organizational projects through this increasingly complex and interconnected world of individuals, groups, associations, clusters, communities, organizations, corporations, nations, religious civilizations, states, alliances of states, and global organizations. It is also needed to detect less than equitable, not always contractual relations in networks, for instance in labour-intensive industries (of which cultural industries are a case in point) and to expose them, to turn them into the valid items for discussion and cultural, political and economic action. This is what social life within formal organizations is all about; this is where the action is in core social processes, where the collective heart of our interactivity and social development beats, where cultural change emerges. This is the social location where individuals do not tolerate asymmetries in relations any more, for instance discrimination against women, exploitation of the young, authoritarianism of those higher up in a hierarchy. We socialize for roles and positions, but we acculturate for dreams, scripts and successful role-playing. For instance, cross-cultural competence is needed in order to evaluate the process of assigning different values (and prices) to the contributions of different 'producers' of food and cultural contents, coffee and songs, steel plates and dances:

> differential distribution of value for labour is similar to that of a 'woman's work', especially their col*labor*ation within the family unit, where the satisfaction of motherhood was considered proper remuneration. Cultural work often goes unremunerated financially because it is assumed that those engaged in it derive spiritual or aesthetic value from it. In a cultural economy like that of a Latin entertainment and new media industries in Miami, there are many collaborators, especially those immigrants and other groups that provide the rhythms, fusions, and hybridities that drive 'content' or, in Castell's words, 'give life' through new musics or situations for a telenovela.
>
> (Yudice, 2003, 213)

This process of interpreting differential distribution of value for labour goes on as piecemeal social engineering in thousands of professional communities, in millions of economic, cultural, political, and social interactions between individuals and groups, and results in changes and shifts in value chains. It is a relatively continuous, but not particularly rapid process: inequalities tend to be preserved and unfairness is very slowly removed and compensated. The temptation to introduce a historical 'shortcut' is quite strong. In fact, socialist movements of the late 19th and early 20th centuries were based on an assumption that they were simply accelerating the process of a change, thus serving as 'midwives' of history, facilitating the birth of something that would have been born anyway, that would have been inevitable anyway – though left to the unaided mechanisms of history, it would have lasted much longer than the patience of trade union and political party members.

Seen through the eyeglasses of cross-cultural competence, similar short-cuts are nowadays slowly becoming visible as they are designed by members of anti-globalist movements (who also want to convince us that these shortcuts are feasible) and negotiated or fought over. The temptation to see the cluster of global organizations (the World Bank, International Monetary Fund, World Trade Organization) and the political elite of the richest capitalist countries (the G8) as the 'axis of evil' responsible for the poverty and exploitation of the 'wretched of the earth' is very strong. It is based on a powerful utopian attempt to create a critical ideology that might, in a favourable political climate, enable a potential counter-elite to take over the government of nation-states and the governance structures of the interstate and intercorporation global system dominated by the Western world.

Of two Cassandras mentioned above, Huntington is the less convincing. Islamic fundamentalists do not offer a feasible shortcut to an alternative non-European modernization. The Muslim world is at present in turmoil, but it certainly is not an 'absolute' enemy, incommensurate 'other', who can be defeated only in armed struggle and with whom no cross-cultural compromise is ever possible. Historically speaking, the Muslim world has shown a greater tendency towards tolerance and multiculturalism than our Christian one, and considerable flexibility in political arrangements. Muslim fundamentalism is a very recent invention, one of the many responses to global expansion of 'the West'. There is no reason to suppose that a peaceful re-engineering of Muslim communities within nation-states cannot happen again:

> What is becoming clear is that Islamic fundamentalism (by no means universally popular among Muslims) lacks intellectual rigor and has difficulty responding adequately to the demands of twenty-first century society. What is needed is an evolving message from the Qu'ran itself, not that of the mullahs reaching back to the phraseology of a millennium ago.

> (Lewis, 2003, 286)

Ritzer, with his warning against the global dissemination of 'nothing' (i.e. of an efficient system that functions in instrumental terms but fails to meet the criteria of value-based rationality, of a humanist interpretation) is more disturbing than Huntington. He may be right in warning us against the feasibility of a consumer utopia – since its establishment would render the Enlightenment project irrelevant and close us all off in empty ritual of 'meaningless' interaction. He writes with a gnawing awareness of the fact that we have to undertake a large scale re-engineering of our own 'Enlightenment' project of the emancipation of mankind. Cultural re-engineering of 'modernity' – understood as an unfinished project, not a ready-made set of universal truths and values – is something urged by most Western thinkers and politicians. Cultural rejuvenation of 'Enlightenment' as a global dissemination of humanist values should be linked, but not subjected to the instrumental rationality of perfectly functioning economic or technological systems. Present-day anti-globalist movements are provoked by what they see as an (economic) 'colonization' of daily life by large corporations, which weaken social bonds, destroy trust, reduce rationality to an economic calculation, and dismantle local communities (which once pulsed with a lively network of voluntary associations and where presently everybody 'bowls alone'). What comes in the wake of Wal-Marts and McDonald's is an empty space of shopping malls, highway-connected suburbs and televised amnesia. *The anti-globalist movements, which are converging and networking on a global scale, take a free ride on the latest digital and satellite-linked communications, rapidly reaping the benefits of the new patterns of socialization that weaken the traditional values and the traditional socialization sites of the younger generation: family, school, the first working environment.* They offer the feeling of a real community in an increasingly 'unreal', artificial and rationalized environment. There is a price to this offer: in order to feel safe from accelerating social change one has to believe that a safe haven is possible to find, and that finding it will not harm other local communities in the world (while we know that disturbing supra-national organizations and networks of nation-states almost certainly will). These movements may be dangerous, not because they might turn terrorist (although there is a minority of their members who feel attracted to extreme, sometimes even terrorist activities), but because they will be filling the ideological vacuum left by the crisis in state-co-ordinated socialization in family, school and a working organization. They will offer 'cozy utopias' to make us feel at home in the universe, at home in the world, in which, as usual, all that is solid melts into thin air.

The most important factor, which provides fertile ground for anti-globalist movements and makes us aware of difficulties experienced in the construction of a cross-cultural competence at all levels, is the fact that changed patterns of socialization in family, school and at work, all of which used to be co-ordinated by nation-states for their respective societies, have influenced the values of individuals, prompting the cultural evolution that is slowly unfolding in front of us. If Whyte's 'Organization Man' from 1962 can be taken as a frame of reference, then a study of the children of Whyte's respondents, *The New Individualists* by Tucker and Leinberger (cf. Leinberger, Tucker, 1991) presents the portrait of a member of anti-globalist movements (not all of the children of the corporate officers of the 1950s became anti-globalists, but those who did, did so in a way that depended on their proudly individualist way). The change from a proud self-made man, who was a good team-player, raised a family and climbed the corporate ladder, to an equally proud member of this Organization Man's children's generation was a very profound one. In the 1960s and 1970s the new individualist, who worked on his or her self-made individuality, who honed his or her personality in a variety of jobs and organizational contexts, emerged and started a career that marked a very radical departure from the career path of his or her father:

> For the organization offspring . . . individualism became synonymous with individuality and with the cultivation of the private self. . . . As the organization offspring came of age in the Sixties and Seventies, they were exhorted to find themselves or create themselves. They undertook the task with fervour, as self-expression, self-fulfilment, self-assertion, self-actualization, self-understanding, self-acceptance, and any number of other *self* compounds found their way into everyday language and life.
>
> (Leinberger, Tucker, 1991, 11–12)

Note that survey questions about Hofstede's dimensions, while remaining unchanged, can mean something different to different individuals, depending on their generational cohort and its particular socializing experiences, i.e. on birth date. Those who are plotted on, for instance the individualism–collectivism scale (some critics would even object to the representative nature of individuals being assumed to render national cultural traits), could understand the questions differently depending whether they had been born, say, in 1930 or 1960, 1950 or 1980.

The baby-boom generation's 'long march' through the institutions and corporations did not resemble a single-company, life-time-employment based, simple upward climb of the ladder of corporate managerial positions. Children of 'organization men' interviewed by Leinberger and Tucker (born between 1946 and 1956, *c.* 40 at the time of their interviews) clearly did not have a safe framework of a single stable company as the stage for their careers. Accelerated change and frequent crises confronted them with takeovers, buyouts, restructurings, mergers, acquisitions, and shake-downs. The emergence of organizational networks replacing hierarchical structures and a proliferation of temporary jobs, positions and projects replacing tenured employment increased their stress. These projects further 'atomised' them in their incommensurable professional settings, roles and enterprises. Pursuing their particular career paths, navigating between networks, platforms and organizations, baby boomers were bound to develop a belief in the instrumental value of organizations. For their parents' generation, life-long-employment companies were much more than instrumental and temporary arrangements for co-operation and accomplishment of tasks. Baby-boomers had to re-define, restrict their commitment to projects, to shorter periods of time, to more flexible networks of individuals. Their vision of organizations was the one of

> permeable boundaries, shifting nodes of power, and relational systems in which stability is continually deferred. . . . One's identity is defined less by job description, as in the old bureaucratic ideal, than by one's relation at any given moment to groups and people inside and outside the organization whose identities are similarly shifting.
>
> (Leinberger, Tucker, 1991, 350)

Leinberger's and Tucker's empirical research was based on 175 in-depth interviews and relied on a comparison of 175 personal 'professional life stories'. Considering the size of the sample, it is hardly more representative than the study of their parents undertaken by Whyte. However, considering the similarity between those 175 professional life-stories and many other cases found in research reports of the past two decades, it is quite clear that a cultural shift has taken place. Different contexts of socialization (less-uniform education within a plurality of paradigms, the socializing influence of political protest, precarious economic developments, organizational instability of employment) produced a different type of cultural identizing: less collectivistic and more individualistic than in their parents' generation, but very inter-subjective, cross-cultural and collectively shared. In spite of professed extreme subjectivity and individualism, and a conscious attempt to be different, even as artificially as possible (as opposed to their parents' generation, who wanted to be very much like the others, as artificially as possible, baby-boomers want to be different, but each of them wants it in the same way).[18] These baby-boomers are different from their parents but in their carefully cultivated differences from one another they reveal a common pattern of collectively individualized cultural identities. To understand those identities and their 'clash' with organizational forms, one has to conduct a re-examination of the theoretical framework of cross-cultural competence (because the shifting context of identizing shifts values along dimensions from generation to generation without necessarily changing the very conceptual definition of a value; the value appears to remain the same, but it exerts a quite different influence on individual behaviour in changed contexts). *Understanding these new, volatile cultural identities and their*

*'empirical testing' in everyday social interactions and in all organizational
contexts is at the core of global cross-cultural competence.*

5 The case of integrating Kazakh immigrants in Poland [with Z. Rejmer]

When speaking of a national cultural identity, we usually think in terms of
relatively stable identities of groups, which share language, territory, history,
and states, and furnish labour for companies and institutions. Less frequent
are studies of the psychic and social effects of cultural identizing. Does, for
instance, a national cultural identity influence an individual, subjective
assessment of one's own psychic well-being and 'happiness'? Does one have
to feel 100 per cent French or Portuguese in order to enjoy life? Does one's
satisfaction with one's life differ from the satisfaction of a fellow-citizen who
feels only 50 per cent French or Portuguese? Normally sociologists do not
ask such questions, except when considering inter-group conflicts (when the
percentage of identifying and being identified with a national group matters)
or relative differences in attitudes towards European integration. When
Therborn was investigating the role of audio-visual 'Americanization' of
European youth, he did so in order to evaluate the overall trajectory of
European integration after 1945. He examined various degrees of pride felt
by young Europeans who described themselves as members of a national
community (cf. Therborn, 1995). He did not examine nor diagnose the
structure of a national cultural identity or did so only indirectly by looking
at studies of responses to a potential decision to abandon the European
Union. The problem was much more acute for those countries that began to
receive relatively new waves of immigrants from the former Soviet Union –
since in their case the very basis for immigration was ethnic and national
identity (e.g. identification with Germany, Poland, Israel). In this case
the 'percentage' of German-ness, Polish-ness or Jewish-ness of the new
immigrants does matter in their immigration and subsequent acceptance
and integration.

A recent Polish study (by Z. Rejmer, 2004) is based on interviews with 53
ethnic Poles who had immigrated from Kazakhstan to Poland in the 1990s;
31 women and 22 men, whose average age was 33.87 and who had been in
Poland 3.3 years on average (cf. Boski, 1992, Grzymała Moszczyńska,
2000). The author is interested in the structure of national cultural identity,
its correlations with age, gender and length of stay in Poland, and in the
possible influence this national cultural identity might exert upon personal
psychic well-being, one's subjective satisfaction with one's life. The results of
her study confirm that there is a considerable influence of national cultural
identity on general satisfaction with one's life. National cultural identity
turns out to be significantly and reliably predictive as far as psychic well-
being of immigrants is concerned. However, the results of her study

also indicate a complex interplay of two different national identities (the 'ethnic' one of the country they immigrated to and the one linked to the 'pre-immigration' country), differences between men and women, and between an 'idealized' national identity versus the 'real' one. Where does the group in question come from?

In the wake of the peaceful break-up of the Soviet Union a number of repressed and imprisoned ethnic groups acquired the right to leave the regions to which they had been forcefully relocated by the Soviet authorities. German, Tartar and Polish minorities are the best-known cases in point. The Polish minority in Kazakhstan developed as a result of mass deportations from Poland's eastern territories occupied by the Russians on 17 September 1939, following the Ribbentrop–Molotov Pact, which triggered the outbreak of World War II. Soviet deportations of Polish citizens and mass executions of the Polish social elites (of which the massacre of some 14,000 Polish officers in Katyń and other prisoner-of-war camps is a particularly gloomy example) were part of a broad social re-engineering and sovietization of the annexed territories. Kazakhstan had already been used as a region to which Poles had been deported after the armed uprisings against Russian occupation in the 19th century (according to Tsarist statistics, 11,000 Poles lived in Central Asia in 1897). Preparing with Hitler for the joint aggression against Poland, Stalin deported 250,000 Poles from the areas along the western border of the Soviet Union in 1936 and settled reliable Communist Ukrainians and White Russians on their farms. Many Poles deported to Kazakhstan died as a result of harsh winters and lack of housing. This act of ethnic cleansing had been overshadowed by the much more bloody engineered famine in the Ukraine, which accompanied forced collectivization in this Soviet republic. In 1940–1 a new wave of deportations of the Polish citizens from Poland's eastern territories (c. 150,000) followed the new partition of Poland executed by Hitler and Stalin, thus significantly enlarging the Polish population of Kazakhstan. Some of them could return in the years 1955–9, when the 'thaw' after Stalin's death enabled the Polish government to secure the return of above 250,000 ethnic Poles from all regions of the Soviet Union. One might say that their life stories were human consequences of a Soviet global project, of which the alliance with Nazi Germany in 1939 and systematic ethnic, professional, generational, and social cleansing 'purges' were significant components.

In 1991 Kazakhstan became a sovereign state, but this did not, however, improve the situation of the Polish minority. Kazakh nationalism led to discrimination against all other nationalities, including the Poles, with respect to education (for instance, the legal profession is reserved for ethnic Kazakhs only), employment, housing, etc. In this situation, many ethnic Poles in Kazakhstan applied for re-immigration to Poland. Of 3,000 ethnic Poles who returned to Poland in the period 1992–2000, two-thirds came from Kazakhstan.

Those new re-immigrants usually came from small towns or villages, had acquired a medium or high level of education and were usually 18–40 years old. Listing reasons for returning to Poland, they mentioned a search for better living conditions, willingness to secure a better future for their children and the emotional appeal of a national cultural identity. Some of them had formed a very idealized image of Poland, not least under the influence of Polish professionals (teachers, priests) who arrived in Kazakhstan to serve the Polish minority deprived of cultural assistance by the former Communist regime.

Confronting the idealized image of Poland with everyday life after arrival often led to disappointment; immigrants did not know the legal rules and regulations, faced anonymous bureaucracies, often had to lower their professional ambitions, suffered a loss of status when looking for employment, and had to cope with their less than fluent command of Polish. Some of the immigrants commented bitterly on their mixed reception by local communities, saying that in Soviet Kazakhstan they were 'the Poles' while in Poland they are 'the Kazakhs' or 'the Ruskies'. On the other hand they did appreciate the 'adaptation courses' – for instance the ones offered by the Polish Humanitarian Action and Warsaw School of Social Psychology since 2002. Generally speaking, children (7–17 years) *assimilated* to the national cultural identity more quickly than others, while ethnic Poles from Kazakhstan who began studying at Polish universities – acquiring their scholarships as young adults 18–25 years old – had more trouble integrating with other students and identizing; thus more often than not they chose the strategy of *marginalization*.[19]

National cultural identity of recent ethnic Polish immigrants from Kazakhstan has been studied with respect to acquaintance with cultural symbols, the personal significance attached to them and strong positive valuation on the one hand, and with respect to the correlative attributes of national cultural identity – for instance, they were asked about hospitality, taking care of the family, cultivating friendships, and engaging in passionate political discussions – on the other. The distinction between *correlative* and *criterial* attributes of national cultural identity was introduced in Boski's taxonomy of criterial and correlative attributes of personal and social identity (cf. Boski, 1992). Criterial identity has been studied via the Cultural Symbols Questionnaire, which included Polish and Kazakh politically significant sites, monuments and buildings, and important dates in national calendars. The Polish cultural symbols included, among others, the following photographs: a view of Cracow (the historical capital of the Kingdom of Poland until the late 16th century), a shot from a film based on Sienkiewicz's patriotic novel about Poland's past (written in order to raise the spirits after the partitions of the late 18th century), the round-table negotiations between the last Communist government and Solidarity (a symbolic moment in the breakdown of the Communist power in Poland), the Grand Orchestra of Festive Assistance (a nation-wide charity collection carried out with heavy media coverage around Christmas/New Year's Eve), a blessing of the traditional Easter food (with painted eggs carried in small baskets to the church), and a portrait of Joseph Pilsudski, who commanded the Polish armies who won independence in 1918 and defended it against the Russian invasion in 1921. Kazakh cultural symbols included the following photographs: *bispermak* (a traditional course in Kazakh cuisine), a portrait of Nikita Khrushchev, a Polish house of prayer in Kazakhstan, *bayga* (a traditional Kazakh game), a dug-out, or the so-called 'Stalin housing' (where most of the first wave of the deported Poles had to live), and a panorama of the Kazakh steppes. The questionnaire on cultural values and scripts accounted for the following cultural dimensions: collectivism, humanism, materialism, liberalism and 'sarmatism'.[20]

Immigrants who had spent between six months and a year in Poland were more adept in recognizing the Kazakh than the Polish cultural symbols. After a year both were recognized equally readily, and after longer periods of time the Polish cultural symbols clearly prevailed and had acquired increasing personal significance. Immigrants gave low scores to the quality of their lives prior to immigration, but the first months in Poland did not score very highly either. However, scores rose with time and all immigrants predicted growing well-being and increasing satisfaction with their lives on a five-year perspective. An interesting discovery was made with respect to the difference between men and women. First, women were more pessimistic than men in predicting their future well-being. Second, men identified with all three prototypes – an inhabitant of Kazakhstan, an imagined Pole and a real inhabitant of Poland. However, women tended to identify with either the imagined Pole or the inhabitant of Kazakhstan, keeping their distance from identifying with a real inhabitant of Poland. While it is clear that women did not identify themselves with a national cultural identity proto-type in which materialism and autonomy (the 'real Pole') prevailed over tolerance and a friendly attitude towards others (the 'idealized Pole'), it is less clear why they did so. What is also less obvious is that women chose a Kazakh identity as a second possibility, even though it is low not only on materialism and autonomy (which would account for their rejection of the real Polish identity), but also on tolerance and a friendly attitude towards others (which should account for its rejection on a par with the real Polish identity). Even more puzzling is the discovery that women in general manifest lower acquaintance with cultural symbols, particularly the Kazakh ones. One possible explanation can be found in the hypothesis that prior to re-immigration, women had focused on idealized attributes of the Polish cultural identity, expecting very warm interactions, friendly relationships, general assistance, and caring attitudes, and found instead a materialist, modernizing culture with autonomous individuals pursuing their entre-preneurial projects, with less time and willingness to cultivate friendly relations with others in their milieu. While men have accepted Poland as a country in which autonomy, independence, entrepreneurship, and pragmatic attitudes are highly regarded (and had already formed this image while still in Kazakhstan), women were less accepting (since they had previously focused on an idealized image and their expectations have thus been frustrated). These results are even more puzzling if one compares them with data from which it follows that women were much better adapted to the new cultural reality than men. How is it possible that much better adapted women were much less 'happy' and 'satisfied', and manifested lower levels of psychic well-being?

One possible explanation concerns the prevailing gendered life-style that female immigrants led in Kazakhstan before their return to Poland. Both in the Kazakh culture and in the culture of the Polish minority in Kazakhstan, a woman plays traditional social roles: she takes care of the household and does not compete with men as far as participation in social and political activities goes. Contemporary Polish culture, however, is highly feminist and women are, at least formally, legally and theoretically, equal to men. They are active professionally and hold jobs or compete with men for seats in parliament, places in university education and top managerial positions. They are expected to perform as well or better than men – to pursue professional careers, fight for their share of power in organizations, etc. Female re-immigrants could thus feel alienated facing these expectations, which, in their eyes, are misplaced and misdirected, since they should be addressed to men. Men, on the other hand, expected a business-like, pragmatic attitude, and accepted it even before re-immigration: they see this cultural identity as compatible with their social obligations and conducive to a competitive struggle.

If acculturation training courses are to be designed in future, one should bear this in mind when addressing gendered audiences. Moreover, it appears that such acculturation courses would be needed not only in cases of low adaptation to the new culture, but also in cases of a relatively high adaptation, but with an underlying problem of frustrated expectations. Finally, one should add that in spite of this astonishing difference between men and women, all immigrants, male and female, declared an increase in their well-being compared to their life in Kazakhstan and are optimistic when assessing their future life chances.

This provides an important clue for social scientists and politicians who are looking for policies and procedures to facilitate integration of large immigrant communities, which are evolving into a new, permanent under-classes in large Western European cities: Turks in Germany, Moroccans in the Netherlands, Algerians in France, and Pakistanis in the UK. Policy-makers must deal with a second or third generation of immigrants, whose integration into society depends crucially on their ability to retain their ethnic identity and to participate in the upward social mobility opened in secularized, Western societies. If women from these substantial minorities can be assisted in reconciling their idealized and actual images of the host country (which includes acculturation training that will help them develop a new, more independent identity and reduce dependence on fundamentalist religious affiliations), if their young generations can be made more optimistic when assessing their future chances (which relies heavily on education and respect in spite of inequality, in Sennett's famous phrase, cf. Sennett, 2003), a considerable source of social tensions and political unrest can be neutralized and many polarizing conflicts avoided (the most obvious ones being connected to religious mobilization by militant Islamic fundamentalists). German, Polish, US, and Israeli experience with their respective immigrants from the former Soviet Union (already reported and analysed in a number of research publications) may turn out to be a very useful contribution to the development of cultural competence in dealing with re-integration through national cultures and new identity-supplying subcultures.

It would be interesting to know if mutual understanding and respect in a world of inequality does, or does not prevail. One possible way of finding out if it does is to look at the actual circulation of ideas about immigrants and their integration in academic communities. If the various experiences of dealing with immigrants and displaced ethnic groups mentioned above are compared and discussed in professional communities of researchers, no matter what 'side' their broader societies are on, and if they are freely available to all interested parties (managers of state bureaucracies, business companies, the media, and local community organizers) then perhaps we stand a chance of breaking out of a vicious circle of endlessly repeating the rituals of apparent integration, while in actuality not living up to our own ideals of equality and fairness.

Chapter 3

Networking organizations

The management connection

> Culture is . . . the structure of values and of the feelings which belong to them, moving through a force field of social action. Politics is the pattern of relations into which the society in question falls, as its members both resist and express its culture. Neither is predominant; either is a tissue of narratives; primacy is a consequence of human effort and accident. Sometimes culture wins out, sometimes politics, either for better or worse.
>
> (Inglis, 2004, 162)[1]

I Organizational cultures by design

Having talked about culture and cultural competence in the context of ends, means and meanings (*the language connection*), and in the context of clashing civilizations (*the global connection*), let us now look at culture and cultural competence from the perspective of increasingly networked and co-ordinated, organized and planned, co-operation and interaction among individuals and groups. Since most of the complex networks in which individuals regularly interact are composed of formally defined organizations (banks and restaurants, schools and hospitals, churches and discos, clubs and associations, but also and increasingly virtual platforms, chatrooms and online communities), and since formal organizations are usually co-ordinated by managers (even the most democratic and non-hierarchic organizations usually distinguish managerial functions and allocate them selectively), we may call this point of view and this angle of approaching the problems of culture *the management connection*. In designing organizational cultures we try to account for understanding and communicating (the language connection), for networking and co-operating (the global connection), and for motivating and leading (the management connection).

Making sense of the world from the perspective of organizing and managing requires a certain skill in balancing the ambiguities between an instrumental view of culture (individual mental software enabling one to co-operate) and a non-instrumental, ethical view of core cultural values (a collective hierarchy of values guiding individual choices and generating positive emotions, thus shaping preferences). An instrumental view of culture leads managers to design organizational cultures in the hope of increased commitment of employees to the strategic goals of the organization in question – no matter what these strategic goals may be. A non-instrumental view of culture leads managers to design corporate codes of conduct they hope will provide regular monitoring of commitment to the core values of the culture into which employees have been socialized; the strategic goals of the organization are then viewed with respect to their compatibility with values. Both organizational cultures by design and corporate codes of conduct belong to standard managerial constructs documented in organizational communications at the turn of the 20th and 21st centuries. Managers see culture either as an instrument for making sense of the world in general and organizational activities in particular, or as a seat of core values reflected in norms and patterns of behaviour. In the latter case managers hope that by monitoring these norms and behaviour in a systematic and transparent way, they will uphold these core values (and gain an additional source of legitimacy for themselves and their organizations). Due to the predominance of 'managerialism' as an ideology influencing the development of the sciences of management and organiz-ation, these two approaches, instrumental and non-instrumental, are often perceived as different facets of the same project. It is not unusual to find them assigned to different roles of the same manager, or to assign all dealings with culture to the Dr Jekyll of a 'leader', while leaving all traditional control functions to a Mr Hyde of a 'manager', as in the following standard handbook of general management:

> What's the difference between a manager and a leader?
> A manager plans, organizes, and controls functions within an organization.
> A leader has vision and inspires others to grasp that vision, establishes corporate values, emphasizes corporate ethics, and doesn't fear change.
> . . .
> Which leadership style is best?
> The best (most effective) leadership style depends on the people being led and the situation. The challenge of the future will be to empower self-managed teams to manage themselves. This is a move away from autocratic leadership.
> (Nickels, McHugh, McHugh, 2002, 227)

Standard managerial studies of leadership also evoke the image of:

> . . . moving away from the traditional control model towards alternatives that emphasize cultural competence, corporate learning and facilitation skills. The success of the new leadership approaches will depend on

aligning people, organizational systems, processes and culture with the new conditions.

. . .

Ideas about leadership are affected by concepts of leadership held within a particular culture or other context in which people find themselves. . . . Without a context, people tend to hold command-and-control as their basic leadership model.

. . .

Leadership is a distributed phenomenon, occurring in various parts of an organization, not just emanating from the top.

(Avery, 2004, 7–8)

The point is to get beyond an ideology that idealizes managers making them appear as leaders, and to understand what is involved in real life, i.e. in emotionally loaded, power-driven, working interactions with other individuals, when managers' idealized cultural self-image and managers' usual control instruments for dealing with employees meet. Creating cross-cultural competence depends crucially on being able to understand ethical choices and ways in which values do make a difference in individual and groups behaviour.

Making sense of the world from the perspective of managing and organizing is influenced by the cultural software of individuals and groups in a number of complex ways. We do not simply make sense of the world by honing our linguistic and analytical skills, and by discovering once and forever 'the world out there'. We continue deciphering and constructing (or re-constructing, deconstructing or destroying) meanings in our communications, and continually redraw 'maps' of reality for ourselves and for others. We do so by also recognizing our duties and meeting our obligations, i.e. by drawing conclusions from our commitment to values and norms or by renegotiating them. We renegotiate by modifying norms, or by rephrasing and reinterpreting values. We do so even if for various reasons we refuse to acknowledge our active participation in renegotiating values, especially if they are sanctioned by religion.

For instance, if we happen to be raised in a Christian culture, we may try to modify the norm of celebrating a single day of the week – Sunday – by refraining from work. A modification is meant to increase flexibility of behaviours. If we want some services to be available 24 hours a day, seven days a week, at least some work has to be done on Sundays as well. Shopping centres are now open on Sundays in most Western countries. This entailed the modification of a cultural norm: the original norm forbade all work on Sundays. In societies where Christian religion dominated time management, it was considered desirable to leave Sunday, singled out as the day God rested after Creation, free from physical effort. On Sundays one was supposed to rest from the work performed during the other six days of the week. Introducing work on Sundays not as an exception (as for railwaymen or policemen) but as a routine for jobs that could be done on other days, and encouraging the general public to go shopping instead of praying and reading the Bible, means that the norm has been changed. The value behind the norm – public homage to God – is still there, but it has been much reduced (to the option of going to a church service instead of visiting a shopping mall). Making the opening times of shops on Sunday shorter than the usual ones on working days (as has been done in Germany, Poland and the Netherlands) means that lip service is still being paid to the original norm, which prohibited Christians from working on Sundays altogether.

Placing old and ailing parents in nursing homes is another example of a modification with respect to a norm, the norm in question requiring one to respect one's father and mother, and interpreting respect as personal care and nursing parents in their old age, spent in their child's household. Needless to say, none of the renegotiations and changes of this norm happens in an emotional vacuum. For those who are brought up with the idea that it is their children's sacred duty to take care of their aged parents, the prospect of delivering a beloved parent to a nursing home, where he or she will be an anonymous patient of a large bureaucracy (and exposed, moreover, to the risk of a legalized euthanasia), is a truly horrifying one. For those of us who believe that the seventh day of the week should be spent reading the Bible and thinking about eternity, shopping on Sunday looks like a worshipping of money and commerce, and a move away from the Christian experience of the passing of time. For those of us who think that personal loving care of one's ageing and ailing parents is a sacred duty in the great chain of life, the act of bailing out of this duty by employing an anonymous bureaucracy is not an option. It is worth remembering that in both cases – when we go shopping on Sundays and when we look for a nursing home for aged parents (and in numerous other ways) – we are in fact managing a change in our norms. It would be strange indeed if our behaviour in the workplace was any different, i.e., if we never negotiated and renegotiated values and norms, either as managers or as employees.

A renegotiation of one of the core values takes place if we either reinterpret a core value or shift the relative position of the core value with respect to others. Religion offers the most obvious examples of values that have either been renegotiated or have changed their position in a hierarchy of values. These examples are most obvious because in religious doctrines values are formulated in the most direct way – as sacred principles revealed to humans by God and meant to be obeyed, not negotiated.

For instance, consider the issue of abortion. If defending the sanctity of human life belongs to the core values of Christian civilization, then those who argue that the value of free choice for child-bearing women takes precedence must be declared wrong. Men and women alike are supposed to accept the sanctity of human life, take it for granted that human intervention should be kept to the minimum, and refrain from interfering with God's ways. The renegotiation of this value begins with the criticism of unequal distribution of burdens. Child-bearing and child-rearing place a much heavier burden on women than men, and in a democratic society it may be argued that those whose duties are heavier should have a more decisive vote in these matters. An unequal share in law-making may also be pointed to: laws prohibiting abortion have been designed by childless men (celibate priests) and voted into legal acts by predominantly male parliaments. Gender inequality in the period of law-making resulted, so the feminist critics may argue, in an unequal distribution of burdens and brutal suppression of individual female freedom. Their stress on female rights may be considered an attempt to modify and reinterpret core values, to change their relative position in a hierarchy, and to redress past wrongs. They attempt to do so by placing individual freedom to choose first, and sanctity of human life second, which is the reversal of the original 'order of priorities' (upheld by celibate priests, who claim that divine gift of life is a higher value than individual freedom) and thus a renegotiation of the value hierarchy.

Helen Prejean, a Catholic nun who opposed the death penalty in Louisiana and wrote the book *Dead Man Walking* devoted to this issue, presented another case for renegotiating a value by explaining the intention of the norm at the time Christian values had been formulated among various tribes in the Middle East. She argued for a different sort of a renegotiation of norms, namely for a reinterpretation of the context, in which they had been formulated in order to understand what was the assumed to be 'the divine intention' in formulating a particular norm for Middle Eastern societies of the time. She quoted the Biblical norm of revenge, 'eye for eye, tooth for tooth', often invoked by those in favour of the death penalty in the US, and tried to reconstruct the way of thinking of the divine law-maker. As a result, she claimed that the norm had been introduced with an intention to *limit* the scope of bloody tribal revenge, so that the vicious circle of increasingly bloody retaliations could be stopped (and not to make it more cruel and painful than the original act, so that it would serve as a symbol of cruel revenge and thus function as a deterrent). If this was the intention, then killing the killer rather than making him (it is, by the way, usually a man) repent with a life-long sentence surely cannot be right from a Christian point of view. Progress can be measured not only in material goods, but also in fact that we do not have to limit ourselves to 'damage control' if tribes or clans continue a vicious circle of revenge, but can think of ways of making a sinner repent and amend his ways, leading him to desire a place in the community he wronged; thus the hierarchy of values should therefore be changed accordingly.[2]

Renegotiations of values, norms and hierarchies is also going on in organizational contexts, which facilitate some ways of making sense of things while 'discouraging' others. Creationism in a Christian church allows us to make sense of biological evolution in a way that is compatible with Revelation; thus the evolutionary theory of the origin of life and species is either weakened to make it compatible with the Bible or rejected. Creationism in a professional association of evolutionary biologists cannot be reconciled with theoretical neo-Darwinism unless one separates the scientific and religious thinking in one's mind by watertight partitions, and is therefore not taken seriously (though there are many biologists who consider themselves Christian and have found ways of reconciling their theoretical views and religious beliefs). Managerialism among professional managers allows them to make sense of organizations as spaces of managerial intervention; a more critical and less flattering approach to organizational analysis – for instance, Critical Management Studies – would have to be weakened in order to make it compatible with managerialism or rejected. Managerialism in a professional association of researchers into organizational, behavioural, social, and managerial problems can hardly be defended on academic grounds, though it may be reconciled with one's views for other, non-academic, reasons. The authors of standard introductions to general management do not usually ask themselves how to reconcile their view on enabling individual workers to increase their knowledge and autonomy at work with the bureaucratic hierarchies of most business companies:

> What does empowerment mean?
> Empowerment means giving employees the authority and responsibility to respond quickly to customer requests. Enabling is the term used to describe giving workers the education and tools they need to assume their new decision-making powers. Knowledge management involves finding the right information, keeping the information in a readily accessible place, and making the information known to everyone in the firm. Knowledge management is another way of enabling workers to do the best job they can.
>
> (Nickles, McHugh, McHugh, 2002, 227)

Or, to quote from a study of leadership that concludes with a selection of features of Organic Leadership approaches:

> The following are most likely to be emphasized: emotion, emotional intelligence, spirituality, systemic leadership, vision, values-based leadership, substitutes for leadership, fostering self-leading employees, using the organizational culture, strategic planning (through the group's sense-making activities), servant leader, socio-cognitive attributions, strategic learning, teaching, mentoring and managing knowledge.
>
> (Avery, 2004, 149)

This list of characteristic features of the 'organic leadership' paradigm includes empowerment along with other 'substitutes for leadership' (understood as command-and-control), and leads us to question at least some of the assumptions of the tacit ideology of 'managerialism'. Since this questioning remains limited to the theoretical discussion of leadership paradigms and does not include a more general critique of social, political, economic and ideological status quo, it is accepted as a professional contribution. Had the authors of leadership studies been more systematically critical, they would have to face the uncomfortable discovery of the influence exerted by managerialism on theoretical choices in the description, analysis and recommendations of themselves and their academic peers. *Is it not surprising that the gradual destruction or neutralization of trade unions, which resulted in a return to a 40-hour work week in the first years of the 21st century (after trade unions had limited it to 35 hours in collective negotiations) failed to elicit research interest among the academic communities in managerial sciences?* Globalization has been analysed from many theoretical perspectives – but not from the perspective of the uses made of Third-World sweatshops in order to increase the exploitation of labour in the First World. De-unionization and de-skilling, of professional work too, are themes that find few sponsors in research communities. It is no wonder that researchers are reluctant to design research projects around these issues. They would have to confront the ideology of managerialism in action. They would have to risk conflict with the community of business managers (which includes not only sponsors of research projects but also the selectors of job-seeking graduates). They would have to face the disturbing proximity of the new knowledge management theories to the rational choice theory, which may have saved the liberal legitimacy of managerialism, but only at a price:

> While reasserting the principles of universalism, reason and individualism, rational choice theorists refashion democratic theory into an individualistic competition that resembles market interactions predicated on self-interest. The early Cold War rational choice protagonists studied the micro-foundations of democratic institutions, seeking to offer a palliative for distress in the form of reconstituted knowledge.
>
> (Amadae, 2003, 22–3)

Mentioning the Cold War in this context is no coincidence. The Cold War shaped business companies, public authorities and the ideology of managerialism (defence of the free world and of individual freedom and entrepreneurship) much more than we are presently aware of. Before more studies are published and before we acquire more insights into the hidden injuries of Cold War (cf. Magala, 2002), let us here limit ourselves to an observation that we are not passively experiencing clashes of civilizations brought together by contemporary political, military, economic, and media networks, and by the increasing frequency with which we are exposed to encounters with 'the Others' due to an increasing variety of project-based networking for longer or shorter periods. We participate in most such encounters either as members of organizations identified with the clashing parties (for instance, if we are citizens of the countries that sent their troops to police Iraq after the US invasion but before the indigenization of the public authorities), or from the sidelines (if our national governments refused to do so or if we refused to support our government's decision – but even then we can scarcely be said to view developments in occupied Iraq as disinterested observers). We do both (participate and observe, evaluate and act), but not randomly and not at will. Our participation and our attitudes are influenced by many factors, of which 'sensitizing' by the media and the cultural 'managerialist' bias require particular attention. How often do we see critical analyses of the disappearance of industrial strikes from the repertory of collective action in the US on prime-time TV? How often do we read about the consequences of the disappearance of trade unions as an alternative to managerial good will in newspaper headlines?

One should point out that from the perspective of managerial connection, the media include not only the mass media (TV, press, internet), but also the media of organizational communication (intranet, e-mail, company documents, managers' speeches, informal gossip). Media frame our attention. In an increasingly complex and 'mediated' social reality, in which our 'maps' of social relations are formed with the aid of multimedia, we become crucially dependent on them. We can see only what the international media let us see, and we are not always aware of the censoring or selecting activities of those who let the media see what they want them to see. Sometimes it is not so much an issue of outright censorship as of the fashionable tide, which simply blocks out the broadcasting time for other, alternative news. A most spectacular recent example has been the sudden turn-around in the US media covering the Pope's visit to Cuba, which could have started a serious review of EU and US policies. The interest of the media was considerable. Potential results of the visit might have been both surprising and predictable. However, immediately after the papal landing, all TV crews left Havana and flew back to Washington, DC. The erotic adventures of President Clinton with a White House intern monopolized media attention and swept all the other issues from the centre of media stage (although the US citizen would have been better served by a discussion of Cuban policy alternatives than by a detailed study of presidential ejaculation or detailed reports of the O. J. Simpson murder case). Likewise, managers who follow a single fad (such as the balanced score card) or fashion (such as business process re-engineering) simply block alternative ways of managing. Leaders disseminating strong company culture during special sessions for high flyers have less time for trade unions, employee representatives or enterprise councils. Managers who are focusing on 'hard' aspects of organizing are less perceptive with respect to the 'soft' ones. Being less perceptive with respect to the soft aspects of organizing allows one to overlook some disturbing socio-political dynamics and political choices disguised as purely technical, functional decisions based on clear and transparent criteria. One can, for instance, defend the view that a decision by Pfeizer to start producing the Viagra pill has been a rational one – a classic case of the market potential of a side-effect of a tested drug being recognized on time, a window of opportunity opened with a profit. It would be much more interesting, though also much more politically risky, to check whether the private and public funds used to finance the advanced search for drugs to save millions from heart attacks and brain strokes have really been put to responsible use (and not diverted to produce a fashionable life-style enhancing drug, whose producer does not intend to share the profits with the sponsors). The limited ability of the former Third World countries to question the pricing policies of pharmaceutical companies demonstrates clearly the urgency and significance of such critical problem definitions. Unfortunately, research communities demonstrate even less interest in researching these issues than the media.

This induced blindness to a disturbing shadow side of business activities is the ideology of managerialism in action. The role of an ideology is to provide a cultural bias that focuses attention and facilitates choices. Nor do we manage dispassionately – ideology is about linking values and norms to passions and emotions. Since all our responses to what we learn are coloured by our emotions, some weak aspects of rational choice theory are increasingly obvious. So the cognitive sciences are increasingly tending to identify emotional intelligence and emotional trade-offs from interpersonal interactions as significant for our orientation in the world and for the choices we make in organizational contexts.[3]

The media also make us aware of the fact that nothing happens at a safe distance from us any more. Modern weapons of mass destruction, pollution, contagious diseases, and contemporary terrorist activities undermine the idea of such a distance, already weakened by air travel and by globally networked mass media. We are heavily networked, very emotional and increasingly formally organized; most of our encounters and interactions with those who attach different meanings to actions and symbols and who belong to different cultural backgrounds are within organized frameworks, under heavy emotional stress and subject to managed scenarios. They are being managed; but are they manageable?

The more complex organizations become and the more flexibly networked they are with others, often equally complex organizations, the more difficult to manage they become. Managers have to pay attention to different cultural backgrounds and local subcultures, which furnish their employees and 'networkees' with different mental software, while employees have to pay attention to unexpected developments and poorly structured problems, which have to be solved, often immediately and at a specific location. More often than not an employee has to respond on his or her own. Unavailable or ambiguous communications with the upper levels of management mean that corporate culture becomes 'what is left when managers are not watching'.

Many of the differences in individual cultural backgrounds, which managers recognize nowadays and acknowledge as requiring managerial attention (e.g. differences arising from gender, age and education, and ethnic, sexual and religious minorities) used to be ignored in the past as a result of an assumed standardization of organizational roles within formal industrial bureaucracies. Cultures were supposed to be solid, monolithic blocks of dark stone. Standardization continues to be an important instrument of managerial control in organizations, but its focus had shifted; one does not standardize individual behaviour as extensively as during the heyday of the Fordist assembly line and Taylor's attempts to find one best way of performing every physical movement. While some digital communications have, indeed, become highly standardized (Q: 'When?', A: 'Asap', as soon as possible), managers of contemporary organizations are expecting and stimulating behaviours that would have been considered disruptive 50 years ago, but which today are cherished as potential ways to break out of an organizational routine and hit upon a new, potentially profitable solution. One does not, therefore, standardize individuals, while one does standardize some of the educational inputs (e.g. by requiring most of the high-potential management trainees to complete an MBA programme at a decent, i.e. recognized and accredited university) and some of the evaluation procedures. One does not, for instance, standardize all contracts, or all employee benefits, preferring individualized 'psychological contracts' and differentiated benefit cafeterias. Nevertheless, one expects equally high levels of loyalty and commitment, no matter what individual mix of psychological contract and benefits an individual has chosen. Hence the career of the concept of 'trust' as a new, culturally induced 'glue', which ideally links all members of an organization and allows them to standardize their mutual expectations.

However, managers, who are supposed to coordinate and 'manage' (supervise, control, direct, lead) many individuals pursuing those complex and formally organized interactions have to rely on compliance and co-operation, the emotional commitment, creativity and innovativeness of their 'subordinates', many of whom are outside of any immediate range of control (either because of their location or because of the nature of their work). This recognition of the fact that – illusions of the ideology of managerialism notwithstanding – actual employees are far less visible and controllable than previously assumed is chiefly responsible for the new versions of enabling leadership. Managers who aspire to be leaders would like to rely on loyal, committed and compliant employees, to be reasonably certain that even when these employees are 'out of sight', their corporation and their managers are not out of their hearts and minds. In order to facilitate this compliance and willing co-operation, to stimulate and motivate innovativeness and effort, managers increasingly rely on 'positive reinforcement' (due to the creative organizational culture driving a professional community of practice and commanding respect and imitation), backed by a generalized threat of 'negative sanctions' imposed from the outside (due to cruel and omnipresent market forces driving towards an unceasing restructuring of every human activity, stimulating take-overs in all areas of social life, and reducing 'redundancy' at all levels of organizational structures). Corporations are no longer solid structures that offer life-time employment; they try to become 'lean and mean', switch their mode of operations, increasingly relying on 'temps' and outsourcing, are continuously re-shaped and re-invented. But in most cases all these trimming down and down-sizing operations are conveniently presented as 'beyond anyone's (read: "immediate superiors', management's") control'.

Managers are usually paid to oversee, plan, monitor, and guide, and more often than not have to run routine administration of large formal bureaucracies. But they like to base their professional identity on a much more idealized self-image of themselves as entrepreneurial and autonomous 'leaders' of employee 'communities', who are capable of designing and implementing new corporate cultures, capturing hearts and minds, firing the imagination of their employees, and turning them into committed corporate citizens, highly motivated to contribute to organizational success.

Managers would like to fit this idealized role model, while at the same time retaining a degree of autonomy with respect to the shareholders and political power holders, to avoid being perceived as 'instruments' of owners and politicians. Managers legitimize their independence and autonomy with their unique expertise, which allegedly enables them to secure a competitive advantage for the companies they happen to manage. They claim their exorbitant salaries are justified by the rising shareholder value of the company, notably due to mergers and acquisitions. This claim is difficult to substantiate, because the sources of any given manager's success can be different from what he or she may think is responsible for his or her 'good luck'. For instance, Jack Welch claimed that his rise to the top of the GE hierarchy of power was due to the fact that he had designed and implemented strong corporate cultures and found ways of inspiring members of a large and globally distributed organization. The corporate culture of GE in the 1990s, according to Jack Welch, was based on three core values: self-confidence, simplicity and speed – and worked because he and everybody else believed in those values, no matter how diversified the activities GE decided to engage in. However, some of his critics claim that GE's financial success in the 1980s and 1990s was based on a very stringent financial policy of immediate sale of less profitable parts of his organization, and purchase of companies that promised to be very profitable. While this policy made financial sense and contributed to the profitability of GE in the eyes of shareholders, it did very little to improve the core productive and innovative activities of GE, so that by the end of Welch's reign GE was a financial superpower but a manufacturing mediocrity. However, in his very own words, a strong corporate culture in the hands of a manager capable of leading a strong management team is the prerequisite for commercial success.

'Objectives do not get you there', said Welch to the MBA students of Harvard Business School, 'values do' – as he proceeded to outline the corporate culture of GE, which has been 'designed to last at least for 10–15 years' and to help employees and managers of a large conglomerate of different enterprises make sense of their diverse activities in multiple locations all over the world. His words are echoed by those of a theoretician of culture, who says that:

> Values condense the general term 'meaning' into something at once more inflammable, more weighted down with historical gravity, loaded up with usefulness, as a weapon or as a medicine. Meanings mean, of course, values do.
>
> (Inglis, 2004, 162)[4]

Such corporate culture (of GE, IBM, British Airways, Citibank, Unilever, or Shell, but also of a small university or of a ring of friends forming a consulting company) has core values, which, if adopted by the entire company – high, middle and lower management in particular – are supposed to contribute to the competitive advantage of the company, both by making company employees more entrepreneurial and committed to the company's success and by projecting an image of a culturally distinct, unique and exciting community on the rest of the world. The degree of internalization of those values by employees can be tested not only indirectly, via a review of the economic results of the company's performance (market share, expansion and growth, profits for shareholders, international reputation and ranking in Fortune's 500) before and after adopting a new corporate culture. It can also be checked with a number of 'socio-techniques' designed to accelerate dissemination and acceptance of the 'designed' company culture and to stimulate innovative behaviour cutting across organizational hierarchies, departments and subcultures. For instance, in the case of GE according to Jack Welch, random samples of employees are thrown together at a 'workout session', where 'ideas flow freely' (which implies that they are not free to flow outside of these artificially arranged workout situations), individuals are 'unleashed' (which implies that customarily they are on a short leash and thus enjoy being let free for once) and hierarchies disappear (with a little help from professional consultants, which implies that normally these bureaucratic inequalities are very strongly felt). Everybody, rank and file, salaried and hourly people are encouraged to 'find a new way everyday', to suggest innovations and to improve every organizational procedure and technology as part and parcel of their daily routine, their daily activity and pursuit, as an inner 'duty' of a committed member of a corporate community.

In a sense, this is an ideal of a classless society translated into the realities of a dynamic business corporation ('classless company') and locked inside a single work setting. Marx promised the proletariat that they as a class will take over all factories all over the world. Contemporary managers appealing to their employees and urging them to make their company more competitive promise individual salvation in the ranks of a managerial profession within a given organizational context. Improve with us and you will be promoted and amply rewarded:

> Work situations generate their own stocks of membership symbols. These constitute the local culture of the stockbroker, the financial manipulator, the industrial manager, the professional politician, and every other occupational milieu. Membership symbols are generated locally within the various realms of work. . . . Business executives and other high-ranking persons do not owe their ability to negotiate membership with other such persons to any great extent to their 'cultivation' in the formally produced cultural symbols, but rather to their use of the symbols of their immediate milieu. Financiers assemble financial coalitions not because of their knowledge of literature and opera, but above all because they talk the language of finance in a convincing way. In contrast to Bourdieu's emphasis on what might be called generalized cultural capital, individuals in elite occupations are successful because of the particularistic cultural capital or stock of symbols that circulate in their immediate network.
>
> (Collins, 2004, 392)[5]

To the managerial mind, the bridge of Babel in a networked society reveals yet another facet. Managers and those who assist them in designing corporate cultures as managerial control instruments are interested in influencing individual cultural competence through the design and implementation of corporate cultures. It is not enough to be loyal to the boss (a principle automatically assumed in all hierarchic bureaucracies); one also has to be converted to his or her corporate culture (a principle automatically assumed in all knowledge-intensive organizations). In a sense, we have returned to the early-modern principle *cuius regio, eius religio* ('the ruler's religion is the religion of his subjects', the principle adopted to avoid civil wars and establish international legitimacy in early-modern Europe), only the religion in question is secularized, localized and changed every 10–15 years, instead of remaining a source of – imagined and re-engineered – stability (as is the case in religious communities, where continuous reinterpretation of the holy books is masked by the stability of the language or institutions, or both). However, the modern return to this principle is far more sophisticated than ever before. This is due to the double 'unzipping' of the cross-cultural competence model based on the Hofstedian framework, this time within the 'Globe' project of a comparative study of 62 societies from the perspective of the culturally endorsed leadership dimensions, led by Robert J. House.

First, House responded to some of the charges levelled against Hofstede's research and assembled a networked team composed of the so-called 'country co-investigators', i.e. 'natives' of a national culture recruited from within academic communities in a nation-state under consideration. Some of the biases have been left untouched: of the ten global cultural clusters (in which people tend to agree on culturally conditioned leadership attributes and manifest a common cultural background) five are European: Anglo, Latin, Germanic, Nordic, and Eastern; while the other five relate to the rest of the world: Confucian Asia, the Middle East, Latin America, Sub-Saharan Africa, and Southern Asia. House has also upheld Hofstede's crucial assumptions on generalizing about the national-level cultural constructs on the basis of a sample of individuals, and about the appropriateness of survey data for measuring cultural constructs.

On the other hand, House and his country co-investigators found that their dimensions of national culture did not always coincide with those of Hofstede or Schwartz, and that sometimes they had to 'unzip' the Hofstedian dimensions in order to understand these differences – for instance in splitting the Hofstedian dimension of 'Collectivism' into 'Institutional' Collectivism (which stands for a pattern of organizing focusing on generalized team work and collective reward distribution at the company level, and has its most visible form in Confucian Asian cultures) versus 'In-Group' Collectivism (which stands for small-group loyalty, pride and identification with an organization at the lowest organizational level, and with a strong loyalty to family, producing both a low divorce rate and informal procedures replacing due process). Needless to say, Hofstede's list of five dimensions has been almost doubled, re-arranged and rephrased, though it still strongly echoes Hofstede's original dimensions. In House's Globe project the list includes:

- Future Orientation,
- Gender Equality,
- Assertiveness,
- Humane Orientation,
- In-Group Collectivism,

- Institutional Collectivism,
- Performance Orientation,
- Power Distance, and
- Uncertainty Avoidance.

House's main contribution to the ongoing discussion on culture and the management connection is his counterintuitive finding that 'there is a negative correlation between cultural values in seven out of nine cultural dimensions' (House *et al.* 2004, 729). Pondering this discovery, House tends to interpret it as evidence for a more complex – non-linear and non-causal – view of the relationship between values and practices. In other words, he assumes that we had all been wrong assuming tacitly (and this goes also for Hofstede, Schein and other established authorities) that if individuals espouse some values, then their behaviour will reflect them: their acts and artefacts will be manifestations of their attempts to implement those values in practice, to obey them while making individual decisions, to follow them as guidelines. This simplifying assumption, all the provisos (e.g. declared versus espoused values) notwithstanding, has to go. As House puts it:

> The opposite relationship may be at work: people may hold views on what should be on the basis of what they observe in action. For instance, in the case of Future Orientation, with very few exceptions, all societies have higher values scores than practices scores – societies report a desire for a more future oriented society. The negative correlation between practices and values occurs because for societies with higher practical scores, the difference between values and practices scores (i.e. the increment) is much smaller than it is for those with low practice scores.
> . . .
> In short, our findings point to the need for a more complex under-standing of this relationship which views it as dynamic and double directional rather than static and uni-directional. What exacerbates the situation is that our findings show that attributes of societal success are strongly related to cultural practices, but attributes of outstanding leadership are strongly related to cultural values. Unless we can better understand the relationship between cultural practices and values, we are unable to explain this complex situation and have little to offer to leaders who are trying to improve their societies' well being.
>
> (House, 2004, 730)

In other words, successful leaders would be those who could design organizational culture and manage cultural practices, that would reinforce cultural values or stimulate the reduction of the gap between values and practices. Needless to say, this new leadership through 'organizational culture by design' game is bound to provoke resistance. Those, who are forced to accept a new organizational culture may do so as part of their socialization (they understand that manifesting commitment to corporate culture increases their chances of promotion), but do not have to share the top management's commitment to corporate culture by design (they also understand that even if they do not believe in corporate values, there is no way managers can prove that this is indeed, the case – that they are not 'converts' but 'heretics in disguise'). They may offer individual resistance to organizational culture, but they may also try to subvert it by collective action. This was clearly the case with the cultural bureaucracy of the BBC exposed to the pressures of a market-oriented project of designing and implementing a new corporate culture.

Another possibility, also noted by House when he speculates on the possibilities of measuring the results of a cultural clash, for instance after a merger or acquisition, is that *a new corporate culture by design, or a fusion of two corporate cultures each with her own distinct design, can trigger some unexpected dynamics, not necessarily detrimental to the company goals.* The resistance to a corporate culture by design changes with time; because of the diminishing importance of trade unions (which could offer a member identification with an alternative subculture) the role of an organizational 'platform' resisting managerial pressures for complete internalization of corporate culture is frequently assumed by professional associations ('professionals' versus 'managers' in knowledge-intensive companies). Loyalty to a professional community offers a welcome alternative to 'thought control' through a corporate culture by design. Academic intellectuals often express their loyalty to the standards of their profession ('we, the men and women of science and scholarship') but are far more reluctant to express their support for a particular university or research institute, or the managerial authority of their deans, rectors and presidents or chairpersons of the university boards of directors. This is one of the most interesting developments within organizational cultures by design: the academic institution of a university has had its corporate culture designed and re-designed a number of times, and nothing suggests that this continuous process of re-designing is over. On the contrary, it is accelerating. The fate of academic intellectuals, of professionals in knowledge-intensive organizations (and most contemporary organizations tend to evolve towards this category) manifests common features.

Let us look at a case in point: a professional bureaucracy subjected to a new managerial policy of control exercised through a company culture by design. It has been imposed through the proliferation of projects for 'task forces' of 'high flyers' recruited from among lower-rank managers.[6] The case deserves our attention because the researchers managed to detect the very level of comparison made by the rank-and-file police officers between cultural values (designed for a reformed public organization) and cultural practices (manifested by the higher-rank policemen in managerial positions while the change projects were implemented). Participants in the project – high-flying police officers – had definite expectations of their superiors and responded to their leadership acts in the course of the whole process of 'bureaucracy clean-up', which has been typical of Western public organizations in the last two decades of the past century and the beginning of the present one as efforts to achieve efficient 'bureaucracy-lite' intensified.[7]

2 The police change project case [with Gabriele Jacobs, Anne Keegan, Jochen Christe-Zeyse, Ilka Seeberg, and Bernd Runde]

Many organizations that had originally been designed as non-profit, professional bureaucracies controlled by public authorities are systematically subjected to a number of clean-up activities, such that their managers are set busy designing and implementing change projects. 'Marketization' and 'digitalization' of the BBC was a case in point. Another is the case of a wave of modernizing projects in European public institutions, which were modernized via change projects borrowed from the business community where they had been applied to business companies. The German and Dutch police forces are cases in point. These attempts at re-engineering, often labelled the New Public Management or the New Management Model, are usually considered from the perspective of their instrumental efficiency: time, cost and quality.[8] Let us, however, look at them from the perspective of the personal experiences of the most crucial part of the large professional bureaucracy involved in most of the change projects.

A multidisciplinary group of social psychologists, political scientists and management researchers conducted research among 'high flyers', i.e. those expected to rise in the ranks to the level of a police captain or higher, making use of their concentration in the German Police Leadership Academy in Münster. Researchers interviewed almost a hundred individuals (98 to be precise, of whom the youngest was 26 and the oldest 43, with the average age 36), asking them to describe and analyse the successful (83) and unsuccessful (69) change projects in which they had participated so far.

Semi-structured interviews led to the specifying of subjectively identified criteria (evaluations) and factors (explanation) which, according to respondents, were responsible for the success or failure of a concrete project. Researchers tried to identify the 'subjective constructs' of these high-flyers among German police officers, i.e. they tried to understand how they 'made sense' of change projects, to which factors (causes, reasons) they had attributed the success or failure of a given project. It turned out that goal achievement (mentioned by 34 per cent of respondents), commitment (19.3 per cent) and satisfaction (13.9 per cent) were the most frequently mentioned criteria of success (or failure). Respondents were quite aware of differences between actual peer and superiors' commitment; they turned out to be sensitive to small signals of lack of interest (patronizing 'smirks') and to a difference between officially stated goals and actually pursued goals:

> Respondents distinguished between the goals as officially defined (e.g. reducing the number of hierarchy levels, introducing a new personnel evaluation method) and goals they perceived as the actual intended aims (e.g. cutting costs, more efficient handling of crime cases, enhancing motivation, but also increasing the level of control over subordinate units, showing off a modern attitude) . . . in quite a few cases projects with no real goals or intended aims were initiated to give the impression of forceful leadership, innovative management, and a modern, dynamic approach to organizing. Quantity seemed more important than quality, and respondents report the gradual emergence of what they call 'projectitis'.
>
> (Jacobs *et al.*, 2004, 21)

This sophistication of respondents was also evident when researchers asked them to identify factors that brought about the success or failure of a given project. A broader class of success 'factors' was suggested, and when a lower limit of at least 10 per cent of respondents mentioning them was applied, five major factors to which success or failure was attributed emerged: support, communication, goals, working conditions, and competence. Support was mentioned by 22.5 per cent of respondents, quoting both hard and soft elements of it, for instance both financial means and emotional empathy. Communication was mentioned by 14.2 per cent, who stressed the importance of who does the communicating, what is communicated and to whom the communications are addressed. Next, 12.8 per cent of respondents considered it important to mention goals, and explained that the success of a project depends on a perceived clarity and relevance of goals. Finally, 10.6 per cent of respondents mentioned working conditions, while competence of the project team was mentioned by 10.1 per cent.

When matching success criteria and success factors (respondents were asked to draw arrows connecting factors to criteria for the project under consideration), respondents came with many interesting observations on apparently small but not insignificant acts of behaviour, which were taken as hints revealing the managers' 'real' attitude towards the given change project. For instance, at one point the police were preparing a programme for children and, following somebody's suggestion, the project participants introduced a colourful parrot as a way of making compulsory instruction by a police officer more lively and interesting for the young audience. When demonstrating the proposed performance, participants in the projects noticed a seemingly banal gesture of one of the superiors – he displayed an ironic smile when looking at the parrot, as if he derided the playfulness that he did not think went together well with the seriousness of the instruction and of the police uniform in general. The commitment among project participants dropped almost immediately: 'After seeing that our leaders smirked at this parrot, our symbol for the intervention programme for children, nobody took it seriously anymore' (Jacobs *et al.*, 2004, 32).

Policemen and policewomen noticed that while encouraging them to manifest creativity in their actions (thinking about a parrot to keep children's attention), their superiors at the same time manifested a somewhat rigid adherence to a 'dignified' code of uniformed conduct. The practice of controlling even the smallest details of conduct from the point of their compatibility with some 'control image' clashed with an attempt to promote new values of open and engaging interaction with target groups. When researchers compared the relative importance of particular factors upon the success as measured by the success criteria, they noticed a very interesting, apparently 'culture-driven' lowering of subjective significance of positive working conditions (i.e. security, salary, status, acknowledgement, perform-ance, responsibility) for 'support' of any given project – although they remained important for 'satisfaction'. At the same time researchers noticed an increase in the significance of 'soft' support factors, i.e. behaviour of superiors (smirks or no smirks) and peers as far as readiness to support any given project went. Soft support factors were associated with a growing significance attached to clear and regular communications:

> Respondents report that employees are even willing to support a project that does not match their own interests if they are convinced of the legitimacy of the goals, if structural and symbolic support for the project is evident and if it is clear that the organization takes the project seriously.
>
> (Jacobs *et al.*, 2004, 34–5)

This culture-driven altruistic behaviour (the ability to disregard one's own interest and to support a project benefiting the entire community) requires managerial maintenance: manifestations of emotional support, regular and clear communications, the ability to admit and discuss mistakes, and the ability to overcome a tendency to gloss over failures and present an idealized version of the change project. In general, it requires critical re-assessment of a heavily quantitative 'managerialist' ideology that stands behind organ-izational cultures by design. Organizational cultures can be designed and core values can be proposed from 'above', but commitment and satisfaction of employees, and cultural practices that can generate and sustain such commitment, cannot. The cultural practices have to be embedded, and commitment has to be won in genuine, not cynical ('smirks') support and in a culture of regular, transparent communications – which is traditionally a problem in most bureaucratic organizations that tend to control and differentiate communication according to the hierarchy, leaving those lower down without sufficient information at most times. The manager as leader recognizing culture-driven commitment is the manager who supports his or her subordinates and communicates with them on a regular basis, even in traditional bureaucracies. He or she sustains and revives cultural practices, rewards or discourages innovations (the parrot!), diminishing the distance between values and practices.[9] This systematic attempt to bridge the gap between the values and practices is particularly important in organizations undergoing radical structural and cultural change – which in business companies means, for instance, changes as a result of merger, acquisition or a joint venture with another company.

3 Cultural due diligence in mergers and acquisitions

> Culture: shared understandings made manifest in act and artefact.
> (Redfield, 1948, vii)

Two companies merge, one company takes over another, or both start a new joint venture. In real life for their employees, the change is that they have to work together with others who do not share their routines, their intuitive grasp of 'the way we do things around here'. Their merger, take-over or joint venture – is usually negotiated at top management levels. Even if it makes very good sense in terms of stock value and market position, there are many uncertainties. First, statistics tell us that at least 60–70 per cent of mergers and acquisitions ultimately fail, i.e. do not result in higher productivity and profits (these are mostly financial statistics, since one assumes a direct correlation between the financial success of a merger, increased productivity and employee morale). Second, we know that entire groups of employees resist change, often conducting their struggle as a 'clash of cultures', sabotaging it or leaving the company (the expression 'we know' does not mean here that we have broad systematic studies, although increasing attempts are being made to assemble a collection of narratives of change from the 'inside' of the organizations involved). Therefore managerial teams responsible for accomplishing a successful post-merger integration are looking for methodological instruments that would allow them to compare merger partners, detect differences and better design the integration process. As of the present writing they have found such an instrument in the concept and method of *cultural due diligence*, applied to the analysis of company cultures and subcultures of relevant merging organizations.

The concept of cultural due diligence is relatively new. According to the Hay Group study of 2004, only 28 per cent of CEOs involved in mergers admitted that their merger teams actually commissioned a third-party objective investigation in order to issue a report on the culture of the companies involved, while almost none realized before the merger that the effects will be felt equally strongly throughout the stronger, active, 'host' company as through the 'targeted' one. Quoting Dutch management consultants from two companies, 'global tmc' and 'unique sources', the authors of the on-line periodic publication, *Europublic*, came up with the following brief checklist for cultural due diligence analysis prior to a merger or acquisition:

> Dutch management consultants *global tmc* and *unique sources* recommend an analysis of seven different cultural elements:
>
> * Organizational strategy (goals, mission statement)
>   *What really matters around here?*
> * Organizational structure (hierarchy)
>   *Is initiative and entrepreneurship encouraged and rewarded?*
> * Leadership style (the 'linking pin')
>   *Who has the most power?*
> * Communication (interaction with others)
>   *What may never be said in your organisation?*
> * Organizational membership (characteristics of personnel)
>   *Do your colleagues really care about the business?*
> * General organizational characteristics (historical context)
>   *Who was the founder of the organization?*
> * Environment (physical and economic context)
>   *What is your present market position?'*
>
> (Europublic, 2004, 1)

This eclectic checklist owes much to pragmatic compromise, as it emerged at the crossroads of academic struggles (paradigmatic competition for peer attention and sponsoring favours on the part of 'hard' managing engineers and 'soft' HR development psychologists) and the practical needs of managers (a race for the most effective and efficient instruments in dealing with complex problems in dynamic environments). It has elements of a 'hard' analysis of structure, line of command and environmental positioning, but also elements of a 'soft' analysis of leadership style, membership commitment and an interpretation of historical developments filtered through collective memories. Consultants want to keep their options open. In an economy in which joint ventures, mergers and acquisitions, and dramatic, unexpected changes are the rule rather than the exception, the race for theoretical instruments with practical significance is steadily accelerating. There are no clear winners, though methodological individualism and rational choice theory are clearly moving to a less dominant position and ruthless down-sizing is slowly losing the status of a dogma in managerial thinking. The Prisoner's Dilemma, once a centre-piece in the empirical foundations of rational choice theory, has become a battleground for a more-balanced, context-sensitive and evolutionarily interpreted behavioural science. Researchers cannot ignore the fact that in spite of all attempts to see it as a 'naked' and 'isolated' building-block of human behaviour, the Prisoner's Dilemma, as with other dilemmas, involves expectations, emotions, memories, and in two-thirds of cases leads to an individually counter-productive 'altruism' (a calculation based on expected reciprocity) rather than personal-profit calculation. Culture and experience 'filter' choices through culturally influenced interpretation 'frames'. Problems noted by individuals are not isolated, but, as Axelrod already observed in his reflections on reiterations of the Prisoner's Dilemma (Axelrod, 1984, Axelrod, 1997; Axelrod, Cohen, 1999), are perceived as linked to the previous and later ones. Cultural memory allows us to generate more 'altruistic' behaviours in real life than classical models of games and economic behaviour would have us believe (given that the dominant theory of decision-making under risk still forms the backbone of most teaching). According to the new approach to context-sensitive 'framing', we should search for

> regularities that are at variance with what should happen if reasoning were strictly logical, based on known rules of probability, or followed normative rules of statistical inference. . . . Inferences about and choices regarding a formally identical problem will be influenced by the context or frame in which it is presented. Frame dependence is inconsistent with assumptions implicit in the Skinnerian model of operant conditioning. In challenging this model, Kahneman and Tversky also challenge the model of learning and decision making underlying the standard economic model, in particular the expected utility framework, the approach to decision making under risk or uncertainty first advanced by von Neumann and Morgenstern in an appendix to their 1944 book on games and economic behaviour.
>
> (Field, 2004, 265)

Cultural due diligence is a concept that promised to 'deliver' by offering a manager or a consultant an instrument to recognize local 'frames' in organizations. The concept of cultural due diligence bears traces both of classical 'managerialist' problem-definition (how to preserve control over subordinates and lower their resistance to change) and of a new concept forged by many different research communities following different investigative paradigms and asking different questions (such as how to allow individuals to make sense of their rapidly changing environment, routines and networked collaborators, and how to upgrade their cross-cultural competence and sensitize them to cultural change). The questions now become how to understand what employees make of their company, especially if they are not constrained by higher-ups in hierarchy? How to reconstruct the evolutionary path of organizational forms, notably as a history of struggles, conflicts and coalitions? How to shift the management mode from an authoritarian one to a more egalitarian one, and how then to generate and sustain altruistic behaviour? How to frame dilemmas so as to facilitate decision-making that meets both the requirements of efficiency and demonstrates long-term compatibility with values? Cultural due diligence means that we are willing to investigate, research and understand the cultures of organizations and the ways individuals make use of those cultures. What, then, is this cultural due diligence all about?

Clashes of cultures and gaps between cultural values and cultural practices are manifested particularly vividly and painfully experienced in the course of large-scale organizational change, of which mergers and acquisitions are cases in point. It stands to reason that if we want two different companies to co-operate closely and to 'merge', 'fuse' or 'integrate' them, we have to understand what makes the people who constitute them different in act, thought and artefact. Cultural due diligence is a term that covers such comparative investigation of relevant company cultures.

Cultural due diligence in mergers and acquisitions has already become a popular concept in the managerial literature: many books are being written on 'breaking through culture shock' or 'creative destruction' of cultures, which yields more diversity rather than less, etc. Under the influence of the practical needs of the consulting community, most of the studies of post-merger or post-acquisition developments are divided into the pre-merger partner-profile descriptions ('what is'), designs for the integrating trajectory ('what should be'), lists of adaptation measures offered to individuals ('how to cope'), and suggestions for a 'change platform' that also acts as monitoring and feedbacking device – for instance, a managerial team of relevant functional managers, or break-through teams of high-flyers from various 'places' in organizations ('how to implement and maintain').

Sometimes more detailed instruments have been developed, as was the case, for instance, with the Organizational Culture Assessment Instrument (OCAI), developed by researchers working with the 'competing values framework' (cf. Cameron, Quinn, 1999). The instrument is a questionnaire, which lists sample statements under six headings; dominant characteristics, organizational leadership, management of employees, organization glue, strategic emphasis, and criteria of success, and asks each respondent to answer twice. Each section has four statements, which have to be assigned some value between 1 and 100: for instance 50, 25, 20, 5 (the sum of assigned values must be equal to 100). The first answer is supposed to give the status quo – to illustrate what organizational culture is like at present.

The second answer is supposed to give an indication of the respondent's preferences. For instance, a respondent may assess a statement in the section on management of employees: 'The management style in the organization is characterized by teamwork, consensus and participation'. A respondent may think that it is only partly true in the present organization, and assign a value of 25 to it, while assigning 75 in the desirable organizational culture he or she would wish to work in. After all the statements have been assigned some values, the answers can be plotted on a diagram formed by two axes, the vertical one running from 'stability and control' to 'flexibility and discretion' (competing managerial values) and the horizontal one running from 'internal focus and integration' to 'external focus and differentiation' (also competing managerial values). To plot the assigned values, an OCAI user places an organizational culture in one of the four quadrants: *clan* (flexible, internally integrated); *adhocracy* (flexible, externally differentiated); *hierarchy* (stable, internally focused); or *market* (stable, externally differentiated). By comparing the two diagrams – one plotting answers about the status quo and the other plotting the answers about the desirable company culture, a researcher can understand what employees think about their company culture and what changes have a chance of being endorsed by them.

When the OCAI instrument was constructed, its authors did not use the language of 'cultural due diligence'. Nevertheless, they had explained their instrument in the following terms:

> We want to communicate clearly that our theoretical model was developed in order to organize organizational culture types, but it does not pretend to be comprehensive of all cultural phenomena. Nor does it apply equally well to cultures at levels other than organizational level – for example national cultures. The framework provides, instead, a way for organizations to discuss and interpret key elements of organizational culture that can foster change and improvement. A major problem in many organizations facing the need to change their cultures is that no language exists, no key elements or dimensions have been identified, and no common perspective is available to help the conversation even get started. Change doesn't occur because it is difficult to know what to talk about and what to focus on. In our experience, this framework provides an intuitively appealing and easily interpretable way to foster the process of cultural change.
>
> (Cameron, Quinn, 1999, 17).

Instruments of this type are quite popular among consultants – suffice it to mention, for instance, the Cross-Cultural Adaptability Inventory (CCAI) designed by Coleen Kelly and Judith Meyers, which is distributed among individuals willing to perform a self-assessment from the point of their potential willingness either to change or to resist change. The authors try to test 'emotional resilience' (ability to cope demonstrated by individuals subjected to a culture clash), flexibility/openness, perceptual acuity (sensitivity that enables an individual to pick up unexpected cues), and personal autonomy (linked to a strong sense of identity and a feeling of empowerment). The statements (the list includes 50 of them) are evaluated by respondents, who assign each of them a value ranging between 'definitely true' and 'definitely not true', and then plot their answers on the CCAI self-assessment profile sheet, where their 'plots' also assume the form of a four-sided figure. (This particular instrument has been published – undated – by Pearson Reid London House and could be found on their website in 2004.)[10]

The authors of this inventory also do not use the term 'cultural due diligence', but the emergence of culture assessment instruments like the ones mentioned above contributed to the emergence of the concept of cultural due diligence itself. Most available books on this topic teach practitioners how to determine critical success factors, either in organizational culture or in an individual's cognitive mapping of organizational reality, and thus provide a normative model of cultural due diligence before, during and after all future mergers and acquisitions a manager or a consultant may face in his or her career.

Organizational culture (whose plurality and complexity is often reflected in the use of the plural: thus organizational culture becomes 'organizational cultures and subcultures') is perceived as a significant factor contributing to the employees' response to a changed work situation after mergers and acquisitions, of which preventing the emergence of a hostile 'us' versus 'them' attitude is essential for the success of the post-merger integration. Organizational cultures are assumed (following Schein, 1985) to have three basic functions: external adaptation (of a company to its environment); internal integration (of employees with each other); and the reduction of fear, anxiety and uncertainty in individuals subjected to organizational changes. This last function is viewed as particularly important and many managerial handbooks on organizational change are being written from the point of view of 'change without pain'[11] and with a clear warning that failing to address these emotionally charged concerns of employees may result in 'deviant behaviour' – in avoiding work, looking for free rides, absenteeism, hiding behind formalities, high mistake rates, high turnover, and loss of initiative ('fatalism'). Competent managers, writes one of the Dutch researchers (following Eisele, 1996), should pay attention to the cultural 'fit' of companies about to merge, to the cultural 'potential' of both partners in the merger and to their own behaviour, namely they should manifest leadership qualities, demonstrate 'charisma' and be attentive to their subordinates. The cultural fit and cultural potential are described in following terms:

Cultural fit, the first general success factor . . . is reflected in, for instance, preferences for style of management, degrees and ways of planning, formalization, reward and sanction modes, time perspective, and growth orientation. The higher the cultural fit between two firms, the less aversion-prone the cultural integration process will be. On the other hand, too much fit can reduce the synergetic effects to be expected from the melting process. It may not be worth the trouble merging with a firm that in face of common problems can add no substantial solutions to the ones already available.

Cultural potential, the second success factor, is equally relevant in mergers and acquisitions as in joint ventures. The term points to cultural traits that guide the way in which relations with other organizations and cultures are generally framed and handled. Eisele (1966) distinguishes four cultural traits that further the cultural integration process: (1) innovative potential, that is, openness to new values and ideas; (2) trust potential, the general tendency to trust others; (3) mutual dependence potential, the tendency to think in terms of two parties needing each other to arrive at common goals; and (4) integrative potential, the tendency to invest in psychical kinship, in sorting out differences, in understanding their meaning, and a preference for co-ordination of behaviour based on shared norms and values.

(Bijlsma-Frankema, 1998, 6–7)

Most of the authors writing on cultural due diligence and ways of guiding, coaching and managing change processes agree that successful post-merger adaptation and integration depends crucially on clearly formulated goals (which inspire employees and provide a sense of direction), translation of goals into norms at the lower levels of organization (which gives employees the feeling of relative safety, of knowing 'what is going on' and being supported by their superiors), and systematic monitoring and feedback (which prevents them from falling into old routines and reinforces the new ones).

4 The case of cross-border Nordic mergers [with Anne-Marie Soderberg and I. Björkman]

Cross-cultural learning experience . . . is a set of intensive and evocative situations in which the individual . . . is forced into new levels of consciousness and understanding.

(Adler, 1975, 13)

The cross-border merger of four Nordic financial institutions, each from a different country – Sweden, Finland, Norway, and Denmark – resulted in the creation of Nordea in 2000. Nordea is the leading financial services group in the Nordic and Baltic Sea region, with 250 billion Euros in total assets and approximately 33,000 full-time employees in 2004. It operates in three business areas: retail banking, corporate and institutional banking and asset management and life. Nordea came about as the final result of the gradual consolidation of national banks and insurance companies into large national players in the Nordic countries. Thus Nordea's creators, four large banks – Merita (Finland), Nordbanken (Sweden), Unidanmark (Denmark), and Christania Bank og Kredittkasse (Norway) – were themselves created as a result of earlier mergers and acquisitions, and had already operated foreign joint ventures in the Nordic region prior to the final merger that resulted in the emergence of Nordea. In a qualitative, in-depth study of the cross-border merger of the four Nordic financial institutions (53 senior executives and all communications and HR managers were interviewed, and company and media documents analysed) the researchers from five Nordic business schools focused on the post-merger integration processes, assuming that this quadruple integration and adaptation process would provide them with a variety of data on coping with multiple national and organizational cultural differences.

The researchers assumed that an organization is not simply a 'container' for texts and talk that merely represents the 'actual works' of a 'real organization'. Rather, communicating is part and parcel of organizing, while organizing also means the framing of the discursive, communicative practices. They thus wanted to avoid reification, essentialism and homogenization, all of which had been associated with the functionalist, empiricist studies undertaken from the 'managerialist' perspective, and to go for two clusters of problems. The first was for the context-bound specificity of utterances and texts performed and issued during concrete events and in particular situations within the framework of definite actions and as part of the organizing processes. The second was the dangerous liaisons between culture and power, power being clearly one of the taboo issues in organizational analysis in particular and in the sciences of management in general (in order to remedy the ideological blindness displayed by most researchers).[12]

Some of the expected traces of cultural due diligence on the part of the headquarters of the new four-fold organization were found: the headquarters were sensitive to cultural stereotyping and expected some friction when managerial teams from different countries were brought together. Therefore the outline of a new corporate culture for Nordea was designed as a cultural bandwagon, which the top management wanted to make attractive enough for all employees to jump on and identify with, thus bridging the gaps between their respective national cultural software. As the second CEO of Nordea, Thorleif Krarup said in Nordea's annual report for 2000:

> A precondition of success is an integrated company with common
> corporate values and branding. All core activities will be linked with
> these values and with the Nordea brand. . . . All employees have the
> right to be part of the company culture and an obligation to live
> according to its values. The employees should know that Nordea stands
> for Nordic ideas which fulfil the customers' dreams and aspirations.
>
> (Søderberg, Björkman, 2003, 140–1)[13]

The difficulty in linking the values of a designed company culture to
the daily routines and social practices of employees were also recognized
(both by the top managers involved and by the researchers they had
approached), although the focus was mostly on the difficulties ('noise') that
perceived national cultural differences might produce in multi-national
management teams within the merged organizations. Some company-wide
integration initiatives undertaken after the merger, meant to link corporate
values and local social practices and so overcome experienced frictions,
indicated sensitivity to other cross-cultural differences, not only the ones
caused by the different national backgrounds of employees. For instance,
the communications and human-resources departments attempted to
build a 'bridge' between company and department cultures within the
new large organization and the Nordea culture by design, and specified its
task as a 'translation' or 'interpretation' of the Nordea values into concrete
procedures and activities of the employees. As a result they came up
with the employee booklet *Making It Possible* and a so-called 'From
Words to Action' process designed and implemented in order to facilitate
the translation of newly broadcasted corporate values into common,
company-wide standards, group and individual practices, and daily
routines.

Distribution of the booklet was not received with equal understanding in
all quarters. In some business units and departments it was greeted with
scepticism, especially if its dissemination was accompanied by a slick Power
Point presentation by a professional consultant with not enough time left for
feedback and discussion with the manager and his subordinates. Some
employees complained bitterly that it is a waste to first invest in employing
highly trained and well-educated employees with university diplomas only
to treat them as a passive audience, which should be managed by issuing
managerial *ukases*. Another factor mentioned by critics of the booklet was
that the top management did not act as change agents. Moreover, they failed
to 'mix their blood' and to set personal examples of upholding the new
corporate values at the expense of the older ones. The human resources
department decided to distribute an electronic survey through the company
intranet, asking for personal opinions about the values in Nordea and about
the value dialogue conducted in their units. The results of the three 'common
culture' seminars organized for all country-based management teams (which

had been meeting in their respective countries face-to-face weekly) are ambiguous:

> It is . . . still unclear if the corporate values have also been translated into different local contexts to be part of a sustainable change of thinking and behaviour. If they have been implemented into common daily practices to such an extent that the employees in the future *'will be living Nordea'* . . . and not any longer use national stereotyping. The HR team responsible for the survey concludes soberly that *'we can make values work'* but *'sustainable change of behaviour can only be achieved gradually and it takes time'*.
>
> (Søderberg, Björkman, 2003, 163)

In one business unit, three 'common culture' seminars were organized by the country-based management teams (which had been meeting weekly face-to-face in their respective countries). The first 'common culture' seminar was organized in the Swedish School of Economics in Helsinki in October 2000 for managers of the four national Markets teams and was considered a major breakthrough in terms of allowing participants to make fun of their national and former company stereotypes. For instance, managers of business units formed across national boundaries could laugh at comparing the top management group (of their bank) to a spider net, while Danish managers from Unibank were told by the other nationalities that their bank was best symbolized by a complex space rocket that could not get off the ground. One of the managers remarked that the establishing of 'joking relationships' helped deal with some future problems.

The second cultural seminar, a two-day event, took place in November 2000. The participants were given the task of defining in advance what they thought should be the guiding values for the cross-border Markets unit. As a result of this common exercise, four values were arrived at: Customer Orientation, Communication, Competence, and Credibility. The third seminar followed in May 2001, with less emotional commitment as routines for the new organization had already started exerting their influence upon participants, who did not have the impression of creating history at the open frontier any more.

In the first cultural seminar discussions of perceived differences in national styles of decision-making (both self-descriptions and ascriptions), a sense of humour and ability to make fun of one's own national stereotype were crucial. Managers discovered that they could overcome some biases, and that they had underestimated the difficulties met in cross-border co-operation. For instance, Swedes considered themselves champions of open dialogue and viewed all others as indecisive, given to too-long discussions with no clear point of decision-making in sight. Danes considered themselves business-like and flexible, while they were distrusted by the others, according to whom they continued to negotiate even after agreement had been reached. The Finns thought themselves action-oriented and with much stamina, while the others found them too formal, hierarchically oriented and bureaucratic. Norwegians thought that one should decide quickly and then open up a creative discussion, while the others charged them with narrow local patriotism and a blind preference for Norwegian solutions.

Even though dichotomies within the organization into 'us and them', both at national level and business area level, dominated the early phase after the cross-border merger was announced, Nordea succeeded step-by-step in creating a rather well-functioning organization, with cross-border departments and project teams and more common practices. A new company name and logo was soon designed, and English was chosen as the corporate language in all cross-border activities. Instead of the top-driven initiative on internal branding expressed in the booklet *Making It Possible*, other means to integrate merging companies and their employees were developed, such as education of cross-border groups of employees, middle managers and senior executives. These facilitated better understanding and co-operation, and created a stronger identification with the new company among the employees.

The researchers conclude:

> A final message to managers aiming at ambitious socio-cultural integration projects between merging companies is therefore that organizational cultures do not exist, if they are not made sense of and discussed by those who should feel attached to and identify with them.
>
> (Søderberg, Björkman, 2003, 172)

5 Knowledge, management and criticism

> Would-be leaders must lead people who will not follow. All a manager or anyone else can do by way of leadership is to become a sort of narrator, joining his or her voice to the other voices in organization.
>
> (Leinberger, Tucker, 1991, 410)

Researchers from Copenhagen Business School found that only by paying due attention to the sense-making practices of employees were they able to understand the socio-cultural processes that corporate designers wanted to influence and guide, thus contributing to the overall post-merger integration. Their methodological focus merits attention in view of the prevailing ideology of managerialism among business and political elites. Viewing organizations exclusively from the top does not necessarily provide the best knowledge about employee interactions. Their methodological focus merits attention also in view of the dominance of functionalism in managerial and organizational sciences.

Viewing organizations as separate, autonomous, individual functional and rational systems filled with individual rational agents (also separate and autonomous), who have to be properly manipulated (managed, controlled, supervised, directed) is dangerously reductionist. The need to redress the imbalance by paying more attention to interpretative, soft, qualitative approaches, which make us sensitive to multiple embeddings, affinities, traditions, and relationships, becomes very important. Qualitative methodologies and the culture-sensitive approach are indeed in need of partisanship in order to compensate for unfair dominance of the quantitative approach among members of academic, ideological and political establishments. After all, this is what democratizing and organizing are all about (behind both the factory and the university door). Rational choice theory and transition cost economics enjoy an institutionally privileged position in access to research funds and career pathing, in expertise and consulting markets, and in the corridors of establishment's power.

Relative neglect of socio-cultural processes in organizations is partly caused by developments in social sciences themselves. Compared say to C. W. Mills' analyses of white-collar workers and the military–industrial complex, contemporary academic output in sociology testifies to a general decline of relevance in sociological studies, justifies the question 'what went wrong?' (cf. Mouzelis, 1995), raises doubts about the McDonaldization of sociological research (Ritzer, 1999, 2001), and arouses suspicions about professional avoidance of politically and morally sensitive issues (Kivisto, 2001, Seale, 2004).

This crisis of sociology has to be addressed if concepts like cultural due diligence are not to share the fate of many a guru and much hype in the sciences of management. Further development of diagnostic instruments have to be based on serious and systematic analysis and in-depth interpretation of socio-cultural processes, which form the mainstream of organizing and managing, and which crucially depend on dense flows of relations, interactions, interpersonal power-struggles, re-evaluations of traditions, and symbolic negotiations. These processes are 'where the action is' before it becomes reflected in budgetary tables, promotional lists and action plans or mission statements. These processes involve the 'production' (or 'creation' in a heroic version of this metaphor) and 'winning' (or 'acquiring' in the business-like version of that metaphor) of knowledge and expertise,[14] and they also involve managerial skills, in the dissemination of information and knowledge and in applying knowledge for gaining power, inspiring individuals and accomplishing goals (Nonaka, Takeuchi, 1995; Nonaka, Nishiguchi, 2001).

This brings us to the knowledge management archipelago. It was discovered not long ago and is being 'colonized' by academics, consultants and managers in the wake of the first wave of general theories of the 'knowledge society', 'knowledge economy', 'information revolution', 'information society' (even 'transparent' or 'weightless' societies) and their consequences: life-long learning theories, the concepts of a learning organization, of a coaching manager and of 'communities' of knowledge, practice and learning. The academic and consulting industries are working at full speed. However, their representatives usually assume that there has been a general shift in the technologies of manufacturing and communication, which makes bureaucratic hierarchies obsolete and allows for more flexible, network-like organizational forms to spread and prosper.

Railroads and the telegraph – so runs this watered-down version of Marx's historical materialism – gave us large business corporations with industrial bureaucracies, standardized mass-production, and military logistics and co-ordination for conducting world wars. In other words, first came new technologies of material production, then organizational and social processes, that grew around them, and then ideas emerged that reflected the ways in which people started making sense of what they had been doing. To put it in a nutshell: 'technology' breeds 'sociology' breeds 'ideology'.

However, all those processes, while increasing the control of the privileged classes over the lower and exploited ones, also simultaneously opened new possibilities for the latter to organize. Industrial workers got a free ride in becoming concentrated in cheap lodgings around large factories. They were available for political organizers and accessible to unions organizing mutual support. The laptop and mobile phone give us, the employees of today, flexible global networks, outsourcing links and a growing variety of organizational forms. They also give us a chance to generate new ideas in order to make sense of what we are doing and what is happening to us. Knowledge management belongs to these ideas.[15] It is a utopian dream of a technology that will set us free, expressed in a politically neutral, managerialist idiom. It is an ideological utopia of egalitarian, democratic organizing ushered in by technology and accepted by managers.

The prevailing view of the evolution of organizational forms is that we are moving away from lofty pyramids of hierarchic bureaucracies and towards flexible, loosely coupled networks of modular organizational clusters and individual professionals. We are doing so not only because some technologies make it possible to individualize communications, but also because we want to break free of the iron cages of industrial bureaucracies. In other words, the new networked utopia makes us see the world of organizations as evolving from fixed hierarchic pyramids to flat, flexible and mobile networks, where managerial control withers away and individual creativity soars (under the watchful eye of a friendly coach, who used to be a stern boss before being reborn as a friendly mentor).

This view is not empirically confirmed by – say – a decreasing difference between salaries of Chief Executive Officers and their subordinates. One would expect that if bureaucracies reduce their layers and become more horizontal, flat and egalitarian (everybody, after all, has access to information via mobile laptops), then not only would knowledge become more equally distributed but also salaries and bonuses. Quite the contrary is true: the salaries and bonuses of CEOs rose dramatically in the last two decades of the 20th century, while employee wages froze or declined and part-time, Third-World wage levels became widespread. If we take the difference between the highest and lowest salary within a business corporation to be an indicator of Hofstede's power distance, then we have to conclude that power distance grew in the past two decades of the 20th century. Organizations became more, not less, hierarchic, privileges of those higher up grew, while waged labour lost theirs. Employees saw their relative position vis-à-vis their supervising managers grow worse (for instance, through a gradual neutralization and attrition of trade unions and enterprise councils). However, this empirical evidence notwithstanding, it is maintained by almost all representatives of organizational and managerial sciences that we are moving towards more democracy and equality of creative, enlightened corporate citizens in most companies and organizations. What does one do if empirical evidence is missing but one wants to sustain an ideology?

If sociological evidence – for instance diminishing wage differentials between employees in the same company – is missing, a technological *deus ex machina* is conveniently invoked. As a result of the simultaneous emergence of interactive, mobile and individualized telecommunications and a parallel increase in complexity and speed of processing information, our knowledge started growing much more quickly than ever before and the process is still accelerating. This overall growth of knowledge requires much more precise and focused management – knowledge has to be both upgraded and lost ('unlearned'), acquired and replaced, transformed, translated, applied, adjusted, etc. Knowledge management becomes very important, managers focus on knowledge transfers as the single most important factor contributing to their competitive edge. So runs the technological story about the influence of new technologies on our organizational and social forms. If everybody has a laptop, mobile phone and satellite links, then a hierarchy of officials managing information flows does not determine one's access to data, does it? Even if 'they' (managers, the ruling classes, social elites) control the TV screens and newspaper pages, corporate PR and annual reports, local radio, intranets, mobile phones and the internet can offer alternative access to independently acquired and disseminated information for 'us' (civil society, local communities, alternative groups, subcultures). The individualized, mobile, personal nature of modern communication devices allows informal peer-to-peer links and relationships between employees to flourish, almost automatically subverting bureaucratic lines of command. Hence a hasty, tentative conclusion: organizations as pyramids are giving way to networks of liberated professionals. Or are they?

In reality this is not an automatic process. Access can easily be denied and tightly controlled, not necessarily on political grounds alone. Nor is it a 'historical' necessity. History can provide us with cases of the use of new mobile technologies to increase monitoring, control and repression – the latest anti-terrorist fingerprinting and photo-taking at the US airports is a very dramatic case in point. Individual professionals (and everybody else) have been liberated not only from the iron cages of industrial bureaucracies but also from job stability and job security. More often than not they had seen their autonomy and discretion limited by Panopticon-like techniques of surveillance and control. Complexity grows, so does our knowledge and the flexibility of our organizational modules, but increased flexibility of organizational form does not have to mean increased freedom of choice for an individual. The ideology of an inevitable technological 'force' transforming organizations *independently* of the will of employees and managers can only be accepted if we turn a blind eye to the socio-cultural processes involving asymmetries of power and inequalities in knowledge and wealth generated by academic and professional institutions. Our superstitious fear of seeing some conflicts as 'class struggles' makes us assume that Chief Information Officers or Chief Knowledge Officers in business organizations have to be – by virtue of their access to the modern technologies that are supposedly liberating us from the oppressive iron cages of former bureaucratic organizational forms – egalitarian democrats.

However, at the very base of these latest transformations of organizational forms there is a paradox, which leaves some hope for those who are under-paid and under-empowered. If evolving organizations and institutions are to deal with this increasing complexity and to participate in the growth of knowledge, they have to train such people in exactly those skills and intellectual frames of mind that had been suppressed in bureaucratic hierarchies – namely, criticism, autonomy and creativity. Organizations must secure equal access to knowledge resources and knowledge development, not limit it to rank and close it to file. Thus a leader and manager must make a conscious attempt to encourage criticism – hoping it will stimulate further competitive growth of knowledge and expertise. At the same time he or she must be aware that these critical skills and this newly won knowledge can become resources in power struggles against him- or herself. This is the paradox that lies at the base of all the knowledge management hype.[16]

A closer look at knowledge management brings us to the newly emerging archipelago of knowledge assets (Boisot, 1995, 1998), the social life of information (Brown, Duguid, 2000; Ciborra, 2002), knowledge management *tout court* (see for instance, Davenport, Prusak, 1998; Lesser, Fontaine, Slusher, 2000; Bahra, 2001), studies of 'communities in cyberspace' (cf. Smith, Kollock, 1999), critical management studies (Alvesson, Willmott, 1996), and even to an attempt to re-write cross-cultural management from a knowledge management perspective (Holden, 2002). All these studies have been written as attempts to cope with the dramatic competitive advantage of knowledge-intensive organizations and an equally dramatic growth in global, individualized, mobile communications. In case of the last author, he bluntly states that he does not want to 'regurgitate' the work of Hofstede, Adler and Trompenaars, but intends to make a fresh start and to see culture not through the eyes of a sociologist or an anthropologist, but through those of a manager taking on global challenges in a globalizing economy.

For Holden, culture becomes an 'organizational knowledge resource' and analysis of culture is related to networking, organizational learning and – indeed – knowledge management. According to Holden, the privileged site of knowledge management and cross-cultural learning is a modern business corporation (presumably assisted by loyal academics serving as researchers cum consultants). It is privileged in the sense that it offers a much better level of observation of culture's consequences than either a society, national or not, or an individual. It is much better equipped to deal with cross-cultural learning and much quicker to exploit empirical feedback than either academic science (which is too slow, fragmented and embedded in paradigmatic traditions) or public authorities (which are too busy trying to strike deals with too-divergent interest groups). As an organizational form, contemporary business corporation is thus far ahead of other cross-cultural learning platforms, according to Holden, because it is continuously busy with 'recreating' organizational culture as a result of global reach and multicultural working forces, marketing demands, global competition, etc. In other words, academics and consultants should not be looking into politician's metaphors of the 'melting pots' or 'salad bowls' of multicultural societies, but behind the factory doors, where multicultural team-working and knowledge-sharing made managers and consultants superior experts in redefining culture and doing business with it:

> cross-cultural management has something to do with transposing values from one cultural ambience to another. But this does not go far enough, partly because values are still signifiers of cultural difference. The task facing scholars of cross-cultural management is to make precisely the conceptual shift . . . major companies have already made in their operations. . . . The core task of cross-cultural management is to facilitate and direct synergistic action and learning at interfaces where knowledge, values and experience are transferred into multicultural domains of implementation.
>
> (Holden, 2002, 58)

Let us inspect Holden's claim from the perspective of the paradox mentioned above, namely the paradox of ambiguous empowerment in the workplace. Is it, indeed, true that culture should primarily be viewed from the perspective of an international organizational resources inventory? If so, then Holden follows the prominent British specialist in international human resources management, Monir Tayeb, who argued for the transferability of national and organizational HRM practices across corporate and national 'fences' in the course of 'the management of a multicultural workforce' (cf. Tayeb, 1996). Interestingly enough, Holden does not notice how close his ideas follow the suggestions of Tayeb, although they are expressed in the book he quoted in the last chapter of his study on re-mapping the domain of cross-cultural management. He lumps her together with newer handbooks of cross-cultural management – Schneider and Barsoux from 1997 is a case in point (cf. Schneider, Barsoux, 1997) – and with older ones – Harris and Moran (cf. Harris, Moran, 1996). The latter illustrates this first wave of books on cross-cultural management, which followed Deal and Kennedy's famous *Corporate Cultures* from 1982 (Deal, Kennedy, 1982). Then he claims that all these authors, Tayeb, Moran, Harris, Schneider, and Barsoux, represent a 'hierarchical perspective of cultural influence, compromise and adaptation', from which a transition should be made towards 'collaborative cross-cultural learning' (Holden, 2002, 306).

Let us examine his claim from the perspective of one of the central dilemmas of contemporary culture in general, and of the organizational cultures of knowledge-intensive organizations in particular, namely commitment to organizations based on inequality. There is an insoluble conflict between two different sets of attitudes a successful socialization and enculturation is supposed to generate in such organizations. On the one hand, successful socialization generates loyalty identification and emotional support, turning a formal organization into a living community. On the other, true loyalty encourages honest criticism, which requires distance and cognitive clarity to facilitate the creativity of employees/corporate citizens. This problem becomes more acute as individuals need to be offered free access to growing knowledge and enough discretion to combine it in a creative way (thus acquiring autonomy and bridging some of the inequality and powerlessness gaps), while at the same time they are increasingly closely controlled by management (thus experiencing increasing inequality and powerlessness gap). *Does the replacement of power metaphors (in descriptions of organizational reality as a 'class struggle' of managers versus employees) with knowledge metaphors (in descriptions of organizational reality as knowledge management, organizational learning and networking) bring us closer to an understanding of organizational evolution and change? Do we succeed when talking of generation, codification and transfer of knowledge, where we had failed when talking of power, resources and charisma?*

Holden's main assumption, which prompted his decision to change the basic theoretical frame for cross-cultural studies, is historical. He assumes that the end of the Cold War, the fall of communist and socialist alternatives to the capitalist economy and parliamentary democracy, the dramatic development of China and of the Asian 'tigers', have changed the context in which all organizations are managed all over the world. He thinks that Hofstede's data have been gathered in a relatively stable and geopolitically stabilized world. This assumption is undoubtedly true. The world of Hofstede's original studies was a world divided by the Iron Curtain and prevented from organizational experiments by the requirements of Cold War mobilization and the ideological propaganda war. There is an element of truth in this assumption: the 'freezing' effect of the Cold War on organizational and managerial options can easily be traced to cultural wars waged with secret funds and under the cover of the Congress for Cultural Freedom in the West and the Peace Congress in the East, and other similar 'front' organizations. Trade unions, which were not directly controlled by the Communist Party, could not emerge in the East until August 1980 in Poland. Communist parties could not take over national state power in the West and a communist president of France or Italy would have triggered a non-democratic response of NATO (cf. the 'Gladio' affair in Italy and CIA support for Christian Democrats). Western Europe has certainly had a social democratic version of a trade-union supported 'participative management' and the 'welfare state' – precisely because in the eyes of military and political planners this demonstrated the viability of a non-communist version of 'capitalism with a human face'. Neither trade unions nor the welfare state have been seriously undermined until a series of crises in the last quarter of the 20th century. The oil crisis of the early 1970s signalled by the emergence of OPEC and the terminal crisis of the socialist countries signalled by the appearance of the Polish anti-communist mass movement Solidarity in 1980 are cases in point.

The same ideological 'propaganda' of tutored economic growth was designed and implemented in Japan, South Korea, Singapore, and Taiwan, although there a purely economic effect was achieved, without accompanying industrial or social democracy. This stability (originating in the symmetry of fear of nuclear attack) disappeared in the period between 1980 (Solidarity in Poland) and 1989–91 (the fall of the Berlin Wall and the dissolution of the Soviet Union). With the disappearance of the Cold War stability, organizing and managing could start experimenting with new cultural resources, not only with the ones closely supervised by nation-states frozen into Cold War front lines.

Holden's assumption echoes the one made by Boisot, whose model of information space is also geared to knowledge management and also supposed to furnish a better explanatory framework for understanding the latest developments in China, or, to repeat the title of one of the comparative studies of post-communist Russian and Chinese developments, 'China's rise and Russia's fall' (Nolan, 1995). Boisot's frame allows us to see the evolution of organizational forms in an information space, i.e. from the perspective of their knowledge management. Changes in organizational forms are presented as movements in the information space due to social and organizational learning processes. Reading Boisot we have to assume that if individuals and societies learn, 'grades' should be given by stakeholders to the organizational forms these individuals and societies generate, because it is through the tracing of organizational evolution that we can reconstruct and document social learning processes. Information space has three dimensions: abstraction, codification and dissemination (to which Holden's 'generation, codification and transfer' roughly correspond). Organizational forms move between the four 'corners' of the 'aquarium' of information space: fiefs (where information is controlled by a single boss); clans (where information is shared by top managers of many companies); bureaucracies (where information is distributed according to ranks); and markets (where information is accessible and transparent – at least in the idealized form of the market). For our discussion, the most important conclusion drawn by Boisot from applying his model of information space to the analysis of data gathered during his stay in China concerns the re-feudalization of former state-owned enterprises.

This re-feudalization means that their organizational forms 'move' in his information space away from bureaucracies towards fiefs, because they operate in markets, in which state bureaucracies turn out to be inefficient. However, Boisot notes the 'iron law of fiefs', which leads the Chinese organizational forms towards a gradual dismantling of state-owned enterprises, and 'a gradual decentralization towards clans' (Boisot, 1995, 426). The Chinese process of social learning how to network in the market eventually led to the spectacular development of a Chinese 'network capitalism' in special zones, coastal cities and other social spaces freed by state bureaucracy. Networking change has not been a simple transition from bureaucracy as the dominant organizational form to the market-oriented company *tout court*. It passed through 'fiefs' (re-feudalization) to 'clans' (network capitalism):

> Neither bureaucracies nor markets can deal comfortably with discontinuous change. They reduce rather than absorb uncertainty by trying to bracket it and convert it into calculable, i.e. codifiable, risk. Clans and fiefs on the other hand, operating lower down the information space, confront uncertainty on its own terms, absorbing it through social relationships that promote trust and commitment rather than a narrow adherence to rules.
>
> (Boisot, 1995, 443)

However, this large-scale lesson in social learning about organizational forms and types of management, is not limited to China. Organizational forms that have been dominant in the West in the past centuries – bureaucratic organizations and market companies – would like to keep the advantages of their impersonal, objective knowledge management, but at the same time want to:

> expand their overall transactional capacities through the internal development of what we have called a centrifugal culture, one in which personal and impersonal forms of exchange can mutually invigorate one another. Many large firms in quest of entrepreneurial renewal in the lower part of the information space are today exploring clan and fief forms of organizational practice through networking and 'intrapreneurial' practices. They are in effect building network capitalism from the inside and, in contrast to the Chinese case, they are approaching it from the market rather than the clan region.
>
> (Boisot, 1995, 443)[17]

Thus the argument about the significance of the end of the Cold War for increasing the accessibility of cultural resources in management acquires its double-edged nature. *The end of the Cold War meant not only the end of the communist type of dictatorships, but also the beginning of an end of industrial bureaucracy as the only privileged organizational form in Western economies.* If IBM had preserved its monopoly, Apple would not have emerged. IBM survives and thrives, but Apple managed to get a foothold in the market, too. Generation, codification and transfer of knowledge – all these processes involve frequent and individualized communications, knowledge sharing, the horizontal exchange of tacit knowledge, decentralization, flexible networking, and empowerment. Marketing managers experiment with relationship marketing, financial officers delegate authority, HRM executives develop psychological contracts and practise outsourcing, CEOs come up with personalized communications and empowerment schemes, logistics experts try supply chain network alternatives, consultants work on corporate culture by design, and everybody speaks of trust.

All agree that a company culture is an umbrella covering multiple subcultures and cultural hybrids, which are continually renegotiated and re-created. Culture is not perceived as solid 'cultural software' with essential values at its core, surrounded by norms that guide us towards the visible 'surface' of behavioural acts and to making sense of the symbols and artefacts around us. Software plus interaction create the background for socially guided individual choices. National cultures investigated by Hofstede, corporate cultures studied by Deal and Kennedy, professional cultures researched by Alvesson, employee cultures studied by Burawoy, managerial cultures investigated by Hope, gender, generation and other subcultures – all of these are social constructs and remain to a large extent tacit until confronted with another culture. These cultures and subcultures become part of our identity; we begin to comprehend them explicitly upon entering relationships and forming networks with the others. All of us carry and re-engineer multiple cultures and subcultures as we relate to the others and interact with them. Culture is perceived as a social construct – Holden chooses the social constructionist approach to culture. He calls for researchers to follow Bartholomew and Adler's plea to replace the hierarchical and essentialist concept of cultural 'black boxes' influencing individuals and requiring their adjustment with the concept of 'collaborative cross-cultural learning'. After all, according to him, culture should be defined as 'varieties of common knowledge' (Holden, 2002, 99) negotiated in 'shared mental space' (ibid., 179). All these varieties may become relevant and salient in one of the multiple organizational contexts, in which inter-actions take place and in which these varieties are being continuously negotiated and renegotiated. Accordingly, he observes

> that so-called cultural 'data' are in fact 'social constructs' made on the basis of the practitioners' and the researchers' own cultural thought patterns and the concepts and categories to which they are socialized.
>
> (Holden, 2002, 57)

It is not difficult to share Holden's assumptions about the significance of the end of the Cold War for the accelerated cultural revolution in management. Freed from the necessity to supply ideological weapons in a potentially lethal war, managers, consultants and employees at large could experiment with new forms of organizing. It is not difficult to sympathize with his methodological choice of a social constructivist approach to the study of culture, either. Privileges bestowed upon rational choice theories (in social sciences) and transaction-cost analysis (in economics and the sciences of management) by the managerial and academic establishments warrant some sympathy for the paradigmatic underdog. However, growing disillusionment with these mainstream paradigms, methodologies and theories prompted many researchers to look for alternatives in qualitative, interpretative, social constructivist, and discursive approaches.

Nevertheless, Holden's canonization of the business company as a privileged platform of social learning with 'shared mental space' and democratic, egalitarian characteristics does have to be taken with a pinch of salt. One of his cases in point is the Danish company LEGO, praised for a strong company culture that employees readily identify with and for creating 'shared mental space' across national borders. In the course of international expansion and networking, the company managed to preserve this strong identity and to transfer it to newly acquired companies outside Denmark. This transfer, according to Holden, is a case of cross-cultural knowledge transfer and the way it was managed a paradigmatic case of a cross-cultural knowledge management. The success of LEGO knowledge management he attributed to the attitude displayed by senior managers and the procedures they followed in order to facilitate creative exchange between Danish designers and producers of traditional wooden and plastic toys, and British designers and producers of software games:

> cross-cultural learning has a greater chance of succeeding when the nominally senior group in knowledge exchanges is not too concerned about imposing values and thinking on others.
>
> (Holden, 2002, 180)

Reading this, one feels that the critical edge of a theory of knowledge management has been blunted: democratic and egalitarian partner-like approach depends on the goodwill of top management. Cross-cultural learning is facilitated by nominally senior managers willingly refraining from exercising their power. Why should we expect benevolent CEOs to show restraint on all or most occasions? The famous toy bricks of LEGO strike us as standardized, modular components of many potential constructions, into which they may readily be assembled and recombined. The ease with which they can be continuously assembled and reassembled reminds us about the growing variety of organizational forms and increased frequency of networking, interacting and communicating between them. We, as individuals involved in companies, networks and projects, interact and communicate with individuals whose socialization followed patterns we are mostly unaware of. Yet we are expected to trust them and to be trusted by them in sophisticated collaborative and competitive interactions. Can we relax knowing that only the goodwill of top managers following corporate code of ethics and issuing corporate sustainability statements prevents them from re-activating hierarchy and power? My guess is that we would like to see a more solid ground for democracy behind the factory and office door and that *translating cross-cultural issues of power and change in organizations into a re-mapped knowledge management domain does not allow for a sufficiently critical distance from our principal object of study – contemporary formal organization.*

It may very well be as Holden says, that a business company is nowadays the best example of the battleground for future cross-cultural co-operation. However, this is far from certain and has not yet been demonstrated in a convincing way. On the contrary, cross-cultural co-operation has also been successfully implemented by and between non-business organizations and institutions. Cases in point can be found in international military alliances, education, health care, and media co-operation. European integration provides a new level of cross-cultural management, half-way between the global and the national (significant parts of the integration efforts are beyond the scope of business companies). But even if Holden is right, if the business company remains the paradigm of an agile, flexible, innovative, entrepreneurial, learning platform, then certainly the explanation cannot be based on assumed self-restraint of power holders. Are business corporations more active learners, creative, flexible and agile only because its managers voluntarily decline to exercise their power, seduced by their new titles as global knowledge workers?[18]

6 The case of the International Federation of Red Cross and Red Crescent Societies [with Thierry Verduijn]

The provision of humanitarian aid to a civilian population deprived of usual resources by a natural (earthquake, avalanche, flood, drought, volcanic eruption, wind storms) or man-made (war, terrorism, forced displacement) disaster is a very difficult and complex undertaking. Organizations dealing with it must be highly knowledge-intensive if they are to respond quickly and appropriately to such complicated challenges. Relief operations require co-ordination of so many actors that both modern information and communication technology and expert knowledge management are required. Without satellite-linked laptops in the hands of relief workers at the border between Kosovo and Macedonia, the relief operation for Kosovon Albanians would have been impossible. Without qualified managers able to assess, design and implement such relief operations world-wide, they would be much less effective and sometimes entirely impossible. With respect to logistics, organization and management, supplying clothes, food, shelter, and medical care for millions of individuals requires close collaboration of humanitarian relief organizations and a large network of suppliers and donors. The International Federation of Red Cross and Red Crescent Societies (IFRC&RC), whose headquarters are based in Geneva, Switzerland, is one of the oldest (it was founded in 1919) and the largest among them. It also acts as a co-ordinating centre and database: 178 national Red Cross or Red Crescent Societies belong to it and they collaborate in order to integrate their readiness for and response to disaster. It is thus involved in continuous knowledge management and environmental scanning (knowledge gathering and evaluation). Knowledge, information and expertise gathered in this way can be mobilized at any time and usually at a very short notice. Since we do not know where the next disaster will strike, the Federation has to maintain an updated database mapping a global network of potential suppliers of relief goods, transport and logistics.

The Logistics and Mobilization Department of the IFRC&RC co-ordinates the emergency relief supply chain, so that rapid deployment of resources belonging to member societies and equally rapid assembling of needed supplies can be secured at any time. It acts as a spin in the web and makes use of flexible, dynamic supply chains, whose elements, like LEGO toy bricks, can be recombined according to the time, place and the nature of the disaster. The Federation primarily co-ordinates the activities of 178 national societies, but an emergency response web also includes other relief organizations (in order to avoid duplicating the effort in the same area), donors (who furnish funds to purchase supplies at short notice), suppliers (who sell food, tents, sanitation, etc.), governments and authorities (which determine the scope of operations and also provide military assistance, if necessary), and transport and forwarding companies.

Management of a disaster relief project follows the emergency response process, which begins with the assessment of a disaster carried out by either the local national Red Cross society or by a cluster of national societies from the region, forming a Regional Disaster Response Team. Either of them can then decide whether to rely on local, national or regional resources, or to call the International Federation for assistance. This decision should be reached within 12 to 18 hours. Should the IFRC&RC be asked for assistance, it will respond by selecting an operations manager, building a Field Assistance Coordination Team (FACT), and putting Emergency Response Units (ERU) on the alert. There are ERUs that specialize in basic health care, logistics, water and sanitation, referral hospital facilities, and telecommunications. The aim of FACT assistance is to send specialist units to the disaster area within 48 hours and to support the local national society in the assessment of needs, and in planning and co-ordinating relief activities. ERUs build up the logistical base for a more systematic assistance effort. During the early hours of a disaster, the IFRC&RC launches an emergency appeal and releases funds from the Disaster Response Emergency Fund. For most urgent needs, relief items from the Disaster Preparedness Stocks are shipped from two global emergency warehouses, based in Panama and Abu Dhabi. Then purchasing/sourcing takes place: both the IFRC&RC and the national societies do the purchasing, with the former clearly in the background, purchasing only those goods that have not already been pledged by national societies.

Two elements of the emergency response process require particular attention from the perspective of knowledge management: the pre-arranged frame agreements with suppliers for the main relief items and co-operation with the United Nations Joint Logistics Centre (UNJLC) in the actual distribution of aid. The main relief items (blankets, tarpaulins, plastic sheeting, jerry cans), which will always be ordered, are provided to the IFRC&RC on the basis of

> frame agreements on product specification, prices and stock availability. The suppliers are selected by means of an international tendering. For each item two or three suppliers are selected to have a global coverage. For other items, the IFRC&RC sends the Requests for Quotation (RFQs) to various suppliers in their database and selects the best suppliers using delivery times, costs and quantity as criteria. If response times need to be really short, the RFQ process is omitted.
>
> (Verduijn, 2004, 190)[19]

Having created the emergency response process for the IFRC&RC, the federation builds additional flexibility into this process by allowing the operations manager to decide if some of the due diligence procedures (such as supplier selection) can be abandoned for the sake of response time. This requires continuous updating and monitoring of new data and knowledge on developments in the field. Flexibility is also required because of the local conditions at the site of the disaster; if the area is flooded, accessibility can change from day to day or hour to hour. Co-operation with the UNJLC provides crucial information about the last-mile distribution of aid, since the UN logistics centre can gather last-minute information on the region's infrastructure, weather conditions and general accessibility, distributing it freely, i.e. through a public, not a commercial website. Finally, all projects of the IFRC&RC are finite and relatively short; their duration is defined before the beginning of the action and when the end date is reached, local resources (field hospitals, water sources) are handed over to local authorities or local national societies, specialists are withdrawn, and the project is evaluated. In conclusion, one may say that knowledge management at the IFRC&RC is strongly linked to the ability of its staff to 'absorb uncertainty' and to continually redesign global networks, building flexibility of managerial response into the particular procedures and the governance structure in general.[20]

However, the real problems of knowledge management in relief organizations lie not in logistics or technology, but in the social and political aspects of relief decision-making. They are connected with the question of power and the prioritization of international aid programmes, both of which manifest and reflect political agendas. The IFRC&RC does recognize the asymmetry between the size of donations and their target populations, which reflects the political agenda of the donors, but can do relatively little about it. In other words, even if a region will – objectively speaking – require more donations in order to meet the target of covering the entire threatened population, it sometimes receives much less than needed, because donors' hidden political agendas makes them support other causes and ear-mark donated funds for specific regions. Sometimes a reverse process also takes place: relief organizations ask for more or less than actually needed depending on what they think can be expected from potential donors:

> One major ethical concern is the selectivity of emergency aid. Relief peaked at US$5.9 billion in 2000, but its global distribution reveals a political rather than moral geography. In 2000, the northern Caucasus received 89 per cent of its UN appeal, Somalia only 22 per cent. . . . Within weeks of the fall of Saddam, US$1.7 billion had been raised in relief for Iraq, while less than half that had been pledged for 40 million starving Africans. Meanwhile, research suggests

that humanities organizations base their funding request less on evidence of objective need than on what they think the market will bear.

(IFRC, 2003; cf. Verduijn, 2004, 197)

One unexpected result of this interest in pursuing hidden agendas is the increasing interest in transparency of relief operations. Donors are interested in tracking their donations through the relief organizations' activities – which means that the latter have to employ more staff ('become more bureaucratic' and more 'hierarchic') in order to provide more precise reports and accounts of their activities and finances. In other words, even though the IFRC&RC and its national societies are relatively small and highly motivated, and have established flexible procedures and assembled global supply chains, they are still required to bureaucratize themselves in order to become more 'transparent' and 'compatible' with their donors, who usually work through large public and private bureaucracies and who suspect loose network organizations of being too random and out of control. Another unexpected side-effect of designing flexible global governance procedures and supply chains is increasing competition between relief organizations for expected future funding and thus their relative position compared to the others. The governance structure for major relief operations created by the IFRC&RC is thus to a certain extent a showcase of contemporary network organization, relying on electronic proximity and on co-ordinating multiple donors, suppliers and transport companies. However, this flexible network is being manipulated by the traditional bureaucracies of the donors and state governments pursuing their political agendas. This 'contaminates' the purely networked organizational structure of the relief organizations in two ways: first, by requiring them to develop their bureaucracies in order to satisfy the tracking, recording and reporting demands of donors, and second, by switching among relief organizations and creating competition between them:

> Hindering the spread of formal collaboration is the feeling that just as organizations could work together to maximise their positive impact on beneficiaries, organizations are also competing to win future grants from donors.
>
> (Fritz Institute, 2003; cf. Verduijn, 2004, 199)

We are thus dealing with a knowledge-intensive organization that is flexible, globally networked, continuously learning, and staffed by highly qualified experts. However, this organization's limits to learning are not linked to the restraint of top managers, but to the conditions imposed by some stakeholders and to competition with other, similar relief organizations. These limitations are linked to critical power factors both inside their organization (stakeholders influencing managerial choices) and outside of it (competition with other, similar relief organizations).

One of the facets of this power-play is the pressure from the majority of organizational forms, which requires even the most flexible and networked organizations to return to more bureaucratic procedures in order to become 'transparent' and 'compatible' with bureaucratic stakeholders. This facet of power can only be neutralized (and thus its influence hampering development of network-like organizations be reduced) if alternative forms of accountability are developed, which do not require a relapse into the old, familiar procedures for guaranteeing accountability and responsibility. At present, such networked forms exist, but they are still more or less constrained by a predominantly bureaucratic organizational environment. Nevertheless, the expansion of network-like forms – if it does happen – will offer convincing empirical evidence that power struggles within and between organizations have resulted in an evolutionary shift in the fundamental building blocks of modern societies, namely, their organizations. If the IFRC&RC manages to invent a non-bureaucratic organizational form to render its activities transparent and make the assignment of responsibilities secure in spite of a volatile, network-like organizational structure (for instance by outsourcing these activities to trusted third parties, acceptable to the stakeholders involved), an important evolutionary step will have occurred.

7 From controlling to coaching: democracy beyond the factory (office) door

There is no question that understanding the power factor is critical in both learning how organizations work and in getting them to accomplish their tasks. However, there is also no question that an analysis of power, very much like an analysis of culture, has been safely tucked away in separate chapters of books on general management and organizational behaviour, and to a large extent ignored in the managerial sciences as a whole. Many prominent authors have expressed their astonishment about power's conspicuous absence from research agendas (Pfeffer) and many pointed out the taboos that surround power, making it 'America's last dirty word' (Kanter). While expressing their surprise at the relative neglect of power issues in the literature on organizational theory, organizational behaviour and organizational development or change, most authors readily agree that focusing on power in research and consulting has become more topical than ever. Reasons for this rising status of power on the ranking scale of topics for research is usually found in the assumed decline of the hierarchic organization and the assumed erosion of the hierarchical bases of managerial authority. As the formal pyramid of organizational structure becomes flatter, authority cannot be taken for granted and future managers have to become Machiavellian leaders introducing less formal ways of 'getting things done' and fighting, i.e. accumulating and using power, to get their superiority accepted and to legitimize their newly won power by converting it into authority.

While Kanter may be right in claiming that power is 'America's last dirty word', one should note at least three aspects of the power issue, which make it less America's and more everybody's 'last dirty word'.

First, power has always been a 'dirty' word for most historically known societies. Neither 'America' nor its contemporaries have a monopoly on making power issues taboo. The transition from feudalism to capitalism in Europe was accompanied by the republican analysis of political power by Machiavelli, who sought to separate the issues of legitimization of power from the issues of efficient and effective use of it. He designed an accessible toolkit to advise free citizens about the managerial exercise of power. No wonder Robespierre admired Machiavelli, having noted in his writings a blueprint for the French Revolution. Moreover, in the course of the 19th century the issue of power had been analysed within the framework of two dominant forms of the political organization of increasingly broad and increasingly networked masses: the state (which became a nation-state), and the political party (which became either communist or social democratic, to mention only those envisioning radical reform of the state and therefore challenging its authority).

The issues of state power and its exercise were analysed by von Clausewitz, who saw the power struggle between states as the most important political game played using diplomatic and military means. Ultimately, the power of a state was, according to him, embedded in a realist threat to use power or its actual exercise. The issue of a political party's power was analysed by sociologists (Michels, Pareto, Weber) and by ideologues of the working class movement (Marx, Lenin, Gramsci). This brings me to the second and third aspects of the power issue, both of which are responsible for making power a dirty word.

Let us begin with the second, which might be called the tacit law of class solidarity of bureaucratic elites. Sociologists have noticed that large bureaucratic organizations – state governments, trade unions, political parties – tend to breed indigenous elites and counter-elites. These may clash but ultimately they form a professional oligarchy, which differentiates itself from rank and file of society, employees and members. Michels spoke of an 'iron law of oligarchy' in trade unions, Pareto of the 'circulation of elites' in modern societies, Weber about the professional communities of politicians and scientists. The elites' relative isolation from the masses and defence of their group privileges does not facilitate open discussion of power issues – that might prompt criticism from below and thus endanger the position of the 'oligarchs' in their trade unions, state governments or political parties. To ignore power issues and focus on legitimizing the ideology in the name of which power is being exercised is much safer than an open debate on power itself. It is safer for the power-holders, but not for those who want to study power issues or to use power against the established elites. Researchers are too often incapable of explaining why power tends to be self-perpetuating and why the list of previously held power positions often constitutes the best predictor of subsequent power positions an individual will be holding in future. Managerialism as an ideology of organizational studies makes power 'politically incorrect' as an object of focus, attention and study, while solidarity between bureaucratic elites ('managing teams') of corporate, political and academic institutions does the rest:

> Considerations of domination and force, of getting one's way against opposition – which is, after all, a part of most definitions of power – perhaps are better left out of sight or discussion. The field's increasing embeddedness in an economic, rational conception of behaviour is nicely coupled with its renewed emphasis on the individual as contrasted with the situation. Both rationality and a focus on the individual in isolation more easily permit neglect of issues of inter-personal influence.
>
> (Pfeffer, 1977, 155)[21]

The third aspect of the power issue concerns the end of the Cold War and ambiguous legacy of the political Left. The end of the Cold War made the deficit of democracy in Western societies much more visible and vulnerable to criticism. During the Cold War, deficiencies in either parliamentary or corporate democracy could be explained as minuscule compared to blatant lack of democracy in Soviet-dominated societies. Once the latter disappeared, this argument disappeared too. The ambiguous legacy is the unfinished search for political alternatives to a class society organized around manageable inequalities. As a result of the breakdown of the experiment with state-socialist societies ruled by communist parties, class inequalities generated by the capitalist market and moderated by parliamentary democracy were not openly countered by an alternative vision of society. They had been, while the idea of a class struggle was ideologically alive on the Left. However, there was a price attached to this ideology. The political Left had been under the direct political and military control of the Soviet power elite (in the Warsaw Pact countries) or under ideological control of fellow-travellers (in NATO countries, especially France and Italy), and it had to keep silent about the Soviet genocide. Martin Amis found the following fragment in an essay by his father, Kingsley entitled 'Why Lucky Jim Turned Right', written when Kingsley Amis was 45 years old. Explaining his continued allegiance and affiliation in spite of his knowledge of the Soviet Communist Party's genocide, he wrote:

We are dealing with a conflict of feeling and intelligence, a form of
wilful self-deception whereby a part of the mind knows fully well that
its overall belief is false or wicked, but the emotional need to believe is
so strong that that knowledge remains, as it were, encysted, isolated,
powerless to influence word or deed.

(Amis, 2002, 273)

This accumulated silence in the face of the Soviet genocide now works
against Leftist alternatives to the liberal state and capitalist markets; the end
of the Cold War removed the institutional alternative to markets and
parliaments, but this removal did not result in a profound analysis of 'what
went wrong' nor in the de-communization of the Russian (and to a lesser
extent other) post-communist societies.

When the Polish poet, Czeslaw Milosz, wrote his critical analysis of the
mix of totalitarian dictatorship and professional privilege used by the Polish
communists after 1945 in order to seduce intellectuals *(The Captive Mind,*
1953), the French philosopher and a member of the Communist Party, Jean
Paul Sartre, called him a 'mad dog on a capitalist leash'. Sartre was ordered
to condemn a fellow intellectual on purely 'formal' grounds, without paying
attention to the 'content' of Milosz's analyses. Once Milosz turned against
the communists during the Cold War, the quality of his analysis became
irrelevant – Sartre was ordered to slander him by the French Communist
Party, controlled by the Soviet one.

The role of Sartre and other leading intellectuals, who were in fact
communist agents of influence during the Cold War, has never been understood nor analysed, let alone explained and assessed. Neither was the fact
that *The Captive Mind* was published with the support of the Congress for
Cultural Freedom, which had been a front for the CIA during the Cold War.
To have both writers' political involvement publicly discussed would
threaten the organizational interests of both the French Communist Party
and the secret network of anticommunist 'precautions' taken by the Western
democracies during the Cold War. One of the possible outcomes of
parliamentary elections in France or Italy during the Cold War might have
been a communist-dominated government – an option the US considered
unacceptable. Revealing these precautions would jeopardize them, as would
public discussion of the French or Italian communists' involvement in
coaching public opinion in Western Europe. None of these was desirable to
the Cold War's protagonists and that is why the legacy of the Cold War
remains a hot issue today. Both writers received Nobel Prizes for literature –
Sartre for prose, Milosz for poetry – but neither spoke of his embedding
in the Cold War power struggles. Nor has anyone analysed a strange
asymmetry: while Western public opinion was influenced by communist
propaganda from the inside, public opinion in the communist-dominated
countries could be reached only from the outside (for instance, by Radio

Free Europe or the Voice of America). Class power in organizations dominating the communist societies appeared much better safeguarded than in their Western counterparts.

Class power in classless societies[22] belonged to the professional party elite called the *nomenklatura*. *Nomenklatura* meant the list of names of party members who belonged to the inner circle of those eligible for important positions in party and state bureaucracies. They exercised power and legitimized it with Lenin's managerial invention, i.e. with the ideological role of a vanguard political party. If classes were always perfectly aware of their own interests, said the Leninists, the working class would have made a revolution without any guidance from above. As it is, however, the ruling classes will succeed in spreading ideological illusions and therefore it becomes necessary to disseminate the revolutionary virus among the working class. Only a ruthless political party stands a chance of accelerating the course of history by training the workers to win the class struggle in their own interest rather than continuing to pull the band-wagon of the middle class, on which they will not be allowed to jump. When a successful struggle for true class interests really occurs, the end of history will follow. Workers will finally take over power from the bourgeoisie. In the meantime, power must be exercised by the party, which, by definition, knows best what is best for everybody. The rest is the history of the Gulag and cynical geopolitics until August 1980, when the first successful organizational challenge to the Communist Party elite's monopoly of the exercise of power in Europe arose.

The emergence of the Polish Solidarity from the strikes in August 1980 led by a simple electrician from Gdansk shipyards, Lech Walesa, led on to free political elections in 1989 and to the emergence of the first non-communist Prime Minister in Soviet-dominated central Europe (Tadeusz Mazowiecki). The independent trade union was a cover name for a huge social movement (10 million members were mobilized within a few months in a country dominated by a hostile communist bureaucracy), which provided an alternative way of exercising power for the disempowered citizens of a communist state. Neither of the first two non-*nomenklatura* leaders in central Europe would have been eligible for power positions if the communists continued to rule unchallenged. One went on to become the head of an independent trade union and subsequently the president of Poland (Walesa). The other metamorphosed from a Catholic intellectual into a round-table negotiator with the communists and subsequently a freely elected Prime Minister of Poland (Mazowiecki). The wave of velvet revolutions in Hungary, Czechoslovakia and East Germany following Solidarity's victory resulted in the fall of the Berlin Wall in 1989. Ultimately, with Central European states liberated from Russian control and with Gorbachev's reforms accelerating the decline of the Soviet system, the Soviet Union collapsed, dissolving first into the Confederation of

Independent States (December 1991) and subsequently into the Russian Federation.

This unexpectedly non-violent and rapid collapse of communist rule provided an important organizational lesson for all the world's managers on the limits to the open exercise of total power, a lesson that was not properly analysed till the present day. The reasons for this relative neglect are complex. First, in spite of the breakdown of the communist system, there was no de-Stalinization or de-communization of Russia after 1999 comparable to the deNazification of Germany after 1945. De-communization would mean that the Left could finally come to terms with communist genocide[23] and researchers would be free to study the archives of the communist parties and secret police forces in post-communist countries. They would then be – among others – capable of understanding the influence of the secret services on the inner circles of the power elites, an issue not without relevance for contemporary democratic societies. As things stand, they are not, and ignoring the shadow of the communist genocide has paralyzed the Left, which has to accept the failure of the communist experiment but is barred by the Russian power elites from investigating its causes and human costs.[24]

Second, most of the managerial techniques employed by the communist *nomenklatura* were not ideologically specific. Failure to come to terms with the legacy of the communist system also prevents researchers from studying the numerous and important learning processes that cross the Cold War lines: even in the situation of the most extreme conflict, both sides learned from one another, as reconstruction of the Cuban missile crisis clearly indicates. Lenin and Stalin seized on Taylorism, considering it a superb method of controlling an enslaved labour force, and admired Henry Ford for declaring that 'democracy stops at the factory door'. Indeed, they improved upon it; in their case it stopped at every door, as soon as one crossed the borders of the Soviet-controlled system. The similarity of control techniques – for instance, those used by special forces or riot police – is ideologically awkward and further contributes to the deliberate neglect of power problems. Should we admit that the slogan 'workers of the world, unite' has quietly been changed into 'managers of the world, unite'? It is, after all, ideologically awkward to read about change management, about vision, values and leadership, and then to compare it to a Leftist dream of the enlightened manager of the revolutionary re-engineering of contemporary society. It is even more awkward to find out that these two exercises of power are, in fact, very similar.

Let us compare a managerial text on power and empowerment from a standard introduction to general management with a political text on the ideologically motivated organizing of the lower classes for their empowerment and conduct of a successful power struggle against their class enemies. First the management text:

Traditional leaders give explicit instructions to workers, telling them what to do to meet the goals and objectives of the organization. The term for such a process is *directing*. In traditional organizations, directing involves giving assignments, explaining routines, clarifying policies, and providing feedback on performance.

Progressive leaders, such as those in many high-tech firms and internet companies, are less likely than traditional leaders to give specific instructions to employees. Rather, they are more likely to empower employees to make decisions on their own. *Empowerment* means giving employees the authority (the right to make a decision without consulting the manager) and responsibility (the requirement to accept the consequences of one's actions) to respond quickly to customer's requests. In co-operation with employees, managers will set up teams that will work together to accomplish objectives and goals. The manager's role is becoming less that of a boss and director and more that of a coach, assistant, counsellor and team member. *Enabling* is the term used to describe giving workers the education and tools they need to assume their new decision-making powers.

(Nickels, McHugh, McHugh, 2002, 221)

Compare this text, in which power issues have been reduced to the matter of empowerment of the employees, and the manager's role has been described in ideological terms that down-play real power and stress the partner-like, peer-like relationship of a manager to his or her subordinates, to a text in which a new organizational form for employees, a collective 'prince', is presented by a philosopher of the New Left (and an academic intellectual as well):

The modern prince, Gramsci wrote, was indeed to have the 'Jacobinist' character of Machiavelli's prince and the disciplined and internationalist character of Lenin's vanguard. But it would also have the religious character of Reformation and the qualities of Rousseau's Lawgiver, founding a new, universal *Sittlichkeit* or moral order. Or, as Gramsci himself put it, the objective of the modern prince was to create '*an integral new culture* which (would) have both the mass character of the protestant Reformation or the French Enlightenment and the classical cultural character of Greek civilization or the Italian Renaissance – a culture which . . . synthesizes Maximilien Robespierre and Immanuel Kant, politics and philosophy, in a dialectical unity which belongs no longer to one particular French or German social class, but to Europe and the world'.

(Sanbonmatsu, 2004, 172)

If a textbook on management belongs to the literature disseminating 'managerialism', then it focuses on reducing the problems of power to the fashionable ideology of empowerment, which tacitly assumes that a large-scale democratization of business organizations has already taken place. No power struggle is mentioned, and this democratization acquires the ideological aura of a natural process – which presumably had occurred under the influence of modern technology, primarily ICT. If a political treatise on making a new political 'subject' (an organization capable of a political power struggle) is written in the context of post-communism, then it is clear that it also focuses on some new organizational form, that somehow could be a synthesis of forms postulated within the European tradition (by Machiavelli and Kant, by Gramsci and Rousseau, etc.). The author also assumes that managers of this forthcoming organizational form would be able to prevent managerialist deviation (because they would be able to stimulate the development of an emancipatory new culture, built 'bottom-up' from the 'best' traditions of European intellectual and political history. He assumes that the organizational follower of a revolutionary political party will not become a victim of the same managerialism that destroyed its communist predecessor. However, apart from envisioning a new emancipatory culture, he offers no socio-technical instructions on how to avoid slipping into managerialist ideology and hierarchical organization.

In both cases, the study of power, in particular of organizational power, is safely cloaked in the ideological language of empowerment (of employees or of working classes). *What makes both incomplete is that neither the accumulation of power nor the effects of the proposed empowerment on the power struggle are taken into account. The effects of empowerment ideology in the present organizational environment are not necessarily compatible with democratization. This is awkward both to the Left (representing employees or exploited classes) and to the establishment (representing managerialism).* The Left is supposed to look for alternative forms of social organization, noting that they do not 'fit' very well with the established organizational environment (both feminist and ecological movements, to mention but two new social movements, have only marginally improved the career chances of women and the quality of air in the world's cities). Moreover, the Left has been forced to note that multinational corporations implement *integral new cultures* worldwide and are much more efficient (in spite of their open search for profits) in levelling the distribution of wealth on a global scale than are international organizations created by politicians. The 'establishment' is supposed to guard the status quo but has been forced to accept the need for continuous change in organizational forms and to preserve the 'openness' of the political power struggle in those organizations. Being fearful of *subversion 'from below'*, the establishment would not like to legitimize social movements by acknowledging they offer cultures by design that compete against corporate ones. But since business companies are continually on the lookout for new fashions and fads among consumers, they have to scout the alternative 'scenes' and to support anti-systemic initiatives (Napster was initially supported by Bertelsman, which also paid the other party in this conflict, the Recording Industries of America Association, in spite of the losses incurred on CD sales by MP3 used for the free exchange of cultural content).

The paradox of power in contemporary organizations is linked to the power of learning – to the question who learns more quickly and reaps the temporary benefits from relatively rapid learning. There is much more to be learned about power struggles from a study of the difference between the highest and the lowest salaries in a business company in the 1980s and 1990s (and from comparing those data to data for the 1960s and 1970s), than from a study of empowerment techniques. There is much more to be learned from the introduction of the new, Panopticon-like surveillance techniques and a part-time labour force than from a study of company documents describing managers as coaches rather than controllers.

Examining the consequences of power struggles in organizations is not impossible – but neither is it easy. The aim of such a study is to overcome the democratic deficit caused by an overdose of managerialism:

> Hardly anyone questions that the self-styled 'advanced industrial democracies' really are democracies, fewer still care to argue that 'the people' actually rule in any one of them, or that it would be a good idea if they did. For in societies where managerial rule is widely practised, democracy appears as inherently crude and hence unsuitable for the task of governing complex and rapidly changing societies. At the same time in those quarters, it is often declared that democracy demands such a high level of political sophistication from citizens as to make it doubtful that it can be mastered by Third World peoples. Thus democracy is too simple for complex societies and too complex for simple ones.[25]

8   A case of panoptic control in a public company [with Casper Hoedemaekers]

One of the classical criticisms levelled against the market economy by its socialist critics was its failure to ensure full employment, i.e. provide equal chances for all members of the lower classes. The Western European 'welfare state' emerged during the Cold War as a democratic response to the paternalist state on the other side of the 'iron curtain'. The introduction of unemployment benefits and the invention of other forms of the social 'safety net' were the response of democratic societies to the challenge posed by full employment in state-controlled economies. The emergence of the new lower class composed mainly of immigrant labour in the large cities of Western Europe in the last quarter of the 20th century gave rise to new inequalities and to a search for new measures to control the damage caused by them. Equally if not more important was the emergence of the secondary labour force, of which temporary employees are the most significant manifestation. However, this coincided with the collapse of the state socialist system, which made full and full-time employment lose its priority status. One of the ways of dealing with chronic unemployment in the cities is to recruit members of ethnic minorities for work in city services. The introduction of job entrance controllers by a large public transport company, Transco[26] in one major Dutch city, is a case in point.

The company employs 3,300 people on a permanent basis, and contracts additional employees through the temp agencies if special projects are being implemented. Entrance controllers, who check tickets at the entrances to subway stations throughout the city, are recruited through the temp agencies and supervised by permanent employees of Transco. The controllers stand in front of the entrance gates and check passengers' tickets before letting them pass through the entrance to the platform. They wear bright green vests and stand in groups of two or three, making them clearly recognizable to the passengers. If a passenger fails to produce a valid ticket, they are supposed to deny him or her access to the platform. All temporary employees are issued a standard set of instructions, including the rules they are to follow and specifying their expected behaviour and appearance. They should not, for instance, lean against the entry barriers, but rather stand in front of the gates with hands behind their backs.

They are expected to stand straight for two hours at a stretch, since they work in two four-hour shifts (from 7.00 am till 11.00 am and 2.30 pm till 6.30 pm), with one ten-minute break in the middle of each. Needless to say, standing straight for two hours can cause considerable discomfort, not to mention boredom, and so employees are allowed to 'kill time', for instance by talking to passengers if business is slow and it is practicable. However, the main problems that cause considerable work stress are linked either to stressful interactions with the clients (passengers) or to the control measures undertaken by the management, including clandestine check-ups on the controllers. The employees often comment on unpleasant interactions and the emotional stress involved. They point out that some passengers seek ways to illustrate their superiority and to send clear signals that they view controllers as belonging to a 'lower class':

> What I think is worse, is when people are irritated. 'You saw me stamp my ticket, are you blind or something?' That kind of thing. That really bothers me. . . . Some people really look down on you. They don't even make an effort to take their ticket out of their pocket or their bag. They just walk right past me. And if you confront them, they're like 'well, I've

paid, haven't I?' Well, how should I know? *They don't even recognize your presence.*
(italics mine – SM) (informant quoted in Hoedemaekers, 2004, 2)

Control is exercised by Transco in two ways. First, controllers operate in teams of five, of whom one is a permanent employee of the company and manages the other four. They stand in front of the entrances together. Second, there is also undercover observation by Transco employees who are dressed casually (not in uniforms) and pretend to be passengers. They check on controllers and report directly to the headquarters. These reports are considered when performance appraisal is conducted and when reports to the temp agency are sent with data on an employee's reliability, responsibility and skill level. These undercover controllers from the company are supported by representatives of the temp agency. The latter also tries to keep track of the performance of employees hired through their services and thus also conducts sporadic checks in order to make sure that no unwanted employee behaviour takes place. On top of these three tiers of managerial control there is yet another method of monitoring actual behaviour at the entrance gates, due to the presence of security cameras. Installed in order to monitor stations and platforms and to respond to petty criminality, these cameras also allow Transco staff to note the behaviour of entrance controllers. Recordings can be used as empirical evidence if incidents occur.

For instance, one of the rules concerns the language controllers are allowed to speak – they are expected to communicate with the passengers and with each other in Dutch and not in their native languages. In an incident in one of the subway stations a controller had made a remark to his fellow controller standing next to him in his native language. The comment has been made at the very moment a female passenger had been passing through the entrance gate and showing her ticket. The woman had interpreted Transco's controller's behaviour as a comment about her appearance, which had deliberately been expressed in a language she could not understand. She turned around and accused him of commenting upon her, at which point the supervisor of the team had appeared. In spite of the fact that the colleague of the accused controller confirmed that a comment had nothing to do with the appearance of the woman in question, the controller who spoke in his native language was fired for breaking the rule.

This quite impressive array of managerial controls (the constant presence of the security cameras gives it an eerie quality of a 'Panopticon'-like system of managerial surveillance) leads to an internalization of the rules imposed by organization. It also leads to ways of circumventing the rules and of modifying them. Employees devise their own rules of the game. Let us begin with the internalization of company rules. Employees contracted as controllers learn to comply:

Perhaps, I always think, make sure you don't lean too much, or walk around, or talk to people for too long in an obvious way. That's important. That's what I think when the day begins, but later I forget about it. I don't think about it any more. But, if I have to say it about myself, I don't think I'm the kind of person that neglects his task, you know. I know, I'll easily pass an inspection.

(Hoedemaekers, 2004, 3)

Subverting the rules of the company and introducing their own rules of the game assumes different forms. First, controllers can prolong their visits to the toilets or their coffee breaks, but second, and more importantly, they can seek and find opportunities to talk to passengers and to establish a more personal relationship. All the employees interviewed in the project expressed their pleasure and pride in the social contact they had managed to establish in spite of a very fleeting interaction, especially with regular travellers whom they met repeatedly at the same location. Interactions available to these controllers are always transitory and superficial, often unsatisfactory or even grim, but at times they offer an escape from the ticket-checking routine. These small conversations make it possible to 'break the ice' between a controller and a passenger, and to establish a more normal, peer-like relationship. Controllers were quite proud of their social skills, which allowed them to escape the routine, exchange a few words, and find solace even in a trivial verbal exchange. They understood very well that this 'small talk' constituted not only a desirable distraction from a dull daily routine, but also allowed them to feel appreciated, to acquire a sense of dignity from being recognized by passengers. Paradoxically, these successful 'escapes' from dull routine and strict adherence to the company rules increased the overall commitment of temporary employees to their job and to the company, and improved their overall performance. From the point of these temporary employees the entrance controller project was a success – their success in a struggle for recognition in spite of unemployment, racial and ethnic difference and social stigmatization. However, their success came at a price; the price of bending the company rules. Could this success be maintained over a broader time-frame?

From the point of the company it was also a success. The controllers reduced the frequency with which violent incidents occurred in subway trains by reducing the number of potentially dangerous passengers (either because their uniformed presence acted as a deterrent or because potential perpetrators were unwilling to invest in valid tickets). Second, while the total cost of the project was €1.5 million, the increased ticket sales (resulting from the reduction in the number of potential free riders) amounted to more than €2 million. Again, the question now becomes whether the over-kill in managerial control (the Transco team leader, Transco undercover controller, temp agency undercover mystery shopper) is sustainable, and if the cost-effectiveness profitability of entrance controllers can be sustained after the effect of novelty wears off.

From the point of view of managing new organizational forms the question of control and supervision looms large. New organizational forms are represented in this case by a Transco project (a much more flexible and temporary platform than an institution) staffed through the temp agency recruiting from underemployed minorities. The central question is the possibility of compromise between panoptical forms of managerial control (the exercise of managerial power in new forms of organization, where employees are not 'fixed' in a single location, but can be monitored closely because of new technologies) and managerial coaching. In this new form of organization employee inputs, compromising these controls but increasing employee commitment have ambivalent status. On the one hand they subvert managerial supervision; on the other hand they are a much more efficient substitute for fear of the manager's invisible eye. Should Transco management follow suit, accommodate behavioural resistance and empower entrance controllers to strike up small talk with passengers? This would allow the managers of Transco to economize on controllers' controllers. Temporary employees acting as subway entrance controllers would not only perform their function (checking the tickets of passengers) but also act as a 'human face' for the company, striking up conversations and maintaining a feeling of community, instead of acting as uniformed instruments of managerial control. After all, small talk on the passenger's way to the subway makes him or her recognize that the representative of a secondary labour force (individuals only temporarily enjoying the benefits of a job) in the company's uniform is a hard-working man or woman, contributing to the passengers' safety and the continuity of commuting services.

Two objections may be voiced at this point. First, does commitment matter in the case of temporary, expendable employees, who will be discarded after the project runs out? Second, what can be done to assure that the verbal interactions ('small talk') with passengers remain at a safe distance from 'harassment'? In other words, can we control the organizational discourse of temporary employees? This brings us to the role of organizational discourse in establishing the social reality of members of an organization constrained by power relationships and creatively responding to them.

9 Manager as narrator; the organizational discourse

Understanding the power of communication and language enables you to utilize words to manage organizations. Take the example of employees. As a manager, you may refer to them generically as employees, but you could also call specific people, on different occasions or in different contexts, 'hands', human resources', 'team players', 'stars', 'deadbeats', 'losers, . . . and so on. Different metaphors not only affect people differently, but also trigger different thoughts. Resources can be exploited and developed, whereas hands are only utilized, and, symbolically, come independent of minds, brains and bodies. By using different metaphors and communicating through them, managers create different realities.

(Clegg *et al.*, 2004, 327–8)

We have discussed many roles a manager plays in controlling, disseminating and even changing and designing organizational cultures. In coaching new employees, a manager shows them 'how things are done around here', thus breaking them into organizational culture by socializing them into accepted practices. While playing those roles, a manager is communicating both with the members of his or her organization and with the external stakeholders. According to Mintzberg's well-known statement on the nature of managerial work, these communicating activities occupy up to 90 per cent of managerial working time. Communicating a vision, a mission, a newly designed organizational culture, requires a manager to be a skilful narrator. He has to know how to 'tell stories'. Paraphrasing the catchphrase of 'managing by walking around', we might say that a manager is expected to be an organizational 'walkie-talkie' – connecting employees by frequent communication and by framing their 'stories' (expressing their sense-making). This activity, spinning narratives, is so important that top managers of large companies who are able to make use of mass media acquire a public status that in the past used to be granted only to film stars or heads of state. Clearly, communication matters, and so does the language in which it takes place. When Enron collapsed, one of the most surprising discoveries concerning the language used by its corrupt top managers was that they assumed names of the fictitious characters of a science-fiction movie, *Star Wars*, cloaking their decisions in coded secrecy. But even without the shock of the Enron scandal, the way stories are told and the way the socialization dice are loaded in favour of managers are now being closely scrutinized, by friends and foes, shareholders and stakeholders, employees, and clients and researchers. This interest in the varieties of story-telling or in organizational discourses has been further fuelled by the evolution of organizational forms (with more frequent, intense and broadly disseminated communications) and the advances in information processing and communication technologies.

The evolution of organizational forms, summed up in a phrase by the transition from the hierarchical pyramid of an industrial bureaucracy to a more flexible, temporary and loosely coupled network of organizational clusters, chains, platforms, and teams, has fed an increasing demand for more intense, frequent, detailed, differentiated, and personalized communication. This demand could arise only in parallel to the increased supply of new information and communication technologies, which made it possible to link satellite networks, personal computers and mobile phones. Attempts to understand these new developments in organizational communications, and in communications to newly mapped stakeholders, contributed to a search for new theories and methodologies that would throw more light on the 'social life of information'. One of them, arguably the most important one, is the so-called *discourse analysis* (sometimes labelled 'critical discourse analysis', or CAD).

The evolution of information and communication technologies aided by digitalization, satellite links, mobile phones, and laptops has contributed to a further dismantling of a concept of an organization as an entity with a fixed and solid location in space and time (it became fashionable to speak of the 'virtual office' and 'virtual organization'). Both these evolutionary processes contributed to the emergence of a new focus of organizational studies – on the language of corporate communications, on the use of symbolic media by the managers, on the role of corporate values and practices. 'Objectives' (of a bureaucratically implemented corporate plan, translated into orders issued to subordinates) do not get you there, as Jack Welch famously remarked: 'values do' (as in the core values of a corporate culture, which can be internalized by individuals and thus motivate them much more effectively).

The 'cultural turn' in organizational studies has provided an additional impulse for researchers to pay attention to how people talk and to what they talk about (stories, myths, even gossip). This cultural turn has been reinforced by the 'linguistic turn' in the 20th century philosophy. Following J. L. Austin's idea that using language is a form of action, we can conclude that communicating *is* managing: issuing performative utterances, we manage others (as in the pronouncement 'I declare you man and wife', which is not separate from action, from the activity of establishing a valid marriage – it is the very core element of such activity (Austin, 1962)). The cultural turn has also been accelerated by the influential theory of communicative action developed by Jürgen Habermas into a political philosophy of liberal democracy. According to Habermas, in monitoring our discourses, our social communications, we can detect the distorting effects that make these communications less free than they could be. Detected constraints usually derive from market forces and public authorities. Both markets and states invade our privacy, our personal space for freely deciding the issues, which a responsible citizen (and a corporate citizen) should have left to his or her discretion. They 'colonize' the world of our personal experience (*Lebenswelt*) and force us to think in terms of accumulation of profits and power. In locating constraints in the market mechanism (which reduces all considerations to a single medium – money) and political process (which reduces all considerations to a single medium – power), Habermas places himself, along with such thinkers as Giddens, Bourdieu, Foucault, Taylor, and Harvey, in the ranks of the representatives of critical social theory.

However, his criticism, though sufficient for legitimizing ecological and feminist movements in spite of their emergence outside of parliaments (i.e. outside the 'legitimate' political system), stops short of more radical political conclusions. The mix of parliamentary representation and market mechanisms may undergo continuous crises, but it is still the best guarantee of the openness of 'the unfinished project of the Enlightenment'. Corporations and governments exercise their influence on citizens, but citizens, though weaker partners in this relationship, are still relatively empowered to be able to express their interests (articulating them differently than politicians would like and forcing these politicians to take sides – as with the issues of sexual minorities, feminism and ecological concerns) and to fight for their values (defending them even if it is detrimental to their material benefit and to their participation in existing power structures).

The guiding ideal of an unconstrained linguistic communication in the symbolic sphere of social and political discourse allows us to 'measure' our distance from this ideal and to struggle to remove constraints. This is the justification for parliamentary democracy, according to Habermas. Unfortunately, it has become questionable in the new period of individualized and mobile mass media and subsequent intensification of the cultural industries. These cultural industries produce 'discourses' legitimizing the powers that be and socializing human individuals into the roles of consumers in a consumer culture. Mass media tend to reproduce large-scale docility and conformity, and left to their own devices they would close off possibilities of critical reflection. Discourse would become a monologue of powers that be. These cultural industries have to be kept in check, to be 'countered' by spontaneous mobilization of free citizens able to oppose their one-dimensional 'discourse'. The role of critical intellectuals – Bourdieu and Foucault in France, Habermas in Germany, Gray and Amis in Great Britain, Fallaci and Magris in Italy – is to maintain the dialogic nature of public discourse, while the role of checks and balances (trade unions, oppositional parties) is to provide instruments and support for such dialogue. Hence the popularity of 'no logos', 'buy nothing days', etc. as instances of successful change of a discourse, a change in 'the grammar of motives' employed in social discourse, 'breaking' the monotony of a monologue of a consumer society, making the society less one-dimensional. The concept of a social communication, that either offers the masses the long monologues of a dictator or limits their choice to a vote for one of the two political rivals who agree on maintaining the status quo in their society, is the concept of one-way authoritarian indoctrination, or equally one-way designed emotional and commercial persuasion. An individual participates in such social communication passively as a receiver, hears only one voice, 'his master's voice' – and cannot talk back. Discourse is totally dominated by those who own the markets and rule the states. Discourse becomes the rulers' monologues, social reality becomes one-dimensional – as Herbert Marcuse, linked to the Frankfurt School's first generation of critical theoreticians, the forerunners of Habermas, once observed.

The background to this turn in the European discourse on management, governance and the politics of organizing in general can be described briefly. Habermas started as an assistant to Adorno, one of the founders of the Institute for Social Research in Frankfurt who had returned from exile in the US after WWII, but his theoretical development was also influenced by the 1968 student revolt. Students of Goethe University in Frankfurt involved the whole Frankfurt School in their protest, but Adorno (who had been central to the school) and Marcuse (who had been marginal) responded in different ways. Young Maoists and other rebellious students horrified Adorno. Young Trotskyists and other revolutionary students idealized Marcuse. Young representatives of the counterculture influenced Habermas' thinking about non-parliamentary opposition in a parliamentary democracy. In a sense, Habermas, by developing a theory of a communicative action, attempted to do for the political and social system what every experienced manager using organizational discourse always does for his or her organization. He tried to preserve the social order, while at the same time lifting some constraints imposed on discourse by this order's inequalities. *If revolutionary disruption is to be prevented but revolutionary criticism used to improve and progress, the marginal, the critical, the potentially innovative and subversive forms of discourse have to be legitimized.* As opposed to Adorno, who did not understand student protest and withdrew from teaching, Habermas tried to understand the rebellious students and their preference for Marcuse's *One-Dimensional Man* rather than Adorno's and Horkheimer's *Dialectics of Enlightenment*. Students saw Marcuse, who told them that they together with the peasants of the Third World were the revolutionary class, as an ideological ally in their struggles against the lack of democracy in academic institutions. Habermas befriended Daniel Cohn Bendit and Joshka Fischer, respectively 'Danny the Red' of the universities in Frankfurt am Main and Nancy and 'green Joshka' of the Green Party in the Bundestag (and now the German Minister of Foreign Affairs). All three made a political career in Germany of the last quarter of the 20th century. Cohn-Bendit articulated cultural policies of multiculturalism in Western cities and became a media personality influential in the entire European Union (he is now a deputy to the European Parliament). Fischer made realist compromises that convinced the 'fundamentalists' among the rebellious 'Greens' and led his party to an electoral victory, becoming one of the architects of the newest stage of the European integration. Habermas, along with Giddens, in the UK, became one of the leading intellectual authorities of the 'liberalized' social-democratic parties of Schröder and Blair.

While Cohn-Bendit and Fischer chose the path of political activism, Habermas remained an academic and followed the path of social critique. He sees the development of European societies as an unfinished project of modernity formulated explicitly for the first time by the thinkers of the Enlightenment and politicians of the French revolution. The project is unfinished because we cannot be satisfied with parliamentary representation (which leaves many constituencies unrepresented) and market allocation of resources (which creates systematic inequalities). Our social – economic, political, cultural – organization must remain 'open' (as in Popper's open society) so that we can respond to new evolutionary challenges and rapid changes in the technological, geopolitical, demographic, cultural, and economic situation. The project must remain open, because we must accommodate non-parliamentary opposition and compensate inequalities caused by the markets with the social plans and policies of the welfare state. All this would be impossible if we did not function as free citizens who are able to use public space and the contemporary mass media for dialogic communication. In exercising our right to constraint-free communication, in openly discussing our values without surrender to the market calculations or fear of repression, we establish the primacy of the world of our personal lived experience (*Lebenswelt*), of freedom.

Habermas compares markets and states to colonial conquerors, who seek to colonize increasingly large areas of our activities, subjecting them to their rule. In asserting freedom of expression, in free dialogic communication, we – as citizens of conscience – defend ourselves against this 'colonization' by 'the rich and powerful'. The role of the critical intellectual in public life (and of a communicating manager in an organization) is thus to 'repair' this dialogic communication and prevent its failure. As Habermas himself puts it in the context of dealing with the sources of contemporary terrorism:

> The spiral of violence begins as a spiral of distorted communication that leads through the spiral of uncontrolled reciprocal mistrust, to the breakdown of communication. If violence thus begins with a distortion in communication, after it has erupted it is possible to know what has gone wrong and what needs to be repaired.
>
> (Borradori, 2003, 35)

In order to understand what dialogic communication might be, we have to analyse the processes of social communication. These are not simply reducible to the sender, who determines the message, to the channel which disseminates it and to the receiver who swallows it gullibly. The sender uses ambiguity, counting on receivers to make choices. The channel modifies or subverts the message (the medium is – sometimes – the message, as Marshall McLuhan once said in investigating the consequences of TV-watching in contemporary societies).[27] The receiver exercises his or her discretion in interpreting, translating, transforming, and using the message in ways that cannot be fully predicted in advance. What results is a new digital and satellite-linked virtual Tower of Babel, a new electronically enhanced chaos, from which, as Barbara Czarniawska aptly observed, quoting George Steiner, a pidgin language might offer a better way out than a new paradigmatic or political revelation, a new Pentecost.[28]

In order to devise a useful 'pidgin' in an academic environment, knowledge should be produced by researchers with 'pluri-vocal' inputs, prompted by different paradigms, working with multiple methodologies. In the case of discourse analysis, methodologies have been imported from sociology, social psychology, anthropology, linguistics, philosophy, psychoanalysis, and literary theory. The analysis of the rhetoric of fiction turns out to provide interesting clues to an analysis of the ideological fictions disseminated by managers of corporate culture and to the recognition of resistance and power struggles within the organizations. This explains, for instance, a sudden re-emergence of Michail Bachtin's concepts of 'dialogic imagination', coined during his analytical studies of Rabelais and Dostoyevski.[29] It also explains the interest in Foucault's analyses of hidden structural frameworks for producing knowledge, geared to the needs of the groups in power, or the popularity of Derrida's concept of critical 'deconstruction' of ideologically 'loaded' announcements of political and organizational authorities.

However, as some authors rightly observe, it is not only the question of utilizing words to manage organizations. Some researchers, for instance Stuart Clegg quoted above, state bluntly that 'by using different metaphors and communicating through them, managers create different realities'. By the same token, by using counter-metaphors and by communicating through them, employees try to change realities and create different ones from those imposed by managers. However, three different views on the role of organizational discourse in management can be distinguished.

- A *moderate constructionist* view, according to which organizational discourse is about the social construction of reality within an organization by its members. However, although discourse analysis offers privileged insight into organizations, organizations include aspects and processes that cannot be reduced to discourse. Therefore one of the main representatives of this view, Mats Alvesson, carefully reminds us that organizing and managing is also about modes of control not primarily targeted on a consciousness and a meaning, but on 'outputs, rules and other constraining measures', which 'also involve cultural control' but do not boil down to an analysis of the language of corporate discourses, and assume institutional and other material constraints in reality 'out there' (cf. Alvesson, 2004, 322). In other words, words matter, but when everything is said, there is still much to be done, since there is a material world 'out there' as well.

- An *extreme social constructionist* view, according to which organizations only exist in so far as they are constituted by an ongoing
  linguistic discourse, because social reality does not exist except as
  socially organized sense-making, socially constructed shared meaning
  and identities. One of the main representatives of this view, Steve
  Linstead, puts it this way: 'Organization has no autonomous, stable or
  structural status outside of the text that constitutes it. . . . Organization
  is structure, but only when structure is recognized to be an effect of
  language, a tropological achievement' (Westwood, Linstead, 2001,
  4–5). In other words, there is no 'there' out there, since every piece
  of reality 'out there' has necessarily to be described in words and
  communicated – thus becoming part of a discourse. In the beginning,
  quite literally, was the word, and all knowledge is based on it.
- A *critical realist* view, according to which discourse analysis should
  respect the ontological primacy of the 'organizational world out there'
  (moderate social constructionists would agree). However, a discourse
  should always be assessed in dynamic interdependence with a structured
  social and organizational world, in which individuals and groups do
  communicate. Individuals and organizations do behave as autonomous
  agents, but not as freely as the idealist implications of the extreme social
  constructivist view would have it, nor so un-freely – under such extreme
  structural constraints – as functionalists and structuralists would have
  it. Each case of the mutual influence of 'soft' discourse and 'hard'
  structure must be considered separately, individually, independently:
  'Interplay between social structure and discursive innovation must
  be analysed dialectically. That is, as a complex and dynamic relationship
  of antagonistic tension and opposition, which is grounded in very real
  material and social constraints that confront actors as obdurate and
  recalcitrant obstacles in their everyday organizational lives' (Reed,
  2004, 415–16).

Extreme social constructivists see linguistic communication as the creative
organizing and managing process that constitutes, undermines, maintains,
and changes social reality. Moderate social constructivists consider material
and political constraints as equally constitutive of organizational realities
(on a par with the creative articulation and communication of interests in
language, i.e. by means of an organizational discourse). Critical realists tend
to side with the moderate social constructivists but refuse to offer general
judgements on the methodological merits of either the material or the
cultural components of organizational realities before concrete analysis of
each empirical case. All three agree that the reconstruction of organizational
discourse and analysis of organizational culture offer privileged access
to understanding organizational processes, but extreme constructivists
collapse culture and discourse, while moderate social constructivists and

critical realists do not.[30] Critical realists see organizational discourse very much like the Marxists saw class ideology: as an intellectual, idealist, 'disfigured' reflection of actual, material, real inequalities and relations of exploitation. Therefore they use arguments about asymmetries of social power linked to social stratification and insist that structuration (a term coined by Giddens) comes before communication, so that class position and place in the organizational hierarchy determine our ways of sense-making and communicating. In other words first you make a career, gain power, occupy important positions in bureaucratic hierarchy, and only then do you adopt a language expressing this power:

> Discourses are positioned ways of representing – representing other social practices as well as the material world, and reflexively representing this social practice, from particular positions in social practice.
>
> (Fairclough, Jessop, Sayer, 2002, 7)

At the same time, critical realists also use methodological arguments based on a realist social ontology and methodology, pointing out that the idealist assumptions of social constructivists blind them to the real constraints in social and organizational life by isolating linguistic communication as constraint-free and treating discourse as a realm of freedom that it is not:

> Language is *a* but not *the* condition of knowledge, since it must be used to refer to something other than itself. . . . Structures are real constraining conditions of action, which cannot be grasped adequately by regarding them simply as effects of systems of representation or 'discourse'. . . . Institutional and distributional positioning conditions agency by defining interests and access to resources. . . . Every case is unique, requiring its own narrative of the temporal process of its formation.
>
> (Parker, 2000, 117–19)

This balanced view, which calls for focus on discourse analysis but within the framework of other, non-linguistic and non-communicative, constraints, allows for a less-idealist and more-realist choice, both in research and in politics. One of the most interesting representatives of the discourse school, David Boje, who has developed narrative methods for organizational and communication research, begins with the assumption that a critical approach requires a reconstruction of those modes of communication, which are suppressed by the dominant forms of ideological control exercised also by corporate authors and sponsors of 'dominant' story-telling. The critical researcher should try to reconstruct other, alternative cases of story-telling, sometimes accessible only in oral form. Fragmented, local, 'polyphonic' story-telling in organizations leads to the reconstruction of 'microstories', which help the researcher assess and qualify the actual influence of the 'grand narratives' imposed by managers on all employees and assess the extent of resistance to this ideological hegemony.

One of the ways of imposing this hegemony is by crafting the narrative plot in complex organizations. The question of who gets to author it is crucial for understanding the way in which organizational discourse is structured and shaped. Boje, who investigated the complex organizational narratives of the Disney corporation, of Nike's and McDonald's hyper-media campaigns, and the corporate publicity policies of casino-hotels in Las Vegas, has sought to interpret the plot of the theatrical stages to which, quite literally, corporations refer. For instance, Disneyland's customers are called 'guests', not 'clients' in company documents and instructions for employees, while employees are 'members' and not 'temps' or 'employees'. Customers appear 'on-stage' in activities when participating in attractions prepared for them, while Disneyland's employees operate 'back-stage' and are involved in 'staging' particular events. These corporate shows either 'enrol' customers in spectacular interpretations of corporately narrated identity or through the media campaigns in which all prospective customers are symbolically 'enrolled'. The role of critical analysts is to deconstruct critically the story-telling disseminated by Disney and McDonalds, and to interpret it as ideological, hegemonic 'messages' serving corporate interests and 'crowding out' the alternative messages of other stakeholders (e.g. environmental activists, trade unionists, health-care specialists, concerned parents, etc.):

> To be hegemonic is to exercise power without notice in the taken-for-granted subterrain of socialization and preparing stories that are ready to hand over to consumptive appetites. Organizations, for example, produce press releases to be distributed and consumed 'harmoniously' as 'common sense' accounts that are designed to be 'taken-for-granted' narratives that do not mobilize resistance or bring attention to ongoing power struggles over institutional sensemaking. In short, hegemonic power operates behind the scenes in acts of socialization, in providing frames that make one's action appear harmonious and neutral.
>
> (Boje, 2002, 79)

Boje suggests that we adopt Derrida's concept of deconstruction analysis in two ways. First, he proposes we accept Derrida's view that deconstruction is something that happens all the time as we engage in multiple communications and analyse stories we hear and tell. When hearing or telling, we are 'stripping' worldviews, criticizing ideologies and laying narratives bare. We are following our agendas, both visible and hidden, manifesting emotions, making and losing allies. We cannot help but reinterpret all stories, communications, pieces of information as a matter of fact. Boje compares this natural, spontaneous deconstruction to the process of entropy, by analogy with the loss of meaning originally intended by the author of the deconstructed message. Apart from the concept of deconstruction as a phenomenon composed of multiple processes around us, he distinguishes deconstruction as an analytical method. The thrust of this method is to detect the instability, complexity, processes, and heterogeneity below the surface of 'official' communications that try to create an impression of stability, hierarchical order, well-structured, functional coherence. The method directs the researcher's attention to the dichotomies and contradictions, the 'rebel voices', 'other sides of the story', and ironic twists of the plot. Some authors speak in this context about 'reading against the grain' (Tietze, Cohen, Musson, 2003).[31]

Critical discourse analysis can be prompted by macro-political concerns. Generally speaking, intervention in a 'class struggle' between those down below and those higher up, between managers and employees is usually coloured by the political sympathies of the intervening researcher or consultant. A simple black-and-white distinction between owners and managers on the one hand, and employees–workers on the other is often blurred nowadays. First, this is because the ranks of management are swelling and the roles of managers become differentiated. Second, it is because the relative weakening of the trade unions and strengthening of professional associations has introduced new complexities to the 'class struggle' at shop floor level. Names such as Braverman, Sennett and Burawoy are often mentioned in the context of an analysis of the new uncertainty and job insecurity, the increase in temporary employment, and the general change in professional career patterns (steady climbing to the top of a bureaucratic pyramid ceases to be the prevailing model). Third, critical discourse analysis can guide the reconstruction of oral histories, and discourse analysis of personal and organizational 'micro-stories' can help in the very simplest context of a daily interaction. Critical discourse analysis can also have a down-to-earth, micro-political significance for managers, trainers and researchers concerned with subtle cross-cultural differences.

After all, as Hofstede once observed, the trajectories of individual socialization change with time. While early socialization is mainly based on subconscious shaping of the core *value* system within a given culture or subculture, later socializing influences (higher education, the workplace) are more linked to the *procedures* with which an individual becomes acquainted. In other words, the organizational socialization of an individual, of which enculturation is one of the main components, is about 'how we do things around here', including 'how to do things with words'. Even words in the same language can – if they reflect different organizational practices and different national values – acquire different meanings.

10 The case of managerial discourse in countries divided by common language or practice: Austria versus Germany [with Frank Brück] and Germany versus Great Britain [with Astrid Kainzbauer]

> England and America are two countries separated by the same language.
>
> (G. B. Shaw)

While the above quotation has been variously attributed to Winston Churchill and to General Patton, it was actually uttered by G. B. Shaw in 1942. Shaw had paraphrased Oscar Wilde, who wrote in 1887 that 'we have really everything in common with America, except, of course, language', and his sentiments are shared by the inhabitants of the Netherlands and of Belgian Flanders, of Spain and Spanish-speaking Mexico, of France and francophone Canada around Quebec, of Portugal and Portuguese-speaking Brazil, Italy and the Italian part of Switzerland, and of Germany and Austria. It is the last case that is particularly interesting here, because we are dealing with the same language, a similar level of socio-economic development and geographic proximity. Nevertheless, in-depth interviews with German managers working in Austria and Austrian managers working in Germany clearly indicate that cultural standards of work-related linguistic communications turn out to be unexpectedly more different than had previously been assumed. Discourse appears suddenly loaded with tacit assumptions about both 'proper' ways of expressing oneself and 'expected' ways of doing things with things (and doing them 'properly'). Tracing these tacit assumptions, hidden by the common language from the view of speakers with different national backgrounds, can be facilitated by discourse analysis. Sometimes this common language is not the natural language of some ethnic group but the discourse of a professional group for instance, trainers offering managerial training programmes in the same domains of knowledge and skills to various national groups of European managers. Then the language and the design of the training is strongly coloured by the expected differences between the nationally distinct groups of management trainees. We shall consider the case of German and British trainers working with both German and British trainees, a case that has been investigated by Austrian researchers from the Vienna University of Economics.

We have seen that global networking, which makes for shifting cultural national identities, can have paradoxical effects in some social settings. This was the case with ethnic Poles returning from Kazakhstan to Poland. Analysing their discourses and the discourses of those who attempted to re-adapt and re-socialize them, we could detect subtle shifts of values and practices in two or three generations. Let us now examine the equally subtle shifts and differences between two national cultural identities linked by a common language but separated by many other attributes, not necessarily obvious to a third-party observer. Adopting the theoretical framework of 'cultural standards' developed by a German psychologist, Alexander Thomas, Austrian researchers from Vienna's School of Economics conducted narrative interviews with Austrians working in Germany and Germans working in Austria. Cultural standards, according to Thomas, are internalized by individuals during socialization and determine perception, thinking, judgement, and actions, reflecting their group, organizational and national identities. In interviewing German-speaking managers who have been socialized in one of the countries in question but work in another, Frank Brück from Vienna University of Economics sought to reveal and reconstruct 'critical incidents'. He focused on incidents in which a particularly striking, unusual, strange, awkward, irrational, inexplicable behaviour of his or her colleagues was encountered by the interviewee during his or her professional career. Because of his location, Brück interviewed 19 Germans working in Austria and five Austrians working in Germany, coming up with a list of six Austrian cultural standards that directly contrast with German ones.

The list opens with the first two: conflict avoidance and indirect communication.

Both are opposed to the German cultural standard of straightforwardness. In a sense, both reflect the respective histories of German and Austrian societies. Austrian society's cultural standards until WWI were developed in a decaying monarchy, which was losing economic and military strength and its ability to hold together different national groups, but maintained a 'façade' of polite, courtly communications and pretentious, exaggerated forms of polite interaction. German society's cultural standards were forged amid bitter class struggles institutionalized in trade unions and fought out in parliament inside Germany. Two bloody wars against other European powers had an egalitarian influence upon mobilized masses. Austrians saw changes and succumbed to the fall of the empire after WWI, but preserved the old-fashioned courtesies in daily communications, as if trying to take the 'edge' off those irreversible losses. Germans saw changes and responded to them directly, as they saw themselves entitled to, even if they were lower in social hierarchy. Modes of discourse preserved these differences well into the 20th century, though both countries have become parliamentary democracies after WWII and both have become developed industrial societies with global connections.

A German manager in an Austrian bank, whose husband had also been offered a job in Austria, described this clash between her husband's expectations and the conduct of his Austrian employers in the following terms:

He got this research assignment, the management of Erich Fried's estate, very well paid. The Austrians wanted him for that position at all costs, after all he's an expert. The contract was planned for a term of five years. Then, because it paid so well, they said the contract had to be renewed every year, but three years were 'not a problem at all'. Then, after these three years it turned out that they should have renewed the contract by February 1, and in April, when he had already received verbal confirmation, they said: 'The contract, no, we didn't extend it.' It was very ridiculous, and I wonder whether this is a typically Austrian situation . . . the fact that for two months he had basically been working without a contract at all, which is really impossible. They should have told him that his contract expired. As I said, this is ridiculous, only think of the insurance coverage, etc. Absurd, but that's how it was! In the end they offered him a different contract, not as well paid, and he accepted immediately, after all I was already there working with him at the time. We talked about the whole situation and said 'so that's what it's like in Austria? That's the other side of the coin'.

(Brück, 2004, 8)

In this case, what struck the German employee in Austria was the lack of a clear and honest warning that the parties can have divergent interests. The wife of the German specialist was struck by an awkward avoidance of direct confrontation, which might lead to a conflict (her husband might have reminded the Austrians that they had initially promised him a five-year long contract). The Austrians finally achieved their aim, but not without creating ambiguity (a contract is potentially renewable) and uncertainty (will it be renewed if the deadline passes?), and after they felt they had removed the danger of conflict (the husband wanted this job anyway) and re-opened negotiations (offering an extension but on new, materially worse conditions). One of the reasons the Austrians avoided direct communication was that these would clash with their idea of decorum. It is not done. One does not behave rudely, one does not behave with brutal directness. The answers should help the other party save his or her face, not embarrass them. A direct, honest answer to the point might reveal the other party's incompetence, failure, mistakes, or inabilities. It might also make it clear to the other party that its bargaining position is too weak to always expect a fair deal. This should be avoided. Persisting in one's German-learned way of responding to clients could be dangerous.

On another occasion investigated by Brück, a German woman working in Austria was struck by the expectation of very indirect communication on the part of her Austrian clients and by their perception of her straightforward and honest responses to their inquiries as 'impolite' and 'rude':

All those phrases like 'Gnädige Frau' ('graceful lady' – SM) and 'Küss die Hand' ('I kiss your hand' – SM) – that was extremely hard, I just couldn't say them all the time. I've always been pretty straightforward and direct, and so of course I would tell them things like 'It doesn't work this way' or 'You can't do that', but they never wanted to hear that. The women especially, they just couldn't take being told things like 'It doesn't work this way' by another woman. There were a number of women who refused to talk to me, and when they got me on the phone, they always said: 'Ah, it's the German voice, I guess I am going to get a rude answer anyway'. But while most women took it the wrong way, men often seemed to think it was the sign of competence. Women generally thought I was too straightforward, or that I was trying to treat them like children, especially when I had to tell them something like 'The invoice is all wrong', or 'You haven't paid yet, when are you going to?' I had the awkward task of asking about those things, especially when there were problems, my boss wanted it that way. But most of the customers wanted to hear flattering remarks, and I just couldn't do that. I couldn't say things like 'Gnädige Frau' or 'Thank you' and 'Please' all the time. I mean, I sort of got used to it and now I do that too, after all I've lived here for 16 years. But in the beginning it was pretty bad, they always wanted to hear 'please' and 'thank you'.

(Brück, 2004, 12)

Such indirect communication, in which one pays due respect to the partner and only secondarily conducts business, goes very well with importance attached to academic titles and hierarchies. The titles 'Frau Chefin' ('Ms Boss' or 'Madam the Boss'), 'Herr Doktor' (both to physicians and to PhDs) or 'Herr Hofrat' (Mr Counsellor to the Court) are in common use and they make up for the gaps left by indirect communication. Using them in daily discourse makes social ranks and differences in power and influence (exerted behind the stage of polite, indirect conversation) visible. Due to this popular usage of titles preceding or replacing names and surnames, even outsiders have a chance of glimpsing real hierarchies. Hierarchies become 'tangible' through the use of these titles, which are also used as doorbell tags with a name and even accompany their owners to the graveyard, where they can be read on their tombstones. Titles locate a person in a social hierarchy and legitimize behaviour by announcing what can be expected from a representative of this social stratum.

A story related by an Austrian student in Germany reveals his pleasant surprise that individuals who are his higher-ups in the social (in his case academic) hierarchy, still offered him partner-like assistance and did not make his lower position 'tangible' to him. It surprised him because he had expected that being his superior in the academic hierarchy, she ('Frau

Professor') would simply get rid of him or make it clear that helping students does not belong to her duties:

> I needed to go to one of the departments at the university one day and the secretary wasn't there. Only a younger woman, and she was really nice. I asked if I could sign up for the classes there and she was very helpful and then even went to check whether there were any grade reports for me. She was really nice! And later it turned out that she was a professor at the department. I thought she was maybe an assistant or something. But when I passed that sign outside, with all the names on it I saw that she was a professor. I just can't imagine anything like that happening at an Austrian university.
>
> (Brück, 2004, 14)

Another difference in cultural standards can be observed by comparing the Austrian *social orientation* and contrasting it with German *achievement orientation*. Austrian social orientation (personal acknowledgement and respect are also paid on the workplace floor, and an engineer's title is not easily shed) clashes directly with German achievement orientation (efficiency is much more important to Germans and they rank rewarding achievement above preserving social and personal equilibrium). Germans want to get things done. The result matters. Do the right thing. Austrians want to get things done in the proper way. The manners matter. Do things right. Austrians think that Germans are too ruthless in exacting obedience and gearing everything to task fulfilment. Germans think that Austrians are too fond of nepotism (satisfying each other's wishes, caressing each other's egos) and prefer to continue a game of social pleasantries (which allows them to push the deadline further and further away) instead of solving the problem. A frustrated German manager in an Austrian bank accordingly complained about the long time it took to fix the problem of a broken fax machine:

> They needed to buy a new fax, but nobody did anything about it. . . . They knew they should, and in a way they did take care of the matter. Someone decided on which particular fax to get, but no one really went and budgeted for it. They only said: 'We need to buy a new fax' and that was it. I just don't get it! They knew it was a problem and that they should do something about it, so why didn't they? I would do something if I saw there was a problem. Sometimes I believe they are all a bit surprised when they are faced with commitment or with someone taking initiative.
>
> (Brück, 2004, 17)

Researchers mentioned also two other Austrian cultural standards, which clashed with German ones. The first is a certain *neglect of rules and regulations*, which made them masters of skilful circumvention of the law. This clashed with the conscientious behaviour of Germans, who saw bypassing the rules and ignoring regulations (for instance, ignoring traffic lights or riding a bicycle without a lamp) as dangerous and irrational. Austrians, in turn, could not understand why Germans are ready to inflict suffering upon themselves and others by scrupulously following the rules, even if breaking them would cause no visible damage (crossing the street on red lights if there is no traffic around).

The second is *supplier-focused service*, which made them less customer-friendly than their German counterparts because they insisted on making clients adapt to the way their service was delivered rather than trying to build the service around clients and their needs and wishes.

Mutual perceptions were definitely coloured by these differences and clashes of cultural standards. Austrians were perceived by Germans as ridden with the 'Southern European mentality',[32] while Germans were perceived by Austrians as being too formalistic, rigid and excessively bound by rules. Can these differences be overcome in the course of special managerial training in cross-cultural differences?

They may be, but cross-cultural training is in itself a cross-cultural event and its design reveals the tacit assumptions of trainers about nation-specific ways of building up a managerial competence. Astrid Kainzbauer from Vienna University of Economics compared the choices made by trainers who were supposed to teach German and British managers respectively. She found tacit assumptions about different ways in which managerial competence is conceived and knowledge acquired in Germany and Great Britain. Such assumptions are clearly culture-specific and linked to the practice of management and management teaching. She interviewed German and British trainers working for German and British managers, and came up with a list of four main families of differences:

- a theoretical orientation of Germans, as opposed to British practical orientation;
- an explicit communication style of Germans, as opposed to an implicit one preferred by the British;
- German task-orientation, as opposed to British person-orientation;
- German ambiguity-avoidance, as opposed to British ambiguity-tolerance.

Kainzbauer found that German management trainees expected their course material to be backed by a theoretical framework and used as a 'base' from which deductive statements about relevant issues can be derived. The British participants did not expect much theoretical detail, and after forming an intuitive and fairly broad theoretical concept went on to analyse empirical results. A British trainer working for both German and British groups of management trainees remarked that with Germans he must be ready to come up with a lot of new information at every point, while in the case of the British audience his attention is turned to 'facilitating experiential activities'. A theoretical model is a useful abstraction, but its completeness and thoroughness are not particularly significant – after all, its usefulness is 'in the eating', not in a description and explanation of theoretical details. The British approach strikes Germans as intuitive and pragmatic, while the German approach strikes the British as pedantic and academic. German trainers usually considered the proper relation of cognitive to the experiential sections of their training programmes to be in the ratio 3:1, while for the British it was 1:4 (according to a study by Schroll-Machl). Kainzbauer sought to check her results by interviewing German students with a record of studies in Great Britain and found that, indeed, they considered their stay in that country as not particularly 'rich' in theoretical information. On the other hand, they noticed that issues have been discussed in much more detail and they were much more in touch with real-life, empirical examples and case stories.[33] Comparing communication styles, she quotes a British trainer complaining after running programmes for Germans:

> British understatement and avoiding spelling things out because it might be too much of an effort mean that I can't be successful with a German group. They simply don't understand what I am talking about.
>
> (Kainzbauer, 2002, 147)

A German trainer expressing doubts about his attempts to train the British also noticed that his 'natural', national-culture bound way of expressing himself was experienced by his British trainees as inappropriate:

> Of course it is also difficult for us to communicate as diplomatically, elegantly and politely as the British. That's one problem with the German language, and I think also when we speak English, we're much too direct. That's always something the British complain about, that even when Germans speak English, they still think in German.
>
> (Kainzbauer, 2002, 148)

Interestingly enough, Kainzbauer tried to apply one of the dimensions of national culture to explain these differences. Observing the number of pages in handouts to management trainees in two German courses (109 and 43 respectively) and the number of books recommended by the trainer, she compared them to the number of pages in handouts distributed during two British courses (18 and 8) and the number of books recommended to the trainees (8 in the case of a German and 1 in the case of a British trainer). She saw it as an illustration of a different position of respective national culture on the uncertainty avoidance dimension. German trainers used to plan schedules of training sessions and their components in a very detailed way, reflecting their efforts to reduce uncertainty in an actual training session. British trainers did not design detailed timetables, and even if they did, failed to take them very seriously if the flow of a session carried them away from the schedule. They embraced improvisation and had no qualms about accepting uncertainty with respect to the direction in which they would eventually drift. A British trainer working with German management trainees noticed that his deviations from the designed schedule were promptly reported:

> For my seminars I always have to prepare a very detailed schedule, and of course I do it, but I don't really believe in it. I merely do it because I know it's expected, not because I think it makes sense. And I know, I hardly ever stick to it in the end, and sometimes I'm criticized for it, not so much if the entire seminar is a success, in that case the schedule is entirely irrelevant, but still the participants notice it. . . .
>
> (Kainzbauer, 2002, 158)

Differences in training discourse, hidden by a common language or the common body of knowledge trainers are conveying, are thus surfacing in various contexts, and revealing the influence of 'cultural software' (national, professional, generational) upon the very mental framework and educational strategies that provide the scaffolding for individual construction of cross-cultural competence. Those experiencing cultural clashes (same language – different country, expats – trainers, theory application – experience buildup) signal it while shaping their cross-cultural competence. In a sense, discovering these cross-cultural differences resembles an angry but revealing exchange between two jury members in Sidney Lumet's *Twelve Angry Men*.

> Why are you so bloody polite all the time?
> For the same reason you are not. This is the way I was brought up.

The way one was (and still is) brought up matters as much as the core values underlying the enculturation and socialization processes. The way one interacts and follows procedures 'exploits' some values more than the others in influencing one's behaviour. Discovering differences in an organizational discourse when speaking a common language or when engaging in common practices is a business for researchers interested in cross-cultural analysis of the Gordian knot of language, knowledge and power, a knot that all of us repeatedly tie and untie with every interaction in companies, organizations and institutions.

Chapter 4

Creative communication
The multimedia connection

1 Media are the message: the shift to digital communication

> In cultural communication, a code is rarely simply a neutral transport mechanism; usually it affects the messages transmitted with its help. For instance, it may make some messages easy to conceive and render others unthinkable.
>
> (Manovich, 2001, 64)

In analysing cross-cultural competence we have already analysed the language connection, traced the global links and the organizational consequences, but have said nothing yet about the multimedia connection. It is usually assumed in theories of communication that we can take the 'carriers' and 'media', 'languages' and 'codes' of communication for granted. After all, do they not come with organizations, technologies, societies, and times? Are they not simply neutral 'instruments' for expressing 'core values' and 'beliefs', for 'sending' and 'conveying' messages?

Needless to say, this is not so, in the long run or even the short run. In the long run, the influence of the media upon the messages is easier to discern, though not from a short distance (we are too submerged in the new media and the realities they construct for us to notice). Some of the media of communication survived their societies and civilizations, allowing us to reconstruct the messages that had been written or pictured. Ancient rulers (managing increasingly complex societies) used to send their messengers with oral instructions. Today, rulers can communicate with coded e-mails and secure telephone connections. Complexity grew and so did the variety of contexts and meanings in which messages were entangled. Human cultures used to be oral – communication was local and happened through the spoken or sung word. Dissemination could occur only if a human being physically approached another. *The invention of writing was therefore one of the first powerful revolutions in cultural media.* It was a breakthrough. Cross-cultural competence (or any other competence for that matter) did not have to be limited to an interpretation of a single perishable utterance and the life-long perfection of individual memorized knowledge and skills. One could cover distances and overcome the passage of time. Plato's writings are among the first communications designed to be written and carried around as signs, be it on a clay tablet, papyrus or paper. They still carry the traces of an oral past; they are written as dialogues or verbal exchanges between human actors, and are meant to be read aloud. Silent reading as a technique of receiving a printed word was invented much later, in the monasteries of European Middle Ages, and was greeted with disbelief as a strange deviation from the accepted mode of deciphering written symbols and converting them back to the spoken word. A monk reading without moving his lips must have been equally strange in his environment as a listener to a Walkman on a crowded bus swaying to the music only he or she hears.

In other words, Plato's ideas were already coded for and disseminated by the new medium, but were still conceived as if they were to be carried by the older one. It is worth noting in passing, that Plato thought oral communication was far superior to communication by the new medium, writing, which he thought destroyed individually honed memory and thus impeded the slow accumulation of spiritual values by aristocrats of the spirit (mandarins, elites, the initiated ones). Writing equalized the chances of those in the lower social strata with those of the higher strata. As far as access to culture was concerned, former monopolies collapsed. Provided they could read and write, members of the lower classes immensely increased their chances of upward social mobility. They did not have to worry about forgetting if they could write everything down and look it up at will. This cultural capital (the ability to write, to collect knowledge in evolving areas of competence, to institutionalize teaching and learning) has accumulated very slowly and gradually throughout the ages, but it did indeed accumulate and in contemporary societies the rate of accumulation continues to accelerate.

The invention of print, important as it was, dramatically increased the speed with which written communications could be disseminated, increased the range of potential receivers who could be reached, but did not change the written medium. Print made writing quicker, more standardized. It certainly made the production and distribution of texts cheaper and more accessible, but the distributed content was still the written word. Print had powerful effects in all spheres of human activity – facilitating religious reformations and political revolutions, scientific progress and the encyclo-paedic ideology of the Enlightenment – but it was a minor revolution. The discovery of the Gutenberg galaxy further increased the number of participants in cultural, social, and political communication, but it was one more episode within the more general, major revolution that had started during Plato's time: the transition from oral to written communication. A real cultural revolution on a par with the transition from oral to written communication was still to come.

Neither was the invention of photography originally understood as the beginning of a new era of mechanical reproduction of visual 'prints'. It was understood as yet another incremental improvement in reproducing images – an incremental improvement upon woodcuts and steel engravings. Mass distribution of photographic prints in printed media did not immediately strike anyone as a radical shift towards purely visual, not necessarily linguistically structured 'images'. Painted 'panoramas' and magic lantern slides – so popular in the 19th century – were not perceived as an early cultural training preceding the invention of cinematography. They belonged firmly to the history of painting and to the growing list of urban attractions. They had never been classified as the 'popular school of seeing images and participating in iconic communication'. They emerged, evolved and contributed to the open-ended evolution of communication. The comic strip's affinities with sophisticated avant-garde film montage (both train viewers in 'reading' images and making sense of them) has also been noticed only recently (and then primarily by specialists theorizing about art).

Gradual enlargement of reach due to telecommunication, which enabled radio and then television and the telephone to transmit messages to ever-growing audiences, and the digitalization through networked computers, resulted in an increased volume of broadcast 'images'. These visual data, according to some theoreticians of organization, started replacing the 'plots' and 'stories' (which had dominated the sense-making activities of organizations' members until very recently) with 'iconic' images and 'photostories'. According to Gabriel (Gabriel, 2004; see also Gabriel, 2005), this may lead to a narrative deskilling among the professionals who supply the 'content' for the 'media'. Should this deskilling become evident, it may provoke a major revision of mass media theories from the perspective of the consequences of changes in the media for the processes of organizing and management.[1]

Indeed, if we compare the written letters exchanged between corresponding individuals with the e-mails they type onto their computer screens, we see a change towards shorter and more compact forms and 'eye-bites'. The contemporary shift towards digital telecommunication begins to resemble the pre-Platonic shift from oral to written communication – although such insight is still limited to few specialist critics and theoreticians in art criticism and visual anthropology (Yannis Gabriel is one of the very few of these exceptions in the area of the theory of organization, perhaps because of his psychoanalytical background, cf. Gabriel, 1999). The insight that we are dealing with something more than an upgrading of existing communications, are perhaps dealing with a qualitative transformation of culture caused by the emergence of new media, is new and very slowly beginning to dawn on research communities in the organizational sciences.

This does not mean that these research communities are not functioning 'properly'. It means that they are functioning without a theoretical framework that would allow us to understand what the media are doing to their users and contents. This delay is quite normal. The growth of knowledge and the complexity of cross-cultural networking pose an evolutionary challenge we have yet to respond to. We are aware of the fact that we cannot wait and see until the invisible hand of evolution, the market or the state ushers in new cultural forms. This 'ushering in' has to be designed, negotiated, adapted, implemented, redesigned, etc. No wonder we are making very little progress in understanding the underground rivers of socialization and enculturation. Do they carry an individual from cradle to grave, from a small brook of the family through a broad river of large bureaucratic organizations to a delta of many organizational rivers networked and intertwined in individual experience and memory? We are not yet quite certain what to do with the cultural consequences of the relatively well-known socialization and education co-ordinated by families, churches and nation-states, analysed in the pioneering work of Hofstede. Since the consequences of mediated culture are much less known and studies of them are only slowly emerging within the institutional framework of knowledge production, these consequences strike us as extremely complex and difficult to grasp.

The emergence of e-mail and SMS is a case in point. In the beginning the general public and most intellectual opinion leaders considered the introduction of computers and the emergence of the internet to be a minor revolution on a par with the re-invention of print (the invention of print had actually been the re-invention: the invention itself, in a different context, had already been made by the Chinese, who had been 'prevented' from exploiting its benefits). This umbilical cord of new, computer-mediated communication that linked them to the printed media proved to be difficult to sever. Screens (of computers and monitors) were (and are) still seen as slightly more versatile pages of a book (texts are viewed by rolling out 'scrolls'); messages sent via the internet were styled as letters (e-mail is still a letter with an address on the envelope and a signature after the 'Yours sincerely').

Slowly but surely, in the last decade of the 20th century, some of these tendencies to see changes in communication media as a minor revolution and not a great leap forward were subjected to revision. There were critical voices telling us that in the latest computer-aided, satellite-transmitted and mobile individualized communications (especially due to increasingly versatile and miniaturized cellular phones) we are moving towards a new medium and new codes of communication, and that these are triggering changes similar to the changes brought about by the shift from oral to written communication. Why is theoretical recognition of this fact relatively slow? In part it is certainly due to the relative atomization of research communities, where a hypothesis about the 'death of a distance' (Cairncross, 1998) translates into unrelated projects about an information society, e-government, telecommuting, digital banking, a virtual university, and computer-mediated communication. Moreover, these research projects with popular labels are partitioned among various departments, institutions, project teams, and paradigmatic schools. To make things worse, some of the most promising research on the new media is focused on 'messages' rather than the 'media'. For instance, quite sophisticated critical and theoretical studies of contemporary art rarely if ever reach other academic audiences, although artists certainly have explored the new media much more thoroughly than any other specialist group of 'cultural experts'.

The academic division of labour would not be standing in the way of examining the impact of the evolving media had we managed to increase the flexibility of research communities and their ability to form more varied networks. Moreover, most of us see the 'new' media through the 'old' ones. Plato saw writing through spoken dialogue, we see digitalized and telecommunicated messages through the written word. The spontaneous, tacit tendency to see the emergent media in the light thrown by the previous ones demands a critical analysis that covers the 'no man's land' between the various institutionally regulated domains of 'winning' and 'producing' knowledge. I have suggested a theoretical name for this project: the 'political economy of the senses' (cf. Magala, 2005), while some researchers speak of the 'political economy of attention' (cf. Franck, 1998). *In a sense, we are repeating Plato's error, although we do not have to. Plato saw the written word as a recording of the real event, the spoken word. We tend to see the virtual reality of digitalized and telecommunicated messages as a recording of a real object – the printed word and the photographed object illustrating the text. We do not have to either.* In other words, we still tacitly assume that digital, computer-aided telecommunication is just a modification of communication based on the printed word. A printed page still prevails as the outer form of data stored in virtual databanks accessed through personal computers – font, paragraph, layout, index, titles, and references repeat the pattern known from book publications. Even if we pay lip service to the ability of information and communication technologies (ICT) to 'flatten' organization structures, we rarely consider the long-term implications of this flattening for the economy and society in general. For instance, we are only beginning to understand the increased risk accompanying outsourcing and off-shoring, and the general retreat from large bureaucratic structures with clear chains of command and responsibility and tested roles in social and political systems. We are only beginning to understand that the shorter and simpler the messages we exchange through the e-mail, the more significant the context and 'hidden dimensions' of communication become. There is no paper guarantee, in 'black and white', so to speak. We are still typing onto screens and printing out on paper pages, very much like we still think that concerned citizens exercise pressure through trade unions and political parties, while media simply report on such struggles, reflecting 'reality out there'. Slogans about the 'fourth' branch of the media, supposedly complementing the tripartite division into the legislative, executive and judicial branches, introduced by Montesquieu, are not disregarded, but neither are they treated as seriously as they deserve. We see media events (Clinton's pre-impeachment hearings, the trial of O. J. Simpson, the funeral of princess Diana, the US presidential elections, etc.) as 'objects' photographed, filmed, described and 'presented' by the media, not as 'events' that the media co-generated, which would not have happened, or would have happened differently, if there were no media.

Almost without thinking we are opening web 'pages' as if they belonged to a written book and not to a virtual website hovering above circuit chips. We are still talking about 'electronic' or 'digital' books, we focus our educational activities around core textbooks with multimedia teaching and learning aids arranged around them. We are very slowly becoming aware of the fact that we have already outsourced quite a number of our cognitive, cultural processes to the new multimedia and new ICT. Ironically enough, neither social scientists nor technological inventors were the first to observe the consequences of this digital revolution and the appearance of 'data cowboys' or 'data dandies'. The first people to become aware of these shifts in the carrier media of cultural communication were those whose sensitivity had been trained in literature and visual arts: artists, writers, poets, and critics:

> McLuhan follows Joyce by being 'abcedminded' and studying the emergence of the 'allforabit' from the earliest stages of writing – hiero-glyphs, ogam, and runes – through the phonetic alphabet . . . to shifts from speech to writing to print and electric media.
>
> (Theall, 2001, 156–7)

The above quotation indicates two early-warning critics: an experimental Irish novelist, James Joyce, and the first theoretician of the new media, a Canadian literary scholar, Marshall McLuhan. The former wrote extremely multi-layered and complex novels, *Ulysses* and *Finnegan's Wake*, which are commonly regarded as virtuoso attempts to remedy the negative effects of the 'Gutenberg galaxy' upon human experience. Print as medium of cultural communication led to sensory impoverishment – only the eye moved silently across a written page, while the tongue and ear, nose and fingertips, remained inactive. Joyce believed that a literary text worthy of its name should address all the senses of individuals and evoke all collective memories of the 'human race'. Noting this attempt to redress the effects of the Gutenberg technology, the 20th-century theoretician of mass media,

Marshall McLuhan, also ventured a hypothesis that the joint effect of mass media and telecommunications, which turn our planet into a 'global village' with their tom-tom like echo of all local events, will result in further 'outsourcing' to 'external' technologies of what used to be at the core of cultural and cross-cultural competence. The Chinese museum of calligraphy in Xian demonstrates unique works by superb artists, who managed to develop 'unmatched' knowledge and skills. Printed communication rendered those skills obsolete and made every printing shop with suitable equipment equally competent in creating and disseminating books, in which the letters and words were exactly alike. To a learned monk used to exquisite manuscripts toiled over by anonymous calligraphers, the new, freshly printed Bible distributed in huge numbers to all ranks of society must have been a heresy, like a McDonald's restaurant to a connoisseur of 'slow food' meals in fine restaurants. No wonder the physical possession of a printed book had been punished by death in some German duchies. Moreover, printed books replaced individual virtuosity with standardized competence. What will the results of moving our communications towards the 'cyberspace' be? Will the virtuosity of present-day 'hackers' be replaced by the standardized competence of the individualized masses of users?

McLuhan thought that this shift will also result in a large-scale 'outsourcing' of some ways of producing and disseminating knowledge, rendering some skills obsolete and demanding new ones (with profound professional and generational consequences). He thought about changes in the very texture of our culture:

> As man succeeds in translating his central nervous system into electronic circuitry, he stands on the threshold of *outering* (italics mine – SM) his consciousness into the computer.
>
> (McLuhan, Powers, 1989, 94)[2]

Our contemporaries (McLuhan died in 1980) are less reserved and speak of developing dataspheres and hard-wiring a global brain, of cyberspace and cyberpunk cultures, spinning tales of technoromanticism, according to which the entire evolution of human societies has made the 'construction of the next dimensional home for consciousness'[3] inevitable. *While not going so far in speculations and sweeping generalizations of the ICT-hype period, one should pay more attention to the type of cross-cultural differences discovered by Astrid Kainzbauer in the very texture and flow of disseminated knowledge and skills in management training. Changing the proportions of experiential and theoretical knowledge may also reflect growing awareness that more theoretical knowledge and more detailed databases are within one's easy and continuous reach, thus prompting our choices in learning and influencing the way in which we structure, package and phase our communications.*

Can these changes be related to a shift towards the new communication media? If so, what kind of changes in cultural and cross-cultural competence will follow this shift? In order to understand them, let us revisit all the previous connections of cross-cultural competence, the linguistic, the global and the organizational/managerial. Analysing the language of the new media, a theoretician of visual culture reminds us of that:

> The visual culture of a computer age is cinematographic in its appearance, digital on the level of its material, and computational (i.e. software driven) in logic.
>
> (Manovich, 2001, 180)

Indeed, the language in which we speak facilitates some communications and makes others more difficult. We have seen in the cases analysed by Frank Brück that Germans speaking German in Austria found it difficult to stretch their language into polite pleasantries, obscuring direct communication; and vice versa, Austrians found it difficult to strip their language of polite forms and get to the point, disregarding the social hierarchy and the emotional part of interaction. According to the so-called Sapir–Whorf hypothesis, also invoked by Manovich,[4] our natural languages create 'moulds' or 'glasses' for perceiving the world and acting in it. Sapir and Whorf's famous example compared an Eskimo language, which distinguishes many varieties of snow (granting each a separate name in their vocabulary) to the single word 'snow' in the vocabularies of most Indo-European languages. In German, French, Italian or Spanish, the single word 'snow' suffices to communicate and interact (as no vital activities, comparable with the ordeals of Eskimos in their climate, warrant such extreme precision in categorizing and describing different varieties of snow). Is it possible that our visual sophistication, reinforced and further developed by the new media, turned 'vision' and 'image' into words, which like the word 'snow' in Eskimo, now break down into many separate words to enable us to make crucial distinctions in our visual environment, our evolving 'iconosphere'?

The visual, cinematographic form of communications, of which the digitalized and satellite-linked messages on our computer screens are the latest version, are clearly being used on a mass scale. Curiously enough, we do not mention them as quite new media very often, and we are much less aware of them than of the print-related conventions, languages and 'media' that have survived the digitalization. Although younger members of our society are socialized in the presence of television, video and computer games, personal computers, and mobile phones with cameras (from an early age, since mobile phones and laptops are already being used by younger schoolchildren), visual literacy and computer literacy are only beginning to be recognized as legitimate components of the tacit curriculae of socialization, on a par with literacy understood as the ability to read and write in one's native language (or in more native languages) and to count. Our explicit curriculae and training programmes list a bibliography, books from which students are supposed to retrieve information, but they do not mention films, TV reports and documentaries, digital sources and databases (or, if they mention them at all, they do so in a separate, usually much smaller section). When do we begin to understand that films, TV documentaries, video clips, and websites and databases are drawing level with the printed word in mediating our communications? When will books cease to be the privileged medium for storing information? Will that moment be a threshold, after which our awareness of the transformation of culture through media for culturally framed communications grow explosively? Note that after WWI it was a novel by Erich Remarque, *All Quiet on the Western Front*, which acquired a 'cult' following in the 'lost generation'. After WWII it was primarily a film, *Casablanca* with Humphrey Bogart and Ingrid Bergman, which became the artwork at the core of generational 'cult' (note that a book automatically directs attention to the author who had written it, while for a film it is to the actors who had been 'showing').

Looking at our communications from this point of view, we have to conclude that the new multimedia communications preserve some of the 'codes' of the printed word, but that they differ from printed texts as the main medium of communication in at least the following respects:

- They are perceived more like a film or interactive video game than a novel with a single plot (as in PowerPoint's mobile images, bulleted points and soundbites replace written pages). They rely to a much higher extent on visual, non-linguistic cues in organizing messages and on in-depth hypertext virtual spaces for displaying information; the medium in which information is stored becomes a combination of the oral, the printed and the visual (photographic, filmic and TV-like) languages (the linguistic connection of the new multimedia).
- They are designed for nomadic masses of individualists in a worldwide search for identities, not for groups easily identified, segmented and serviced. Most of these identities have to be invented and anchored in diverse institutions and networks, since 'natural' career paths disappeared along with the immutable bureaucratic organizations of a hierarchically stratified society. Multimedia communications rely to a much higher extent on individualized mobility (from an immobile cinema-goer to an itinerant mobile phone cum palmtop user) and the global reach of telecommunications, interactions and continually evolving infrastructures (the globalization connection);
- They are much less hierarchical, much less anchored in a single cultural tradition and more future-oriented in their functioning. They stimulate mobility, individual initiative and navigation through the newly emerging 'cyberspaces' (with the aid of 'Netscape Navigators' or

'Internet Explorers'), without a single compelling principle of organization and management, but with a strong preference for pluralism and
non-traditional forms of governance (the managerial connection).

New language, new reach, new forms of organizing and managing. The
differences detected by Kainzbauer in her comparative studies of German
and British management trainees are an interesting case in point. German
trainees display respect for the printed word, which they had acquired in
their educational system. The British trainees display their spontaneous
preference for experiential learning and see learning as submersion in the
simulated reality of a problem-solving situation created by the trainer.
Increasing usage of video films and computer-simulation games in managerial
education testifies to a growing recognition of the necessity to recognize in
our educational activities the transition to the new media of communication.
Experiential learning in the virtual reality of computer-supported training
programmes was expected to develop in an explosive manner. This, in short,
is what a transition from a printed to a digitally screened medium promises,
or seemed to promise, until a breakdown of the ICT hype around 2002.

However, a year before the stock exchange crash of some of the 'dot.com'
companies (though not all of them), Rosbeth Moss Kanter had already
noted the extremely young age of the internet entrepreneurs, who went
almost immediately 'from diapers to dollars'. Listening to the generational
and revolutionary rhetoric they had used, she was reminded of the countercultural and anti-Vietnam war protest movements in North America and
Europe in the late 1960s. She had used the label of 'e-culture' to describe the
counterculture of the late 1990s and warned (as a sociologist by training)
that one should not worry about the Digital Divide, which presumably
separated the personal computer and internet users from non-users, but
rather about the Social Divide. Classes are here to stay and inequalities
between them will outlive the digital revolutions. Other researchers also
noticed that new communication technologies 'are not being used to the
extent we imagined, by the people anticipated, nor in the ways we expected'
(Woolgar, 2002, 21).

Nobody predicted, for instance, the 'dot.com' crash of 2002, nor the
spectacular rise and fall of Napster (and other exchange platforms for music
based on MP3 technology) – a cultural barter trade forum for millions.
E-culture, as all cultures, has social embedding and social consequences. The
presentation of these consequences in and through the new media enables
one to simulate the effects of national, professional and individual cultural
'softwares' upon communities and organizations. This is why *the efficiency
of managerial training and the depth of theoretical insights orchestrated as
experiential learning in cross-cultural competence building programmes
might profit from the uses of films and simulation games, if we recognize
that they are not simply 'illustrations' of the theories printed in the books,*

nor are they simply innocent, mirror-like 'simulations' of reality. They are mirrors, windows and frames at the same time.[5] They are mirrors, because they can use images and sounds to create virtual reality 'reflecting' the realities of empirically distant situations. They are windows, because they allow us to look at reality through the eyes of a creative artist, who analyses reality as he allows it to flow in front of the viewer, so that particular aspects of these flows are visible (for instance, power games or emotional exchanges). Finally, they are frames, because they can be used by viewers as frames of reference for observing 'culture in action', 'cross-cultural shocks' and their consequences.

Let us now consider some cases in point, a few instances of cinematographic 'virtual realities' of cross-cultural clashes and their consequences. Perhaps in granting cinematographic masterpieces a status equal to that enjoyed by books, we may hope to increase our awareness of the 'grand shift' and of the major transformation in the communication media, which is bringing about consequences that we cannot perceive at the moment, let alone define, predict, control, and 'manage'.

2 The uses of extremes: *Merry Christmas, Mr Lawrence* (N. Oshima)

The thing, above all, that a teacher should endeavour to produce in his pupils, if democracy is to survive, is the kind of tolerance that springs from an endeavour to understand those who are different from ourselves.

(Bertrand Russell, 1950, 121)

The Japanese film director, Nagisa Oshima, lives in France and has produced a number of films that are considered to be in the top class, along with films directed by Louis Buñuel, Federico Fellini, Ingmar Bergman, Orson Welles, and Stanley Kubrick. Among his best-known films we find *Empire of Senses, Max, Mon Amour* and *Taboo*. His historical war film, *Merry Christmas, Mr Lawrence*, is an adaptation of a novel *The Seed and the Sower* by the Anglo-Dutch author, Laurens van der Post. However, it is a film, and not a novel, and when used in the classroom situation for students on the course on cross-cultural management (which I had conducted for the past five years at the Erasmus University in Rotterdam for students from 60 countries all over the world, including Japan), it works by submerging them all in the 'virtual reality' of a small camp isolated in a tropical jungle during WWII. This total isolation of the Japanese camp for Allied prisoners of war, where the action takes place, makes for a particularly strong effect; viewers have the physical feeling of being imprisoned by hostile, unpredictable forces beyond their control in a place from which there is no escape. The film is beamed onto a large screen in a dimmed lecture hall, and students are immobilized while the film moves reality in front of them; the events of the plot unfold before the viewers' eyes against the background of Java in 1942. Music for the film was composed by Ryuichi Sakamoto, a Japanese pop singer, who also plays one of the three main roles, along with his British equivalent, David Bowie, and another British actor Tom Conti. Casting leading pop stars in the two main roles of, respectively, the commandant of the camp, Japanese Captain Yunoi and a late British arrival at the camp with leadership qualities, Major Celliers, had been a conscious choice of Nagisa Oshima. The Japanese director wanted to stress the artificial, artistic, theatre-like, aesthetic, and virtual nature of the film (after all, most student audiences know very well that David Bowie has not died in a Japanese camp, but continues to sing to thousands of fans). This feeling of artificiality is strongly reinforced by Oshima's observing of the principles of Greek tragedy; the unities of place, time and action are broken only rarely and without lifting the feeling of seamless continuity in a nightmarish viewing experience.

The first break occurs at the very beginning, when Captain Yunoi participates in a session of a Japanese military tribunal in Batavia and saves Major Celliers from execution. The second occurs on the eve of the expected execution of two British prisoners (Major Celliers and Colonel Lawrence, played by Tom Conti) for a crime they did not commit. During their last night together they lay each other's souls bare, make intimate confessions, and thus also demonstrate their individualized cultural 'software' patterning, which has shaped their actions, choices and lives. Introspection involves imaginary travel in time to the critical incidents that shaped their inner monologues, their personality, their character. These two confessions are a sort of a self-psychoanalysis. The third break, the one provided by Yunoi, is made during a conversation with Colonel Lawrence and involves a departure from the principle of 'keeping up appearances' here of a 'shining warrior' with no conscience or remorse. It turns out that Yunoi belonged to a generation of young officers who overthrew the civilian government in Tokyo in 1936 and hoped the Emperor would back them. He did not, the coup failed and most of the rebellious officers were executed. Yunoi survived only because he had been fighting in Manchuria at the time, but he lost all his friends and felt ashamed to have been 'unjustly' separated from his comrades and spared by fate. The fourth break is an epilogue in Batavia a few years later, in 1945. Apart from those four brief episodes, the camp is the stage and all events happen on this stage (it is also one of the very few films with no female characters).

The *plot* is relatively simple and dramatic. Life in the camp follows a daily routine, until a Korean guard is discovered having sex with a Dutch inmate. He is brought to Sergeant Hara, substituting for Captain Yunoi who had to travel to the military tribunal in Batavia. Hara calls for Colonel Lawrence to witness his handling of the incident. Having humiliated the Korean guard, Hara allows him to begin committing hara-kiri. Lawrence is appalled, but

Hara is determined to finish the act by beheading the wounded soldier. He is interrupted by the return of Captain Yunoi.

Yunoi had just been present at a session of the court-martial of a captured British officer for leading native guerrillas against the Japanese invading force. During the interrogation it turns out that the officer was trying to survive with a few of his soldiers, who had been killed in the same battle in which he was captured. Yunoi also learns that Major Celliers had been tortured by his Japanese captors, who wanted to obtain military information from him. When Celliers bares his torso and demonstrates bloody scars on his back, Yunoi, ashamed of his fellow-officers and attracted by a handsome enemy, decides to defend him. The trial was supposed to be a sheer formality, but the tribunal cannot reach a decision and the prisoner is sent back to his cell. In the morning, he is taken to the execution hall, tied and faces a firing squad. Only after the soldiers fire does he learn that they fired blanks, knowing that the tribunal had pardoned him and sent him to Yunoi's camp.

In the camp, Celliers is recognized by Lawrence, who had fought alongside him in Africa. The Japanese place the new prisoner in the sick bay to recover, while Yunoi asks Lawrence to take special care of the exhausted man and to stay close to him in the infirmary. The routine of camp life resumes; Captain Yunoi performs daily samurai exercises in martial arts, and the official representative of the prisoners, the highest ranking officer, routinely refuses to give him information on the military specializations of the inmates, quoting the Geneva convention. While the two engage in rehearsing the same dialogue, demanding information and refusing it in the same formal phrases, Sergeant Hara and Colonel Lawrence chat more informally, trying to ease the daily life of the inmates and to understand what the 'other side' thinks. Lawrence is the only Allied prisoner who speaks some Japanese and had been to Japan before the war. Sergeant Hara asks, for instance, if Lawrence does not feel ashamed of being captured and having revealed his real name to the enemy, and if it is true that all Allied soldiers are homosexuals. Lawrence asks why Hara allows a Japanese soldier to commit hara-kiri and why is Yunoi so intrigued by Celliers. Lawrence replies that being captured is not shameful but belongs to fortunes of war, and that homosexual incidents happen when men are deprived of the company of women and are herded together. Hara answers that he is not overseeing an execution, but has mercy on the poor soldier's family. If he reports this hara-kiri as a death in action, the widow will have the right to a state pension. Hara has also noticed Yunoi's interest in Celliers but has no explanation for it (although he, like Lawrence, suspects homosexual fascination, which he feels too ashamed to admit to anybody else).

Celliers recovers and assumes the role of a natural leader of the prisoners. When inmates are forced to fast together with the Japanese in order to mourn a deceased Japanese guard, Celliers defies orders by collecting and eating flowers. Yunoi understands that this is a direct challenge to his authority and throws Celliers into a separate cell, feeling disappointed and rejected. When Japanese guards capture an illegal radio Lawrence is also taken to the cell and told by Yunoi that he will be executed for smuggling the radio into the camp. When Lawrence replies that both of them know he is innocent, Yunoi answers that someone has to be punished in order to satisfy his sense of symmetry and harmony. At night, one of the Japanese soldiers decides to fulfil Yunoi's wishes and kill Celliers, whom he sees as responsible for Yunoi's dangerous softness. He kills another Japanese soldier who refused to give him the keys to the cells, and sneaks in. Celliers manages to defend himself, collects Lawrence and sets out to escape. They are quickly caught and brought back to the cells. Both Celliers and Lawrence think that this is their last night and share stories about their lives. Celliers recalls failing to help his younger brother who was subjected to brutal initiation rites in a British public school, and expresses his feelings of guilt – his inner life has been shaped by remorse and repentance. Lawrence recalls meeting a woman during the fall of Singapore, who remains in his memory as a promise of life after the war. Suddenly, at midnight, they are called to the commanding officer's office. Captain Yunoi is out of the camp, and Sergeant Hara is drunk because it is Christmas. 'Merry Christmas, Mr Lawrence', says Hara, 'get back to your fellow inmates'. He pardons them, saying that he is 'Father Christmas'.

When Yunoi returns, he metes out a disciplinary punishment to Hara, but is obviously relieved that Celliers and Lawrence survived thanks to Hara's ingenious cross-cultural trick. However, very soon a new conflict breaks out between the arrogant British commanding officer representing the prisoners and Yunoi. This time all inmates are assembled on the parade ground and Yunoi takes hostages, announcing he will execute them if the military specialists among prisoners are not reported to him. Celliers again takes up the challenge, walks up to Yunoi and kisses him passionately on the mouth. Yunoi raises his sword to kill Celliers, but cannot bring himself to do so. Torn by public exposure of his secret longings and by the impudent challenge to his official authority, he faints.

Yunoi is replaced, the camp evacuated, Celliers condemned to death by being buried alive. After the war, Lawrence visits Hara in a death cell in the military prison in Batavia for Japanese soldiers found guilty of war crimes. It is the last night in the life of Sergeant Hara. Yunoi has already been executed. Lawrence shares Hara's last moments and they exchange memories of the camp. He says that Hara is a victim of people who think they are right, very much like Hara and Yunoi had once thought that they had been right. When Lawrence gets up to leave, Hara suddenly shouts 'Merry Christmas, Mr Lawrence' and smiles. They part.

The *cross-cultural differences* as illustrated by Oshima and discussed with students can be presented under the following headings:

- The contrast between the Japanese national culture, strongly collectivist on Hofstede's dimensions and disciplining individuals through public shame, and 'western' (British, Dutch) national cultures, strongly individualistic on Hofstede's dimensions and disciplining individuals through individual guilt.
- The contrast between acceptable behaviour of symbolic figureheads (CEOs) (they have to proudly uphold the values and observe the norms of their national and professional culture), and of the second-rank managers of daily cross-cultural encounters, who are allowed more leeway in understanding the 'enemy' and accommodating foreign culture;
- The contrast between the empathy and cross-cultural competence demonstrated by Hara and Lawrence in an extreme case of a 'clash of cultures', and cultural relativism as a gradual development of cross-cultural competence following genuine, unbiased curiosity about the other culture, personal interest in an individual from a foreign culture and increasing frequency of non-hostile cross-cultural encounters.

When asked about the main differences between the core values of the Japanese and of the British as demonstrated, respectively, by military codes of conduct and expected 'honourable' behaviour when facing an enemy, students usually contrasted Japanese collectivism to British individualism. 'The Japanese society is based on honour and belonging'; 'The Japanese have a collective conscience'. In the case of British soldiers, 'individualism is more common'. 'When captured, they still hope to escape and fight their enemy'. The Japanese were expected to 'fight until the last man, in contrast British troops were not, instead they were encouraged to save themselves if faced with an unbeatable opponent'; 'In Western culture people have more respect for their lives, they value it in all individuals, and therefore they try to save as many soldiers as possible'.

Interestingly enough, some students, especially those from India, Pakistan and Indonesia, often mention the role of colonial troops that were used to protect British soldiers, because the British allegedly failed to 'perceive the colonial troops as their own soldiers' and used them, especially the troops from India, to protect their own 'boys'. Deployment of colonial troops is seen, together with the preference to surrender or escape, as the self-serving behaviour of a colonial power:

> In the centre of the British value system stands the human individual and its rights. In the British view these rights are universal and have to be valued at all times, even in times of war. As long as the individual is white and civilized – for African, Asian or Indian these rights obviously cease to be universal.

Another added that a 'prime example is the dramatic rescue of soldiers out of the surrounded city of Dunkirk'. It would be interesting to discuss the film with Japanese, Indonesian, British, Indian, and Dutch students, using such remarks as input for an analysis of the national cultures that were 'invisible' in the movie ('Indonesian 'natives', Korean 'colonial troops').

Answering the question about the difference between second-rank managers, like Sergeant Hara and Colonel Lawrence on the one hand, and symbolic figureheads, like Captain Yunoi and Major Celliers on the other, students stressed different expectations of their constituencies. Hara and Lawrence 'were able to exploit ambiguities and gaps in formal regularities since they were not highly respected characters'. Yunoi and Celliers were seen 'as role models and their behaviour would have influenced the behaviour of their troops'. They would have found it difficult 'to bend the rules' and to 'exploit ambiguities in formal regulations' because 'they are in the centre of attention at all times'. Some students pointed out an organizational background to this difference: 'For Yunoi, to give an order is relatively easy, just naming the objectives and expecting them to be carried out accordingly. Execution by Hara instead relies in some point on co-operation with the prisoners in the camp.' They point out that Hara's and Lawrence's mode of functioning depends on a rough and ready reciprocity, which in turn facilitates a more flexible approach to the rules, and makes life 'to some extent easier for both sides'.

When comparing Yunoi and Celliers, students were asked about the roots of their personal identity. Yunoi identified strongly with a group of samurai-like ambitious young officers, who organized the failed coup d'état in Tokyo. He felt that symbolically he had failed them. Celliers forged his identity in a psychoanalytical inquiry into his failure to rescue his younger brother from a humiliating initiation ritual. Students pointed out the function of personal guilt and public shame in both cases: 'Captain Yunoi feels shame because of the failed coup-d'état, which was a group activity'. Moreover, he 'thinks of himself as part of the group [the samurai-like officers] instead of seeing himself as an individual'. The difference between Yunoi and Hara on the one hand, and Celliers and Lawrence on the other, has led students to trace some analogies in modern business companies and public organizations. Some students see the division of labour between a symbolic figurehead, who should address the stakeholders outside of the organization, and a hands-on manager as the one who should be addressing the various groups within the organization, as 'natural'. Students quoting an example of the Spanish San Miguel brewery in Malaga state that:

> the so-called hands-on manager, who operates among his/her employees, has tight relations with the employees and employees tend to listen more often to this boss. The strategic figurehead has the function of dealing

with external perspectives and will behave less according to the operational culture of San Miguel, simply because he is not operating in this environment.

Class difference between Sergeant Hara and Captain Yunoi has not escaped student viewers, either. Sketching an analogy between the film duo Hara–Yunoi and the situation at a French company or university, they noted a difference between a French manager or professor who graduated from a *grande-école* and his assistant who does not claim such a pedigree:

> Having studied at and graduated from such a prestigious university means you come from the upper class of society. Therefore you have a name to uphold and a status to defend.

However, 'an assistant of such a manager or professor does not have the duty of maintaining the mental picture that is behind those *grand-école*'s alumnae and is able to work under fewer constrictions. He/she can be much more open about new theories and practices. It is therefore easier for a "hands-on" manager to bend the rules a bit or be more critical or "avant-garde" '.

Most students tried to find a compromise between adherence to the core values they had been socialized into and a perceived need for flexibility and tolerance in cross-cultural encounters. They said that 'we must stay true to our core values taught us by our parents and the surrounding society, yet we must be flexible enough to adapt ourselves to other ways of thinking and looking at things from a different perspective'. Some quote Colonel Lawrence, who when responding to an angry question from Captain Yunoi, 'Am I right, Lawrence, am I right?' answered 'No, you are wrong, Captain Yunoi. We are all wrong.' Some point out that words are not innocent and that a pinch of cultural relativism defends against defining actions as 'right' or 'wrong' with nothing in between. They suggest that calling them 'different' instead of 'wrong' gives less ground for a feeling of superiority. Empathetic understanding, as demonstrated by Colonel Lawrence, is approvingly quoted as an instance of an ability to maintain one's identity and core values, while at the same time preserving freedom of manoeuvre in negotiating with the other party: 'Try to understand what values and beliefs are the groundwork for a culture and be flexible when applying your own values in your judgement of this culture.'

Finally, students who watched the film were asked about its potential use in managerial training: 'Would you use the film by Nagisa Oshima in a training programme for the managers of a multinational corporation grooming mid-managers for a joint venture with a Japanese company in Indonesia? Why?' The answers were almost evenly split between positive (slightly more) and negative (slightly less). Those who would have used the film in training usually argued as follows:

I would definitely show this movie as part of a training session along with other workshops explaining differences between two cultures. It is believed by most of the managers that in case of a failure in a merger of two companies with different nationalities, culture is the main reason. And this movie, through its approach, shows very well the differences in values that two cultures have. The Japanese are a very traditional society and the decisions in Japan are made very slowly and in accordance with the majority's opinion, although the respect towards the leader and older people comes first. Also the Japanese put a lot of emphasis on honour, trust and reputation, the feeling of shame and public humiliation being unbearable and the worst punishment. And because this movie puts all these cultural features in the spotlight by comparing them to the British culture, as representative, more or less, of Western civilization, we would definitely show it to mid-managers.

(Catan, Death, Flores, 2004)

The arguments against showing the film to management trainees were usually presented like this:

No, we would not use this movie for a training program. It is a movie set in a totally different situation than that of a day-to-day business. The way people act during a war does not show you how people act in a modern company. Also, the movie was set during the Second World War. This was 60 years ago and since culture is constantly changing, this movie is not a good reference point for modern day Japanese culture. Although some basics of Japanese culture that are still present today may come forward in the movie, like praising conformity more than individualism, it is a violent movie with ritual deaths and beatings, which is not something you should show managers wishing to understand the Japanese better.

(Dogra, Haandrikman, Li, Lian, Mubarik, 2004)

Responses of Japanese students indicate that they are far less concerned about the 'cruelty' of the film, which is often pointed out by European students as the main reason to avoid showing it to managerial audiences. What troubles the Japanese students is what they perceive as the 'anachronistic' samurai ethos. They often point out that the generational difference between them and the protagonists in the film, makes the 'cultural software' of Captain Yunoi and Sergeant Hara 'anachronistic', 'dated', and so less relevant for understanding the behaviour of contemporary Japanese managers (and of the next generation of these managers, to which they belong).

Nevertheless they agree with non-Japanese students that the artistic power of the cinematographic medium, augmented by the genius of an exceptional film director, contributed to its powerful effect on the audiences. They intuitively realize that the film is a delicate artistic argument for *fairness in comparing national cultures and national patterns of socialization*. The rituals of a British public school can be more brutal than the rituals of a Japanese warrior caste, and a simple sergeant in the Imperial Japanese Army can have a more profound and subtle grasp of the cultural significance of a Christian holiday (a gift of life) than the majority of the Christian characters in the film. The apparent formality of Japanese interactions can cover the very informal and partner-like collaboration of Yunoi and Hara, while an apparent equality of the Allied prisoners of war can hide class differences and an ongoing power struggle. Class differences are evoked, for instance, in a scene, when the commanding officer disparagingly reacts to the name of Lawrence's public school, which he considers not 'classy' enough compared to his own. The significance of the friendship between Lawrence and Hara can be measured in the numbers of deaths avoided. Hara, like Lawrence, demonstrates a very honest, open-minded curiosity about the 'others', in spite of the fact that they had been defined as 'enemies' and that he has a monopoly on the use of violence. This 'message' and the wealth of the 'medium' speak for the didactic uses of *Merry Christmas, Mr Lawrence* in a classroom situation or a cross-cultural training context.

3 Power and ideology: *Underground* (E. Kusturica)

> The Austrian pacifist . . . took too seriously all the babble about hundred-year-old myths and passions, and did not see that the Serbs and the Albanians themselves far from being 'caught' in these myths, manipulate them.
>
> (Žižek, 2002, 235)

Emir Kusturica, born into a Muslim Bosnian family of Slavic origins, won a Palm d'Or at the Cannes film festival in 1995 for his dramatic tragicomedy about Yugoslavia's recent history, *Underground*. His film was based on a story by Dusan Kovacevic, *Once Upon a Time There Was a Country* and the film is, to a certain extent, a pastiche of the first soundless films. The titles of successive episodes are written in old-fashioned script on a screen as if they served as the soundtrack. Documentary scenes from WWII and the death of Tito are mixed with the 'plot', giving the appearance of documentary evidence. Finally, the narrator sits at a table talking directly to the viewer in an artificial 'happy ending' to the film. Clearly, we are witnessing a dramatic history of a country, but told from the perspective of three individuals with strong passions and dramatic personal histories. They form a triangle: a young petty thief and communist activist, Marko; his friend Blacky from the Belgrade gangster *demi-monde* (whom Marko enlists in the party); and the woman they share, Natalia. The rhythm of the story is punctuated with Balkan music played by a gypsy *klezmer* band. I had used this film in an MBA course on 'Global Networks of States and Markets' at the Rotterdam School of Management during the final years of the war in Yugoslavia. Course participants, usually junior managers and management trainees in their early thirties, found the experience of seeing this film a convenient starting point for a discussion of some side-effects and consequences of globalization and of the decline of the communist system.

The plot. It is 1941. The German army has invaded the Kingdom of Yugoslavia. Some of the provinces welcome them as liberators (Croatia, Slovenia); the largest, Serbia, organizes resistance. Marko, a communist activist and a petty criminal, persuades his gangster friend, Blacky, popular among the lower classes of the city, to join the Party. Bombs shatter the Belgrade zoo, the people remove the rubble and suffer under martial law, but the two friends continue to rob banks and German military transports, proclaiming their patriotic duty to resist but profiting from their shady business-as-usual. They share a lover, Natalia, a young actress from a Belgrade theatre, who bets on all horses and also enjoys the 'protection' of a Nazi officer. Blacky kidnaps the actress from the stage of the theatre during a performance watched, among others, by her 'protector', and throws a wild wedding party on a river boat. These open challenges to the occupying power attract the attention of the Germans, so Marko decides to hide Blacky and his people in an underground cellar. He himself remains above the ground, conveniently keeping Natalia for himself. The underground community led by Blacky in the basement of a house in Belgrade develops its own rhythm and rituals, producing weapons for resistance fighters above the ground and receiving food and supplies from Marko in return. Partisan sentiments enable the people to accept their existence in an underground cave. So it is no wonder that Marko finds no particular incentive to tell the inhabitants of the basement that WWII has ended and continues broadcasting war communiqués and air raid signals to them, maintaining their underground status quo for years. He clearly belongs to the communist *nomenklatura* (the privileged inner circle of party officials eligible for attractive jobs in state bureaucracies), and enjoys the power, privileges and profits from the underground slave labour, troubled only by Natalia's moral uneasiness and her increasing hatred of her own complicity. Finally, Tito dies and after a ceremonial train ride with his coffin through all the republics, the breakdown of the Yugoslavian federation begins. The underground community breaks out from the underground (but not from ideological prejudices fed by years of propaganda) and wakes up to a civil war. Blacky and his son happen to stumble upon the site where a film about Blacky's heroic actions during WWII is being shot. Marko wrote the screenplay, the actors resemble Blacky and Marko, and some wear German military uniforms; one looks like Natalia's protector. Blacky and his son take this rehearsal of a film scene for a real occupation and shoot an actor, then find themselves in the middle of civil war.

History repeats itself, but this time as a bloody farce. Taking ideological illusions for reality may be dangerous. Film, like all media, is not innocent. All the underground caves, where the population lived for 50 years, burst open, people come up and fight, surrealist underground tunnels appear to link the centre of Berlin with Athens and Belgrade, Rome and Sarajevo. Refugees, UN trucks and truckloads of arms for all parties flow through the tunnels under the old continent. Blacky's son gets killed, Blacky becomes a warlord killing Croatians, shoving the UN soldiers aside, while Marko emerges as an international arms trader, doing lucrative deals with all combatant parties, until one of them decides to terminate him as a 'profiteer'. It turns out that it was Blacky who ordered Marko's execution, without knowing that his soldiers had captured Marko and Natalia. When death and destruction dominate, the happy end arrives: the narrator tells us that 'once upon a time there was a country', and the protagonists of the story, resurrected for the occasion and seated as if for a wedding reception, are set on an island just separated from the continent and floating peacefully away. This floating island has the shape of a Bosnia-Herzegovina and disappears to the strains of lively dance music played by a gypsy band.

The metaphors. The most important metaphor is that of the underground. It is, quite literally, a cellar, the basement of a house, where protagonists hide from the Germans searching for them 'on the surface'. But it is also Plato's cave, with an ideological twist. The inhabitants of the cellar do not have access to 'reality' 'out there', but are dependent on manipulated communications controlled by Marko. They are kept underground and disciplined to believe that it does not make sense to break free because the country is still occupied by the enemy. They continue to believe this, falling victim to an ideological illusion orchestrated by Marko (using the sounds of air raid alarm sirens, war communiqués from the military headquarters, melodies popular in the 1940s, food arriving in military containers). Ideologies are a very specific cultural form – they are usually a product of holders of organized power (in this case of Tito and his communist *nomenklatura*). They are, quite literally, 'organizational cultures by design'. They also keep individuals in a 'cave', imprisoning them through conscious manipulation of their world views, through the structuring of their beliefs, channelling of their passions and coaching of their feelings. The lessons of communist management have not been lost on contemporary media wizards. As Walter Benjamin observed in the 1930s, in contemporary democracies only a dictator and a film star can win and exploit media attention.

There are also two metaphors of mediated reality: the scenes in the Belgrade theatre during the German occupation and the scenes during the shooting of the propaganda film about Blacky reinforce the ideological message of Marko. Both of them show the artificiality of art and the manipulation of symbols and emotions in ideologically tainted communication. Both of them are also a metaphor of the complicity of all of us, as consumers of images and clients of the media, in maintaining the ideological illusion, in keeping individuals and societies (including ourselves) in the underground (or virtual) 'cave'.

Student responses. Students, probably under the influence of the media coverage of Sarajevo and other fronts in the Yugoslavian civil war, stressed in their comments not only the ideological function of the underground ('the undemocratic system in the former Yugoslavia', 'skilful manipulation of war memories by the ruling class') but also a more psychoanalytical one. They considered 'underground' to be a dangerous collective sub-consciousness of sorts, a symbolic location of barely tamed or wild, dangerous human impulses that surface in the moments of crisis.[6] Some of them even claimed that Kusturica's showing of a bombardment of the zoo in Belgrade was highly significant: the escape of wild animals symbolized the releasing of wild human instincts 'buried deep inside every human being from the beginning of evolution'. In war, according to them, the principle '*homo homini lupus*' is confirmed more often than in times of peace. Others pointed out that being underground for a long time led the inhabitants to create their own culture, without the reality checkpoints they would have had under a democratic system.

Some students mentioned Plato's cave and commented upon the people in the underground community getting a 'deformed sense of reality'. In one case, a student even referred to an economic 'underground', a grey sphere of the national economy, and wrote that:

> in non-democratic countries the majority of economic activities are conducted in an 'underground' circle among members of illegal networks which exploit suppressed and desperate people.
> (Leyer, Fourne, Maak, Helterich, Hamer, Heusbergen, 2004)

Those who focused on manipulation noted that in order to control the ideological purity of the message one has to make sure that individuals do not have independent access to global media (the internet, TV, foreign press). To a certain extent, claim some students, every country has some version of its own 'underground' (if people are limited in their media access to those media controlled by local politicians). South Korean students added that Kusturica's *Underground* is one of the best-selling videos in their country and were pleased to encounter it during the course (it would be interesting to hear the opinion of a North Korean student, if we had one at the Erasmus University in Rotterdam).

Generally speaking, in spite of the complexity of symbolic imagery, the rapid pace of the film narration and the presence of many subplots and metaphors that can be understood only against the background of some basic knowledge about the Balkans in general and former Yugoslavia in particular, students did not seem to have too much trouble in following the fable-like, ironic narration, or relating the metaphors to communist ideological control. Some of them found the last scenes of the civil war, with UN soldiers standing by helplessly and with uncontrolled warlords repeatedly declaring that a war is not a war until brother kills his brother, very disturbing, but agreed that they were extremely well integrated in the aesthetic flow of the narrative. They also understood that a general wedding-like feast at the end of the film, the artificial happy-end with dead protagonists returning to enjoy life, symbolizes the willingness to forget and forgive and to try to drift back towards Europe. Last not least, *Underground* lasts almost three hours and it is quite telling that viewers do not ask for a break nor do they leave the hall before the end.

The critics. All films that touch upon contemporary political reality immediately become partisan. Can partisan films be used in a legitimate didactic process? Are they not part and parcel of political propaganda? Kusturica's film is no exception to such criticism. Critics have often pointed out that his film is very strongly pro-Serbian. Marko and Blacky are a Serbian and a Montenegrin, and both fight on relentlessly in occupied Belgrade, while the Slovenes and the Croats welcome Nazi troops, Muslims and Croats steal weapons and money from the resistance fighters, and Natalia makes personal collaborationist arrangements with the representative of the occupiers. Serbs are presented as the only true representatives of Serbian, Yugoslavian, Balkan, and by extension, a progressive European and truly Christian spirit. They are also spontaneously virtuous, stubbornly fighting for their ideals, while the others (including the weak and corrupt UN soldiers) prefer compromise and accommodation.

Most of the critics found the documentary footage highly biased. Why was there no footage of recent war crimes committed by the Serbian army in the bombardment of Vukovar, the shelling of Dubrovnik, the systematic destruction of Sarajevo during the three-year siege? Why did Kusturica not show the nationalist farewell to the Serbian troops leaving Belgrade to decimate unarmed Bosnian and Croatian populations?

Another type of criticism focused on what some critics saw as the aesthetic 'anaestheticism' offered to the viewer, who is free to see the film from a safe distance as a visually pleasing 'story' and forgets about some morally suspect consequences of national identity ('the spiritual purity of national identity'):

> This mythical image of 'the Balkans' is faked, mediated by Western gaze, it already involves a cynical distance. . . . The political meaning of *The Underground* does not reside primarily in its over-tendentiousness – in the easy way it takes sides in the post-Yugoslav conflict (heroic Serbs against the treacherous, pro-Nazi Slovenes and Croats) – but rather in

the very depoliticized aestheticist attitude. . . . The impossible position of enunciation characterizes the contemporary cynical attitude in it, ideology can lay its cards on the table, reveal the secret of its functioning, and still continue to function.

(Žižek, 2004, 1)

Most of the students responding to questions after seeing the film did not have these doubts; they perceived the film as pacifist, anti-nationalist and focused on the ideological and economic manipulations of the 'evil' *nomenklatura*. Marko, as their highest representative, succeeded in prolonging the ideological illusion of the war and enslaving the unlucky citizens in underground sweatshops. There was no escape from this ideological underground; literally, there was no escape, except into a civil war. Students noted the re-enacting of the ideological bias and prejudice from WWII (Blacky calls his own people *Chetniks*, the Croatian soldiers *Ustashes*, using the names of the military formations from the 1940s). They noted that Marko's indoctrination imprinted nationalistic stereotypes on the citizens' minds. They noted that ideologies are organizational cultures by design. But they did not find cynicism, of which the director had been accused by the critics, nor did they notice any affinities between the making of an ideologically 'correct' war film and contemporary PR techniques. The broad, epic range of the symbols and metaphors, and the vivid, quick narration did not favour in-depth analysis of the influence of an organizational culture by design upon individuals. Disturbing questions about our susceptibility to the cynical aesthetization of politics (the selling of political candidates and their programmes) and economics (the aesthetic overkill in advertising and the design of shopping malls) are difficult to raise when a shower of vivid images impedes articulation of an independent judgement. Sound-bites and image-bites delivered rapidly by multimedia operate differently from the printed word and sequential unrolling of an argument. Perhaps this is indeed one of the morally disturbing consequences of the development of the new media with their cinematographic 'montage' of vision.

4 Dynamics of socialization or democracy behind the factory door: *Twelve Angry Men* (S. Lumet, W. Friedkin)

Can one respect the value of democratic openness under present conditions while also being politically savvy, even relentless in naming and struggling against those forces and constituencies that presently block most meaningful forms of democratic accountability and participation?

(Keenan, 2003, 190)

When the first meeting of the International Association of Cross Cultural Competence and Management took place in Vienna in 1997, participants from Austria, Italy, the Netherlands, Belgium, Poland, and Great Britain all agreed that in designing a film clinic for training programmes in the managerial sciences, one should not omit this film. Teaching organizational behaviour, organizational learning and cross-cultural negotiations classes, according to the founding members of the association, would be greatly facilitated by viewing and analysing *Twelve Angry Men*. Indeed, the film, based on a TV theatre script dating from the Cold War, can be viewed as a penetrating and dramatically attractive presentation of the virtues of democracy and consensus-building in every organizational setting. After all, managers on both sides of the Iron Curtain tried to persuade world public opinion that only in their factories, offices and courts of law could true democracy be found (while in their adversary's case, as Henry Ford famously remarked, it stopped at the factory door).

One of the classic films about the shaping of a collective mind over a 'real life case', this film takes us into the locked jury room where the twelve members of the jury have to decide if a Latino youngster is guilty of murdering his own father or not. In the 1957 version of the film, directed by Sidney Lumet (and based on a literary text, namely the TV script by Reginald Rose, which had been broadcast in 1954), all members of the jury are white males. In the 1998 re-make by William Friedkin, some members of the jury are black or Latinos and there is more age differentiation, but they are still all male (although the judge, who appears briefly at the very beginning, is a woman).[7] The entire action of the film takes place in the same locked room, with the same twelve male actors. There are no flash-backs to their memories; everything happens as if on a theatre stage with an unchanged set.

The plot. After hearing the arguments for the prosecution and the defence, the twelve members of the jury retire to their room to decide on their verdict. Most of them have been convinced by the arguments of the prosecution that he is guilty. As they settle down to discuss the case, most of them point out that the knife, with which his father was killed, had been purchased by the boy a few days earlier, that a neighbour saw him running down the stairs, as if fleeing, immediately after the murder, and that another neighbour actually heard and saw the murder from the opposite side of the street. When they take a preliminary vote, it turns out that eleven out of twelve vote 'guilty', but one member of the jury, a middle-class architect, Mr Davis (played originally by Henry Fonda and by Jack Lemon in the re-make) refuses to do so. When questioned, he answers that he does not know if the boy is guilty or not, but would like to discuss the case before deciding. How can he believe beyond reasonable doubt that the boy is guilty if the other jury members have already made up their minds and view the due process of law as a mere formality?

Reluctantly, the other members of the jury begin a discussion, in which the complexities of their personalities and attitudes towards society, justice and due process become evident and strongly influence their perception of the evidence and reconstruction of the crime. Violent verbal clashes over interpretations of events and biased judgements of character influence the course of discussion as much as rational arguments and pieces of evidence brought back from the courtroom. Mr Davis begins to undermine the conviction of the majority of his fellow-jurors that the boy is guilty of murder by reconstructing the events and discovering flaws in the prosecution's arguments. Is it possible that a knife bought and presumably lost by the boy is not the knife found on the murder scene? Davis managed to find an identical switch-blade knife in a pawn shop in the neighbourhood. Is it possible that an old man, who lives one floor below the victim, actually heard the crime, got up from bed and managed to reach his front door in time to see the boy fleeing from the murder scene? Considering the old man's limp, he would have needed more time to actually get up, walk to the front door and open it just in time to see the fleeing murderer. Could the neighbour on the opposite side of the street see the murder scene through the windows of the passing subway train? Could she have heard shouts from the other side of the tracks in spite of the noise made by the speeding train? Considering the fact that she wore glasses and a passing train makes a lot of noise, neither seems likely. Davis does not limit himself to the rational arguments; he is also generating emotional support for his 'cause' and demonstrates the bias and prejudice hidden behind formal adherence to the rules and procedures of the jury.

Consecutive votes reveal growing support for his 'reasonable doubt' about guilt, at the expense of a group of jurors still ready to uphold the 'guilty' verdict. Hidden agendas, cultural backgrounds and personality differences surface, clash and fill the jury room with dramatic confrontations, flaring of tempers and racial slurs. Davis criticizes the unfairness of the court proceedings: in spite of the appearances of a formally fair trial, the court-appointed public defence lawyer did not do his job properly and failed to exploit the gaps in the prosecution's case, which had put the defendant at a disadvantage. Moreover, he points out that the past history of a lower-class teenager with a record of petty crimes and offences biased both the neighbours of the victim and the other jury members against him. Davis himself is not free of doubt: one of the members of the jury asks him what will happen if they vote 'not guilty' and then it turns out that the boy had in fact murdered his father? Davis takes note of this possibility, but does not give up persuading his fellow jury members. Finally, all twelve members are swayed and vote 'not guilty'. The jury has reached its verdict. They leave the room to communicate their decision to the judge. They remain anonymous; only two of them exchange names when shaking hands at the end.

Ideological message. The main reason why the virtual reality of a single location – the locked jury room – works as a simulation game for the audience is that we do not know any better than members of the jury whether the boy is guilty or not. We have to live with uncertainty, knowing that the best we can hope for is to listen to as many different voices as possible and to acknowledge reasonable doubt. We have to try as hard and honestly as we can to falsify all proposed 'theories' or 'verdicts', but keep in mind that it is the honesty of the search for truth and the democracy of the process that matter, not absolute certainty about 'the truth'. In other words, when following the jury discussions and assessing pieces of evidence and witnesses' reports, we too are left to draw our own conclusions. This uncertainty makes us feel that in watching the jurors we are actually participating in an experiential learning class in organizational behaviour, where we can see the difference between the structure of an organization (the jury selected in a court case) and actual processes (the dramatic struggle to reach a verdict), between the task orientation (the judge will not accept a hung jury) and the relationship orientation (guiding the discussion, managing emotional support for 'our' voters), between the formal equality of the jury members and the actual inequality in intelligence, education, empathy, and social skills. One of the members of the jury assumes the role of a manager who takes care of formal proceedings (calls for votes, asks for pieces of evidence, decides about practical issues, etc.), but his authority remains formal and fragile, since Mr Davis emerges as a born leader, with a vision and mission (to get rid of bias and prejudice, and to consider the boy's case with due diligence) and with a natural authority (of a compassionate and intelligent, educated individual with strong moral values).

Watching the dramatic proceedings of the jury, a viewer is also aware of the organizational learning that takes place in the jury room. Jury members who demonstrate extreme bias and prejudice are ostracized and isolated, so that their influence upon discussion can be minimized and the damage controlled. If subjected to open, democratic scrutiny, their prejudices can be identified and neutralized. Morally repugnant behaviour (for instance, willingness to sacrifice the 'truth' for the sake of a timely finish, thereby enabling one member of the jury to get to a baseball game on time) is rebuked and corrected. Cases of different opinions are handled with increasing efficiency and resolved by addressing not only the rational but also the emotional and cultural issues. Finally, all members of the jury bring with them their own cultural 'software'. These include negative stereotypes ('they breed like rabbits'), biases ('slum dwellers grow up to become criminals') and prejudices ('if we get a chance to kill one of them, we should not waste it'), which form the underside of strong social identities. The members of the jury manifest them in 'real life', illustrating the complexities and difficulties of managing a multicultural workforce in a contemporary organization.

Characteristically, there is a shift in the main thrust of bias and prejudice between the two versions of the film. In Lumet's version, European immigrants are considered 'strangers' in the American paradise; a car salesman whose baseball tickets are burning a hole in his pocket complains that a Swiss watchmaker – still wet from the boat crossing – is trying to 'tell him how to run the show'. In Friedkin's version, the Latinos, immigrants from Puerto Rico or Mexico, are considered the main threat to the American way of life; a fanatical black ex-Muslim urges the need to finish 'them' off, before they finish 'us'. In a multicultural society, torn between a vision of the dominant culture's 'melting pot' (still dominant when Lumet made his film) and a vision of a diversity of co-existing cultures in a 'salad bowl' (praising the values of diversity when Friedkin filmed his re-make), clashes between members of the jury are lessons in domesticating potentially violent subcultures and in management across cultural differences.[8]

The steadily growing popularity of *Twelve Angry Men* and its growing reputation as an excellent virtual simulation of a real-life cross-cultural management is also based on a pragmatic belief in the liberal vision of a 'just' society. Equality of all is symbolically expressed by the random selection of jury members: in a democratic society, all citizens are said to be equal and equally ready to perform their civil duties. In actual 'real life' situations and contexts, inequalities surface anyway, but their influence upon due democratic process can – this is the message of the film – be successfully countered. Emotional outbursts, fierce arguments, disturbances of organizational routines – all these can be tackled via proper procedures and appeals to sovereign individuals. Society is daily constructed by autonomous individuals in interaction patterns managed by leaders upholding the vision of a liberal society with a free market, responsible officials and independent judges. There may be cases of unfairness, of lack of due diligence, of negative stereotyping, and discrimination – but in all these cases a change, an improvement, a remedy are available if citizens exercise their rights within properly designed organizations and with morally and intellectually responsible leaders. The future is ours, fellow citizens (it does not belong to the 'comrades'); if we succeed in preventing bias, prejudice, negative stereotyping, and discrimination from subverting the 'unfinished project of the Enlightenment',[9] we shall live up to the ideals of liberty, equality and fraternity.

This strong, almost didactic message of the film owes much to the background of the Cold War (which thus seeks to provide an ideologically appealing legitimization of liberal democracy in its American version).[10] Emotionally effective dramatization of a single episode in the interactions of a group of random individuals brought together by the invisible hand of democratic society makes it particularly suitable for studying processes and complexities that artists can visualize better than social scientists.

Contrary to what some theoreticians claim, democracy should enable individuals to work together in spite of lack of trust, familiarity and understanding:

> Trust represents an intangible form of social capital. . . . Loosely speaking, social capital is the ability of people to work together easily and efficiently based on trust, familiarity and understanding.
>
> (Buchanan, 2002, 201)[11]

The protagonists in *Twelve Angry Men* do not trust each other's motives, are not familiar with each other's social milieu, and need time, effort, management, and leadership in order to accomplish their collective task. In spite of these difficulties, in spite of the ongoing power struggles, and in spite of the clash of cultures and subcultures, they succeed in bringing a unanimous verdict to the judge. Their success is to a large extent a success of their leader, 'the leader of their cause'. He stirs their 'melting pot'. They accomplish their task, gain knowledge, hone skills, practise moral judgement, and become better citizens. The true leader knows how to make use of the chances and opportunities created by democracy and is determined to make his use of them fruitful. The need for both management and leadership in a democracy is one of the strongest messages of the film. It is this message that makes *Twelve Angry Men* particularly suitable in enhancing the learning experience of students in schools of management. As a virtual film clinic for students of business management, the film can be used in courses on organizational behaviour and human resource policies, leadership and cross-cultural management, business ethics and corporate social responsibility.

The list of courses and specializations in which the film can be of use indicates another important property of this dramatized story about the members of a jury. The movie 'simulates' an organizational reality and 'creates' a virtual reality of an organizational process – allowing the viewers to make use of knowledge and skills developed and disseminated under different academic headings but assembled and re-configured by a manager in a concrete organizational context. In a sense, it *is* a simulation game. *Twelve Angry Men* can be viewed as a dramatized case that unrolls before our eyes and allows us to watch and identify ourselves with the protagonists, to 'put ourselves in their places'.

Conclusion
Managing cross-cultural competence

> Year after year we are becoming better equipped to accomplish the things we are striving for. But what are we striving for?
>
> (Bertrand de Jouvenel)

For viewers of the original version of *Twelve Angry Men*, the answer to this question was simple. An evil empire had plunged the free world into a Cold War, and 'we' (Western market democracies led by the US) were fighting for freedom and democracy. In the film we can see how freedom and democracy curb our vices and reward our virtues – something dictatorship and slavery cannot do. But after the spectacular breakdown of the evil empire of the Soviet Union, the answer could no longer be drawn from an FAQ databank of a propaganda war.

It is impossible to answer de Jouvenel's question without the kind of competence necessary to compare values without a simplifying toolkit of ideological black-and-white distinctions. Moreover, having identified our values, we still need to decide on our priorities: which values would we like to honour first? The 'we' in most of our projects and interactions, organizations and institutions is becoming more complex and heterogeneous. Compared to the first version of the film, in the second there are three different social and psychological types of African-Americans, two different 'Latinos' and the judge (a person in a position of authority) is a woman. The leader is still a white, educated, upper middle class professional, but his authority is not taken for granted and the others do not pay him the same 'instinctive', 'automatic' respect the manual workers did in the first version. He wins by demonstrating his courage and competence, not by his class origins. Merit and persuasion matter more than power and status, although the latter look better than prejudice and humble roots.

Moreover, it is not only that there are more of 'us'. There are also more doubts about what we stand for and what we are striving for. It appears that a board reading 'Under construction' should be placed in front of values and the hierarchies in which we situate them. Black-and-white distinctions do not suffice anymore. Can the truth about what happened to the boy's father be established beyond reasonable doubt? Is the final decision of our jury a genuine solution to the dilemma of the boy's guilt, or is it a shady compromise, covering over the inadequacies of our minds and institutions? Capitalist democracies turned out to be historically, economically and politically 'better' than communist dictatorships. But is a welfare state in Europe with permanent structural unemployment better than a 'liberal' state in the US with less welfare and less unemployment but more underpaid jobs, which keep the working poor structurally poor? Creating and adding value is not only about profits of a corporation; it is also about giving reasonable hope to those who cannot make ends meet.

Truth, Goodness and Beauty – carved in marble over the arched entrances to the opera houses of Europe – are subject to criticism and described as changeable and relative not only in daily life but also in the specialized domains of culture: in science, in morality and in art. Truth is limited in space (to a research community accepting a paradigm) and time (until a new discovery, invention or paradigm emerges rendering the old one obsolete). The values of Goodness and Beauty share the same fate. Social groups and communities clash over the answer to the questions about what is 'good'. Is it good to facilitate a terminal patient's suicide? Or is it better to assist him or her in their last journey to an inevitable end, assuring him or her of the importance of saving his or her soul? Should we support abortion, because it allows female individuals to decide freely about their own body? Or should we see abortion as the unnatural act of terminating a barely started life that is not ours to take? Should we grant homosexuals the right to marry, recognizing that they are equal to heterosexual persons, or should we respect the negative attitude of a majority of voters? Is it better to legalize soft drugs, thus making them less attractive to organized crime, or should we stand firm and condemn them as lethal poison? Should we allow individual possession of firearms (as in the US), or issue them only to authorized members of the public services? What is better: freedom of expression or the protection of religious sentiments? The list of contested issues is very long.

Contemporary artists do not produce works that point to some hidden, distant but single and clearly defined ideal of beauty; they confront us with ourselves, our social selves, our multiple selves. They make us feel 'estranged' from 'normal' reality by pursuing – to use Zygmunt Bauman's term – the strategy of 'defamiliarization' of our increasingly artificial and increasingly 'beautified' ('aestheticized') environment. What makes this 'defamiliarization' different from Brecht's 'strangeness effect' designed for a politically committed theatre and devised between two world wars, is that Brecht wanted his audiences to feel estranged from capitalist society, to mobilize them for a class struggle on behalf of the have-nots. Contemporary artists do not mobilize us for a single ideological cause. They mobilize us against routine, normality and stagnation, keeping up our generalized willingness for change. Defamiliarization fulfils the important function of opening our options as change agents in all locations and at all times.

What kind of competence does it take to understand, appreciate and evaluate contemporary interactive art, installations, performances, and other forms of artistic creativity woven into our daily activities? What does Jenny Holzer mean when she places unobtrusively among film titles on a billboard outside a theatre in a large city the claim that 'If you behaved properly, communism would not exist'? As critics phrase it, 'One dominant trend in contemporary art is the questioning of the sociality of which the observer of art is a part' (Schinkel, 2004, 14).

The games artists play have become as sophisticated and as interactive as the games played by moralists, specialists in ethics, social scientists, and humanists. *Science may be a privileged supplier of knowledge products for contemporary organizations, but neither art nor religion have been pushed out of the marketplace of ideas.* Cross-cultural competence also requires an ability to purchase ideas, concepts, frameworks, and evaluations from their representatives.

Cross-cultural competence allows for successful bridging of differences in identifying, naming, prioritizing, and implementing values. The growth in the complexity and interconnectedness of contemporary individuals, groups, organizations, and entire societies requires frequent reflection on 'what we are striving for' (culturally articulated values and beliefs) and which 'equipment' (organizationally determined managerial instruments) we need to succeed in our striving. Cross-cultural competence cannot be reduced to the content of a crash course in doing business with non-Western partners. It is not another word for acquaintance with the list of differences between 'the West' and 'the rest', although awareness of such differences is part and parcel of it. Cross-cultural competence as presented and explained in the present study should be understood as the ability to detect, understand and exploit cross-cultural differences manifested in all processes of organizing and in all managerial activities.

The word 'exploit' here requires particular attention. Cross-cultural competence depends crucially on:

- *Creativity* in bridging differences in perceiving, communicating and implementing values and beliefs. Hybrid recombinations, 'bastardized' variants, compromise constructs increase overall levels of serendipity, flexibility and adaptability. Creativity is social evolution's random (serendipity), 'genetic' (hybrid recombinations) drift (adaptability). Without creativity there would be no increasing pool of 'cultural variety', from which evolutionary selections could be made by societies looking for ways out of unpredictable future situations.
- *Criticism* in detecting ideologies and methodologies that lurk behind these differences and which flow from the ongoing power struggles,

the most sensitive processes of organizing. All resources can and are being mobilized, and all domains of culture ransacked for ideological arguments by the powers that be. *Not only religions or television can function as the opium of the people. So can a positivist methodology or a managerialist doctrine, provided they contribute to the distorted representation of inequalities and power relations.* Criticism safeguarded and negotiated at all times determines not only the growth of knowledge (sciences and the humanities) but also the growth of the GDP (new technologies) and the development of democracy (the deficit in both representative and participative democracy in the media age has to be worked upon at all times). Criticism enables us to select better means of preventing this deficit from growing and to avoid a too one-sided selection of organizational solutions (which would dangerously reduce variety in our culture, as was the case in totalitarian societies of the 20th century).

- *Moral autonomy* of cross-culturally competent individuals to decide what they prefer, perceive, communicate, and implement. Achieving and maintaining moral autonomy between the Scylla of fanatical dogmatism on the one hand and the Charybdis of cynical relativism on the other is a criterion of 'progress' in the history of human societies. A virtual *agora* remains an *agora* in spite of being virtual – and it is on the *agora* that we argue about progress and decay, development and decadence. The evolution of human societies with cultural traditions differs from the evolution of natural species in that not all evolutionary choices are morally acceptable and not all are politically negotiated. In a sense, we are dinosaurs with a conscience and a voting right – including the right to vote ourselves out of existence.

Cross-cultural competence is not a new capability of human individuals. Prominent individuals managed to develop cross-cultural competence in the past (Marco Polo is one case in point and so is Bartolomeo de las Casas). However, in our times cross-cultural competence is needed and being developed by increasing numbers of individuals. It is becoming increasingly explicit and is frequently subjected to inter-subjective analysis as we discover many more cross-cultural differences than we had suspected when designing our organizations and patterning our interactions. Not all cross-cultural differences are 'manifest'. In fact, some of the most important ones are not. Poor M Jourdain in Molière's *Bourgeois Gentleman* expresses his astonishment when told that he had been speaking prose all his life without realizing it. It was not manifest to him that ordinary speech belonged to 'prose', while artificially altered, linguistically processed and aesthetically pleasing speech (subjected to more formal constraints) was called 'poetry'. More importantly, nobody told poor M Jourdain that in trying to acquire the cultural sophistication associated with the former upper classes, to which he had been promoted by the collective (French revolution) and individual (market success) action, he was in fact successfully creating a cross-cultural hybrid. In acquiring the cultural 'software' of the aristocracy he had so admired in pre-revolutionary times, he was not becoming 'one of them'. He was becoming 'like them' – but remained a bourgeois with an aristocratic cultural 'outfit'. He was acquiring the cultural identity of a new upper segment of the middle class, expressed via the artefacts of the former upper classes, which were continuing to lose their political and economic resources but whose cultural capital turned out to be very attractive to the *nouveaux riches*. Nobody warned him that his new cultural identity, which he had been acquiring at such expense, will never be comfortable to wear, will never convince him or others about his cultural sophistication and superiority, will always look like a cheap imitation compared to the cultural competence of the upper classes in the past, and will always be available to increasing numbers of the 'enriched' middle class. Cross-cultural competence is not neutral from the perspective of the class and status differences between social groups and individuals.

Like M Jourdain, most of us have been making cross-cultural comparisons and exploiting cross-cultural differences all our lives, although we have not always been aware of it. For instance, we have not been aware of the fact that our media-saturated environment has trained us in processing mostly visual information at the expense of all other information, including the oral/auditory kind. In a virtual *agora*, we follow our eyes first, and the image is mightier than the word. We have trained and conditioned our senses to provide increasingly complex visual information, so that a photograph or a film become as 'natural' to us as a book used to be, or a long epic poem recited aloud before there were books. Creative use of multimedia (in science, education, entertainment, and the arts) makes us realize (i.e. visualize, 'sensualize', perceive with our senses and not just understand via our theoretical concepts) how multidimensional our realities are, in how many multiple realities we learn to move simultaneously. Thus we learn more about the elementary particles constituting our cultures (and about secret weapons of mass appeal and persuasion constructed with knowledge about them).

Like M Jourdain, most of us have been choosing paradigms and methodologies and forging loyalties to professional communities, although we have not always been aware of the broader implications of our choices for stabilizing or destabilizing the powers that be. For instance, most mainstream quantitative researchers, when asked why they consistently promote a very neopositivist doctrine of science (and tacitly agree to suppress qualitative approaches, discriminate against the 'interpretativist' ones), answer – genuinely surprised – that this is simply the way things have to be done if one wants to safeguard one's professional career and the continuity of a common body of knowledge. They appear to believe in 'safety in numbers' – both those crunched in analysing data (number of data) and those of crunchers (number of researchers) assembled around them in research communities of practice. *Exposing the artificiality of this presumed continuity of professional practice as a social and political project contributes to the awareness of the methodological and ideological pedigrees of cultural constructs. We learn more about the force fields framing the evolving continents of culture if we include the scholarly and scientific edifice of 'knowledge' in our analysis instead of taking it for granted.* We learn to heed the ironic warning that Bruno Latour, paraphrasing Jean Jacques Rousseau, sounded by saying that although 'scientific disciplines are born free, everywhere they are in chains'. Researchers still accept the epistemology constructed as a 'war machine' for both 'Cold War' and 'Science Wars', and follow the illusory ideal of a perfect hierarchy with 'science is number one' at the top (even though they seem to overlook the possibility that physics may have been replaced by molecular biology as the 'queen of the sciences', that the trend is now towards biochemistry and may perhaps go towards neurosciences, so that the hierarchy itself is also tentative and temporary).[1]

Last not least, like M Jourdain most of us remain largely unaware of the emergent inner 'core' of our personalities, motivations and aspirations. We turn out to be a parliament of selves rather than something with a single 'ruler', a single 'self' and 'identity'. All of us dream of upward mobility and self-development, and all of us try to rationalize and emotionally experience our devotion to core values. Few of us, however, are able to persuade our different selves to vote for a single project in the parliament of our 'selves'. All of us are socialized into cultures, shaped by institutional frameworks and their subcultures, all of us choose and continuously repair, develop, tune, and hone our identities and cultural competence. We like to imagine that at the intimate heart of our individual projects of cultural identity, we (our innermost 'selves') sit down to judge and decide in the 'closed rooms' of our sovereign moral autonomy (so brilliantly visualized and dramatized in *Twelve Angry Men*). We hope that our cross-cultural competence will enable us to peek into the closed rooms of others, from different social strata and professions, from different societies and different epochs. We hope to be able to feel empathy when following others, watching their rituals and hearing their arguments. We hope to understand their negotiations or at least to map our own democratic deficits, flaws in moral reasoning, and emotional shortcomings.

We started our reflections on cross-cultural competence by considering the linguistic metaphor and investigating the 'language connection'. This brought us to the socially privileged language of the 'scientific construction of knowledge'. We continued our reflections with an analysis of the rapid increase in cross-cultural encounters due to global networking on many levels and in many areas of our activities. This brought us to two different scientific 'prophecies' about the future: prognosis of a clash of civilizations (especially between rival 'truths' – 'Western' and 'Islamic'), and the prognosis of convergence towards McDonaldization (every social activity will be simplified and rationalized, rendering alternatives obsolete and meaningless in face of the only 'truly rational' way of doing things). We concluded our reflections on cross-cultural competence by considering the 'medium is the message' metaphor and by investigating films as an example of the 'multimedia connection' that is bringing us closer to a virtual reality of hybrid value connections between science, religion, art, and the media, producing – among others – infotainment and edutainment. This brought us to the virtual *agora* of contemporary societies of spectacle, which surrounds us with images and sounds, and transforms our cultures by doing so, for instance by making us reveal our value calculations much more frequently and in much more detail, and forcing us to keep these calculations and reflections transparent and open.[2] It is time to bring all these connections together.

In order to develop cross-cultural competence we must study language and media, the global networking and exchanges, the processes of organizing and managing, that involve power and ideology. This can be done only in interdisciplinary project teams that do not bow to the narrow professional ideologies of research communities. Needless to say, from the perspective of professional academic hierarchies, which depend heavily on bureaucratically defined specialization, interdisciplinary research always carries with it the danger of marginalization and loss of professional status. A researcher who conducts interdisciplinary research loses his career anchor, his institutional embedding. Hence the attempt to reduce problems best tackled by interdisciplinary teams to conceptualizations contained within a single discipline. The attempts on the part of cognitive psychologists to claim problem areas from sociologists, economists and philosophers is the most recent utopian case in point. What gets lost in an attempt to reformulate a problem area best conceptualized by an interdisciplinary team is the complexity and tacit ideologies involved. Tacit ideologies are the most obvious obstacle in the way of the single-discipline and single-paradigm approach. Power is usually legitimized through culture into authority. Cultural legitimization of power is called ideology. Ideology is one of the most important of culture's consequences and one of the most demanded cultural products. It can, in turn, cause entire cultures and subcultures to become 'ideology's consequences', or at least to give them an ideological flavour. This is what researchers start discovering once they study the influence of the Cold War on contemporary culture (particularly science and the arts), on the ideology of managerialism, or the relationship between cultural production and economic activities.

The ideology of managerialism has undergone chameleonic transformations in the course of the past 100 years. It started off as a justification for the activities of a Taylorist foreman with a stopwatch and ended up as praise for a networking coach acting as a peer and offering team support. Researchers have discovered that our cultural climate has been heavily influenced by the overheating of the political atmosphere in the radical student protests of 1968, by the sudden disappearance of the Cold War's ideological Ice Age (1980–9), and by the blowback of the neoconservatism in the last two decades of the 20th century. Freeze (Taylorism), unfreeze (student protests and countercultures), re-freeze again (neoconservatism). It is not only the physical climate of our planet that changes: so does the political and ideological one. The ice melted, a thousand flowers bloomed, communism broke down, populist capitalism emerged – but throughout all these 'climatic' changes our creativity, critical sense and moral autonomy had to be re-established in every organization, in every context.

This is the challenge of postmanagerialist, cross-cultural competence in a new, rapidly evolving environment, where there are no clear poles of an 'Evil Empire' in the East opposed by an 'American Dream' in the West[3] and with no clear-cut distinction between 'Left' and 'Right' politics in parliaments, governments or the governance structures of contemporary societies. *Cross-cultural competence – of the kind we are trying to construct in our research, teaching and consulting activities, the kind that increasing numbers of individuals are accumulating in countless interactions, the kind we are tracing through new conceptual frameworks and theoretical models, is an emergent discipline among the managerial sciences. It is located between the fields of organization theory, organizational development, human resource management, and communication studies; it maintains close links with sociology, cultural anthropology, social psychology, cultural economics, and the other disciplines in the social sciences and humanities.*

The theory of cross-cultural competence is still under construction, as is the entire academic field of cross-cultural studies. Perhaps we should stress the comparing at the expense of the comparison? A crossing of cultures as part and parcel of managing processes at the expense of cross-cultural management as a ready-made toolkit for first-aid emergencies? Perhaps a name for what managers do should be 'managing' and not 'management'. Perhaps it should remain a fluid and hybrid 'gerund' rather than become a solid and homogeneous 'noun'? After all, one of the predictions about the future of organizational development tells us to expect hybrid improvisation rather than intentional, deliberate design, and vibrant, local cultures rather than dominant imperialist Westernization:

> In turbulent periods, orderliness is limited to short-lived transactions, intelligence is reduced to local expertise, and determinacy covers only those events close together in time and space. While no one questions that it would be desirable to have grand and stable designs in times of turbulence, the organization is not sufficiently homogeneous to support concerted action, nor is the environment sufficiently determinant to

encourage accurate, long-term prediction. Instead, the way out of the turbulence may lie in continuous improvisation in response to continuous change in local details. Designing replaces design.

(Weick, 2001, 88)

Cross-cultural 'competing' (or competence-building) replacing competence? Gerund replacing noun? Hybridizing and bastardizing our cultural 'ideoscapes' happens daily in our globally tele-broadcast media. Making organizations more flexible and improvisatory has already become the regular policy of most companies and institutions. Managing them with a learning and coaching approach in mind has already transformed the ideology of managerialism, smoothing out some of its authoritarian consequences and eroding its hierarchic core.[4] Between the Scylla of fundamentalist absolutism (there is only one Truth and one Priority) and a Charybdis of total relativism (anything goes), growing numbers of individuals are socialized into the world of multicultural experience and multicultural inequalities. Conflicts, to which these encounters and inequalities will inevitably lead, have to be tackled by cross-culturally competent individuals.

Are we educating them at our universities? Bringing them up in our virtual *agoras*? Socializing them into cross-cultural competence in our societies? Shaping with our theoretical inquiries? Are we aware of the fact that in measuring and comparing incommensurable values, we might, to use the words of Arjo Klamer (a Dutch economist whose chair in the economics of art and culture belongs to the very few interdisciplinary islands in the archipelago of research institutions) 'devalue the goods measured' (Klamer, 1996, 24)?[5]

After all, we live in an age of measurement and incommensurability. We live in an age of measurement, because we want to 'fit' knowledge produced for bureaucracies into a standard form that allows us to compare everything, including values. We live in an age of incommensurability, because values are embodied in many products of our culture, including the artistic and religious ones, and acts of measurement often destroy the very values they seek to measure.[6] We have to arrive at a 'parliament' of subcultures, where differences can be negotiated and options made transparent to the governments of passion and executive organizations shaped by power interests.

This, in the long run, is what cross-cultural competence is all about. It grows in the shadow of power and passion.

Notes

Introduction

1 The expression 'the view from manywheres' was introduced by Richard A. Schweder in his book devoted to the problems of cultural psychology with cross-cultural theoretical interests (cf. Schweder, 2003, iii).

1 The ends, means and meanings of culture: the language connection

1 The only categories in which Nobel prizes are granted are physics, chemistry, biology, medicine, and literature. In 1969 economics was added to the list, and some of the winners are either close to the qualitative critics of cultural bias in human behaviour (Amartya Sen and the questions of democracy, freedom and development) or developed concepts used within cognitive sciences, economics and the sciences of management (Herbert Simon and 'bounded rationality').

2 It comes as no surprise that the introduction to Lawrence's and Nohria's book has been written by E. O. Wilson, who closes it with the following words: 'Finally, the four-drive model will also be of interest to scholars because it has been conceived from an independent approach to the study of human nature. Its conception of broad instinctual categories can serve as a valuable reference point for future studies by both social scientists and biologists' (Lawrence, Nohria, 2002, xvi).

3 Geertz claims that there is an accelerated production of new paradigms and sub-specializations in the academic communities: 'Paradigms, wholly new ways of going about things, come along not by a century, but by the decade, sometimes, it almost seems, by the month' (Geertz, 2000, 188).

4 Schweder sharply observes that 'it would appear that the bygone and miscon-ceived idea of a reductive 'social physics' is going to be replaced with the fashionable new idea of a reductive 'social biology' based on a set of universal truths generated out of cognitive neuroscience, human genetics, biological anthropology, and a species-typifying cognitive psychology. (As an aside, the expression 'it is not rocket science' has not yet been replaced in popular discourse by such phrases as 'it is not brain science' or 'it is not genetic engineering'. Perhaps this is just a case of cultural lag and the popular recognition of a shift in scientific prestige from nuclear physics to microbiology is only a matter of time. Or perhaps the public is waiting to see whether the human genome project is going to realize its quite benevolent medical dreams or will turn out instead to be a eugenics nightmare or just a very expensive dead end' (Schweder, 2003, 299).

5 Hooker comments on the Wittgensteinian view of language, adding that 'cultural practices generally receive their meaning . . . the same way language does' (cf. Hooker, 2003, 70).

6 This linguistic turn in the philosophy of science, which prompted comparing all codes to natural languages, was prompted by the first linguistic revolution of the 1960s. It has been popularized by a fashionable school of theoretical thinking in social sciences and humanities, called 'structuralism', which urged the search for structural and formal analogies in diverse domains of life and culture studied by various disciplines. Interestingly enough, the social sciences were undergoing a second, less turbulent cognitive revolution in the 1990s, and the present quest for biochemical foundation of thought and behaviour in the quantitative social sciences is one of its manifestations.

7 'A necessary condition of functioning effectively in a second culture environment is to acquire relevant basic social skills through behavioural culture training, mentoring and learning about the historical, philosophical and socio-political foundations of the host society' (Ward, Bochner, Furnham, 2001, 271). The authors add: 'The content of the training curricula should be based on a job analysis of the KSAAs – the knowledge, skills, abilities and attitudes, required to function effectively in the destination cultures (ibid., 269).

8 The same author pleads for an interdisciplinary integration of psychological and anthropological research on culture understood as a process of meaning-making (psychological, symbolic) in a broader social context (sociological, anthropological), warning the academic puritans who refuse to mix with the representatives of other academic disciplines that 'we could never understand an individual's mind and ways of creating meaning outside its context, and we should assume essential differences in the respective processes from context to context' (Ross, 2004, 171).

9 'The West is seen, in effect, as having exclusive access to the values that lie at the foundation of rationality and reasoning, science and evidence, liberty and tolerance, and of course rights and justice' (Sen, 2000).

10 'Weber's *Wertrationalität* (rationality based on values, on interpreting ends rather than calculating means – SM), far from being expelled from a disenchanted world, remains part of our lifeworld, which cannot be reduced to the bargain-hunter's bazaar' (Archer, Tritter, 2000, 54).

11 Benjamin Lee Whorf had defined the purpose of linguistic inquiry as a quest for meaning, but the successes of structuralists in dealing with the grammar and phonetics of natural languages led to a serious disregard of the much more difficult semantic aspects of languages, which were not supportive of the 'mentalist' and 'cognitive' claims in science. A natural semantic meta-language (NSM) presents a rival paradigm in linguistics and has implications for the study of culture and the so-called 'cultural scripts' (cf. Anna Wierzbicka, 1997).

12 This tripartite division into science before 1940 (with the corporate laboratory as the primary location), science in the WWII and the Cold War (1940–80, with the research university as the top production facility), and science after 1980 (with industry hybrids working for global privatization), has been suggested by an economist and historian of science, Philip Mirowski (cf. Mirowski, 2003, 8).

13 Theories of cultural scripts seek to identify and compare norms regulating the expectations of members of cultures and organizations with respect to each other's verbal, intellectual and physical behaviour (speech, thought, action) and even their experiencing of emotions (there are scripts regulating being in romantic love, experiencing the loss of a close person, becoming angry or happy, etc.) This requires interdisciplinary co-operation with cognitive anthropology,

cross-cultural psychology, psychology, and sociology of culture, etc. Most of the relevant debates are presented in a block of periodicals, including *American Ethnologist, American Anthropologist, Journal of Linguistic Anthropology, Ethos, Culture and Psychology, World Psychology, Cognitive Science, Cognition and Emotion, Philosophica*, etc., and some are filtering into the mainstream managerial sciences (Kets de Vries, Yannis Gabriel, Burkhardt Sievers, Bart Nooteboom).

2 Clashing civilizations: the global connection

1 Robert O. Keohane, 2003, p. 131.
2 One does not have to be a representative of a particularly critical school of social or managerial studies, nor to prefer a qualitative approach in order to voice criticism of global inequalities. For instance, a quantitative researcher from a mainstream school of economics concludes his statistically based investigation of income inequalities between nation-states with the following comment: 'Latin America has so far grown with the largest excess inequality of all regions in the world. In fact, from this perspective, Latin America seems to be living in a distributional world of its own, acting as though it were on a completely different planet. As the likelihood is that all over the Third World political oligarchies would like to appropriate such a high share of national income, the key question that still needs to be answered is, why is it that it is only in Latin America that they manage to get away with it?' (Palma, 2003, 129).
3 Walsh quotes the British Prime Minister Harold MacMillan, who said in Strasbourg on 16 August 1950 that 'We have not overthrown the divine right of kings to fall down to the divine right of experts' (Walsh, 2003, 367).
4 The term 'political economy of attention' was introduced by the Austrian social geographer, Georg Franck (cf. Franck, 1998).
5 Samuel P. Huntington, 'The Hispanic Challenge', *Foreign Policy*, March/April 2004. Needless to say, the author claims that Mexicans, as African-Americans before them, lack the work ethic and have too-high fertility rates.
6 Paul Feyerabend, an *enfant terrible* of the Popperian circle of philosophers of science who introduced the extreme relativist principle 'anything goes' in order to demonstrate the ideological nature of research programmes in institutionalized science, argued that 'the knowledge we need to understand and to advance the sciences does not come from theories, it comes from participation' (Feyerabend, 1987, 284). Feyerabend quotes an Iranian scholar, Majid Rahnema, who claims that the overall effect of the expansion of modern educational bureaucracies has been to turn knowledge from a common good into an inaccessible and scarce commodity, thus implicitly reinforcing states and markets: 'Before the present school system came into being, for thousands of years education was not a scarce commodity. It was not a product of some institutional factories, the possession of which could bestow upon a person the right to be called 'educated'. . . . Now, only those certified by the school system, according to its self-devised criteria, could have the right to teach. Education thus became a scarcity' (ibid., 298).
7 Some authors would argue that the very concept of a 'global culture' is a non-sense: 'Culture refers to very local stuff – as in, those idols worshipped in a given temple, the crops grown in a specific field, the mind (or at best class of minds) educable in a given pedagogic practice, or the stuff that grows in this or that petri dish. To speak of "culture" in a global sense is to speak nonsense – particularly so when the culture in question is the purported totality of global cultures' (Lemert, 2003, 299). Lemert notes, quite correctly, that 'it was only very late in

the nineteenth century that the idea of "culture" as a sustained order of common intellectual habit came into use', and that even in the *Oxford English Dictionary* 'culture refers to very local stuff' – as in the passage quoted above in note 7.

8 In Pontecorvo's film *Quemada*, about a fictitious island in the Caribbean, a revolutionary leader of the oppressed black slaves emerges as a result of British intrigue against the Portuguese. When he refuses to accept a purely political change after victory and demands that economic exploitation also be terminated, he is captured and executed. On the night before his execution, while talking to a sympathetic British adventurer who helped him achieve his leader's status and offers him the last chance of escape, he describes the difference between his native culture and that of the 'white man': 'we know where we want to go, but we do not how to get there, while a white man knows how to get everywhere, but does not know where he wants to go'.

9 Ritzer quotes Georg Simmel, who was among the first European thinkers to observe the acceleration of cultural change (although he thought this change was limited to cultural forms and resembled a change of fashions more than a much more profound reshuffling of values and norms): 'Simmel is concerned with the "tragedy of culture", which for him involves the growing gap between subjective (the ability to create cultural products) and objective (those cultural products) culture. Because of the division of labour and the specialization of individuals, objective culture proliferates at an exponential rate while subjective culture grows little, if at all. The result (and the tragedy) is that people increasingly lose the ability even to understand, let alone control, the objective culture proliferating around them. Thus, Simmel depicts a world in which people are increasingly alienated from, and oppressed by, their objective culture' (Ritzer, 2004, 192).

10 One of my former Dutch students, the daughter of Turkish parents but born and raised in the Netherlands after their arrival in Rotterdam, has recently published a collection of essays on her uncertain identity, a 'me', who is torn between the Dutch 'we's' among whom she grew up and studied and the Turkish 'we's', represented by her parents and the relatives she met on holiday trips to Turkey. She recognizes the possibility of choice between the two and calls herself 'Dutch of the first generation', as opposed either to her parents, whom she calls 'allochtons' (by origin), or to those of her peers who have chosen to identify themselves by their Turkish origins, whom she refers to by the same name (albeit they are allochtons by choice, having turned against the possibility of assimilation and adaptation) (Umar, 2004).

11 Hofstede, interestingly enough, is a nominalist. According to him, theoretical concepts are useful fictions, artificial scaffolding to let us see and influence reality better (and to be rejected as soon as they outlived their usefulness). He often repeats (for instance in his response to criticism expressed by McSweeney) that culture does not exist, nor do values: 'they are constructs, which have to prove their usefulness by their ability to explain and predict behaviour' (Hofstede, 2002, 91–2). Moreover, he outlines an interesting possibility of differentiating between culturally defined ends and means: 'The practical consequences of the fact that the national culture components relate primarily to values, the organizational component to practices, are far reaching. Values (as we measured them) are hardly changeable (they change, but not according to anybody's intentions), while practices can be modified – given sufficient management attention' (ibid.).

12 Hofstede is quoted only once in this volume of contributions to a project sponsored by Harvard University's Academy for International and Area Studies, namely by Daniel Etounga-Manguelle, the president and founder of the Société

Africaine d'Etude, d'Exploitation et de Gestion (SADEG), a former member of the World Bank's Council of African Advisors. He is the author of the study, which poses a rhetorical question in the title: 'L'Afrique – a-t-elle Besoin d'un Programme d'Adjustement Culturel?' Etounga-Manguelle quotes Hofstede's French book (Bollinger, Hofstede, 1987) and concludes that 'If Europe, that fragment of earth representing a tiny part of humanity, has been able to impose itself on the planet, dominating it and organizing it for its exclusive profit, it is only because it developed a conquering culture of rigour and work, removed from the influence of invisible forces. We must do the same' (Etounga-Manguelle, 2000, 77).

13 Even within the 'Western' scientific and scholarly communities there is a subtle difference in status assigned to various national contributions, which boils down to a ranking of German, French, Italian, and Spanish, and other theoretical contributions below those by the Anglo-Americans, a process tackled only marginally by social scientists (cf. Lamont, 1992; Lamont, Thevenot, 2000).

14 In an autobiographical note on his own values, Hofstede writes: 'I completed a university education in the Netherlands and after that worked for half a year incognito as an industrial worker; thus I learned to some extent how an organization looks from below. I am a Protestant Christian but do not claim absolute truth for my faith; I know too well how conditioned we all are by our cultural environment. I believe in the equality to God of all mankind, and my image of an ideal world is one without fear (Hofstede, 2001, 523–4).

15 'Findings from new research based on a sample of students at leading European business schools indicate a significant convergence of national values. The four value dimensions of Hofstede were used as the basis of the research. The findings show a number of important differences between male and female students, raising the question whether divisions of gender are more important than those of country. Italian and Swedish women, for example, may have more in common with each other than with their fellow males' (Gooderham, Noordhaug, 2002). One should note, however, that the sample of respondents in Gooderham and Nordhaug's study were all MBA students. Perhaps this student population has already become so standardized and 'prefabricated' that their national backgrounds have been pushed back in identities constructed with future global assignments and multinational employers in mind. However, although more convincing arguments would be needed to question Hofstede's framework, the argument about gradual convergence along gender or age lines requires more systematic attention from the research community.

16 Cf. Joinson, 2003, 186. Joinson suggests that socializing rather than marketing is the core function of the internet: 'In a comparison of the revenues of content and network providers, Odlyzko argues that although content may be glamorous, it is not the key to financial success. For instance, the US telephone industry (providing connectivity rather than content) had revenues of $256.1 billion in 1997. In comparison, the whole of the US motion picture industry had revenues of $63 billion. While Odlyzko is not arguing that connectivity is the largest part of the US economy, he does point out that people tend to spend more on connectivity than on content' (ibid., 187, cf. also Odlyzko, 2001).

17 'A true understanding of the logic of another culture includes comprehension of relationships among values and how values relate to one another in a given context' (Osland, Bird, 2000, 70). These authors introduce the concept of 'value trumping' to describe a conscious decision to revise the hierarchy of values in a given context: 'Schemas reflect the underlying reality of cultural values. For example, people working for US managers who have a relaxed and casual style,

and who openly share information and provide opportunities to make independent decisions, will learn specific scripts for managing in this fashion. The configuration of values embedded in this management style consists of informality, honesty, equality, and individualism. At some point, however, these same managers may withhold information about a sensitive personnel situation because privacy, fairness and legal concerns would trump honesty and equality in this context. This trumping action explains why the constellation of values related to specific schema is hierarchical' (ibid., 71).

18 'In their individualism they see identity as culture, in their organizationalism they see culture as identity. For individuals, the unique convergence of artificial systems in the person yields personal identity. For organizations, corporate identity is dispersed in artificial systems that converge nowhere. Thus, the organization is no longer endowed with a psyche, but is seen as a culture in which the identities of members are dispersed and out of which those identities are partially constructed. . . . Because they are at home in networks and shifting relationships, and because they value what they do over where they do it, they see any particular organization as only a temporary node in a larger network or as a subplot in a larger narrative – and they are always prepared to change positions in the network or to find another subplot they feel more comfortable in. For them, legitimacy is an ongoing daily construction, and they are ever ready to heed the siren call – from whatever source' (Leinberger, Tucker, 1991, 406, 415).

19 Rejmar quotes Grzymała Moszczyńska, who has applied Berry's model of acculturation according to which individuals exposed to another culture or growing up in a multicultural environment usually adopt one of the four dominating acculturation strategies: assimilation (rejection of the old culture, acceptance of the new one); integration (both cultures preserved); separation (rejection of the new culture, sticking to the old one); and marginalization (placing oneself outside the mainstream of both cultures) (cf. Berry, 1990).

20 While humanism (a disinterestedly friendly and helpful attitude), materialism (instrumental rationality, profit-driven), collectivism (the group interest comes first), and liberalism (individual independence of traditions and tolerance for innovation, in sex and morality also) are easy to comprehend, 'sarmatism' is a particularly Polish dimension, named after the mythological ideology of the Polish gentry, which found its legendary roots in a nomadic tribe of Sarmatians (a tribe of this name actually did exist in pre-Greek times, but had little in common with later inhabitants of central-northern Europe). Boski defines 'sarmatism' as 'resentment and distrust of those who succeed, anarchistic interpretation of liberties, low co-operativeness, and excessive hedonism' (Boski, 1992).

3 Networking organizations: the management connection

1 Inglis addresses the issue of the intricate interplay of culture and politics: 'The deep difficulty with culture . . . is its all-or-nothingness. The corresponding exigency of politics is its collapsing absolutely everything in front of power. Make a fetish out of power and all you can stand on is the powerlessness of principle: do the same with culture and your only principle is one of moral super-ciliousness. Politics is the practical business of societies, and power only one of its quantities. Culture is the evaluative activity of everyday life, and efficacy is not really an issue. Let us say that culture may operationally be defined as dominant-values-plus-explanatory system' (Inglis, 2004, 163).

2 Helen Prejean lost her case, both in the individual action for parole for a particular prisoner from a death row and in collective mobilization of public support for abolishing the death penalty. In most states of the US, the death penalty is in place and is applied on a regular basis. An interesting example of a culture clash connected to this issue emerged in an avant-garde campaign of Benetton's advertising genius, Olivier Toscani, who photographed inmates of death row and posted their images outside Benetton outlets in Sears' stores in the US. Families of the victims of these inmates were outraged both by the publicity for convicted murderers and by the instrumental management of these images for advertising purposes. As a result, Sears cancelled the deal with Benetton and closed their outlets in Sears' chain stores in the US. Taking risks in games of cultural sophistication and provoking moral outrage does not always make good business sense (though it did in Toscani's previous billboard campaigns, which were also provocative in playing with religious and moral values, for instance depicting a priest and a nun kissing passionately, and a black stallion mounting a white mare – all this on giant billboards advertising Benetton in large cities).

3 There is a tendency in contemporary social sciences to attribute at least some forms of intelligent human behaviour to our biological and evolutionary 'roots', i.e. to the collective experience already observed in animal societies, cf. *Machiavellian Intelligence* (Byrne, Whiten, 1990) or their follow-up study (Byrne, Whiten, 1997). The problem with these attempts to ground an evolutionary explanation of brain development and explain cognitive skills via socio-biological theories listing the neural consequences of all collective behaviour of a herd species, is that they are reductionist. It does not suffice to say that the human intellect develops because we acquire social expertise (with the core skill of subtle manipulation of others within a social group), and to reduce 'the social' to interactions within a collective of physical, material, biological individuals. Machiavellian ideas have been found in all animal societies where the power struggle is intense. However, only a human wrote *The Prince*. Machiavellian ideas have been found in all human civilizations (cf. the writings of Lao-Tze or the book of Arteshastra). However, only in one did his book receive a sequel, *On War* by von Clauswitz, which sought to translate Machiavelli's theory of the acquisition of individual power into a theory explaining the acquisition of power in a world of modern corporations and organizations. Socio-cultural determinants of these developments can hardly be explained by referring to attempts to ground all explanations in the competitive nature of organisms in group life. Attempts to deduce ethics from socio-biological mechanisms appear to be a rejuvenated form of social Darwinism or E. O. Wilson's version of sociobiology, rather than any genuine breakthrough in understanding organizational behaviour and managerial influences upon it.

4 This pragmatic twist to the concept of value as if it allowed us to translate meanings into action by adding emotional and political 'push' to the cognitive content (meanings) is an interesting new development in theoretical approaches to culture prompted by managerial concerns.

5 Pierre Bourdieu introduced the concept of generalized cultural capital in order to explain the class differences not only in economic property and political power but also cultural sophistication. Bourdieu's famous study *La distinction. Critique sociale du judgement* has been translated – quite tellingly – into German as *Die feine Unterschiede* or 'subtle differences', but in fact the differences he is studying are not so subtle – they are linked to classes, not organizations, as the basic differentiating and identifying factor in social life, although they are, indeed, much more subtle than the crude Marxist idea that cultural production

reflects the class position of the sponsors and controllers of social processes, and thus always produces ideological justification for class domination on the part of the capital owners, while de-legitimizing the attempts of the working class at resistance and revolutionary mobilization.

6 One of my MA students conducted a similar project in one of the regional police corps in the Netherlands, and her results coincide with the results reported by her German colleagues (cf. Han, 2003).

7 The expression 'bureaucracy-lite' is ambiguous. It points out a tendency to avoid an impression of inefficient and overstaffed public service, while preserving accountability and line of command.

8 *Neue Steuerungsmodell* as a blueprint for the modernization of public administration in Germany. This model aims to restructure the relationship between city councils and the administration: less micro management on the part of the city councils, more discretion and more leverage for the administration. Goal attainment, performance and quality were increasingly subject to control on the basis of performance and cost–quality indicators, along with other data collected by a professional controlling body (Jacobs *et al.*, 2004, 11).

9 The authors conclude that in future inquiries into the management of change one should focus on research 'that integrates the mundane aspects, the daily mistakes and obstacles of change projects' and which 'is both necessary and timely given the spread of projects from a traditional engineering context to a variety of different contexts including, increasingly, non-profit and governmental organizations. Second, we argue that the social and behavioural aspects of change projects, which are often relegated to a secondary position behind technical and managerial aspects, should gain more prominence in studies of change management projects' (Jacobs *et al.*, 2004, 3–4). Their conclusions coincide with the mounting criticism of methodological individualism and rational choice theory grounded in a biologically interpreted 'code' of individual human conduct. Arguing for the evolutionary origins of altruism and methodological falsehood of individualistic assumptions of the Prisoner's Dilemma, the author of a recent book on altruism and reciprocity in the behavioural sciences claims in a conclusion entitled 'The invisible hand and the blind watchmaker' that: 'At the bedrock of universal culture, as at the bedrock of universal grammar, we find evolutionarily designed *hardwiring*. In both cases, cognitive modularity is central to understanding the functioning of these legacies, and in the former case, and perhaps the latter, group selection is a necessary mechanism in this design process. In both cases, historical explanation begins *earlier*, in delineating the evolutionary processes that produced the human genome' (Field, 2004, 331).

10 Cf. http://www.pearsonreidlondonhouse.com/ccai/ccaiproduct.htm The Cross Cultural Adaptability Inventory is offered in sets composed of a manual, a self-assessment set, action-planning guide, multi-rater kit, facilitator's guide, and a 'cultural passport to anywhere'. Colleen Kelley and Judith Meyers are identified as authors but no dates are given. The cost of the preview package is $52.00 and the total cost of a complete package is $170.85.

11 'Change without pain' is not a fictitious title; a book with that title has actually been written by Eric Abrahamson and subtitled 'How Managers Can Overcome Initiative Overload, Organizational Chaos, and Employee Burnout' (Abrahamson, 2004). Among the tips he gives are 'Encourage a culture of homogeneous diversity' or 'For an organization to have the capacity to recombine itself, it has to be made of subcultures bound together by common culture. That is, it must balance within itself the opposite poles of strong homogeneity and diversity. The cultural diversity encourages the creation of

the varied elements to be combined, whereas the homogeneity makes the combinations possible' (Abrahamson, 2004, 196). Generally speaking, the author looks at culture from the perspective of the genetic metaphor and wants his change master to be a master *recombiner* of cultural 'genes' – cloning, customizing and translating corporate culture, destroying the old one and recombining its elements with the new one, and making sure it is expressed in behavioural norms.

12 The fact that power issues are conspicuously absent has often been remarked, but little has been done to remedy it, as if this taboo was still being very strongly enforced. As Jeffrey Pfeffer once noted: 'Power has a bad name in social sciences and is most often conspicuous by its absence from literature. It is not just Williamson (e.g. Williamson and Ouchi, 1981) who has critiqued the concept and argued that it was neither necessary nor useful for understanding organiz-ations. Courses about power and influence in schools of administration started only in the late 1970s and still exist in comparatively few institutions. . . . Although power may have always been important and certainly is becoming more so as hierarchical bases of authority erode under the environmental changes described above, power as an idea does not fit very well with either our conception of organizations and individuals as being rational utility and efficiency maximizers or with our social values that emphasize cooperation and deemphasize inequality in the access to social resources' (Pfeffer, 1997, 137).

13 The media were even more dramatic. An advertisement in the international press showed a man fishing on a frozen lake – fishing for 'Nordic' ideas for Nordea. The caption was: 'Believe it or not, this man is busy harvesting our greatest natural resource, and it isn't fish – it's ideas. . . . We are the reflection of our region and its most important natural resource, ideas. We bring a clear Nordic outlook and approach to the market places of the world. We are looking forward to doing business with you . . . the Nordic way' (Søderberg, Vaara, 2003, 153),

14 Steven Fuller has observed that the new domain of knowledge management still displays the ancient Greek uncertainty as to the leading metaphor about acquiring knowledge: a military/aristocratic or an industrial/plebeian/bourgeois one. The military metaphor sees knowledge as a clearly defined goal, while the industrial one sees knowledge as something that is 'perpetually generated and accumulated, so that, as with money, one can never have enough of it. . . . Knowledge managers attempt to reinvent the military side of the military–industrial metaphor. But now the material stakes are higher than they have ever been, and what it means "to do most with the least" has accordingly become more complicated. There are opportunities here both for an intelligent democ-ratization of inquiry and a mindless "natural selection" of knowledge producers and products' (Fuller, 2002, 253).

15 This belief that a laptop computer plus a mobile phone with global satellite connections will deliver to us a more egalitarian society full of entrepreneurial individuals co-operating in flexible networks smoothly evolving around successive creative developments curiously echoes a cruel illusion of Lenin, who had declared that communism is the power of the workers' and peasants' councils plus electrification of the country. What makes them similar is an underlying Marxian belief that history moves like a layer-cake: first material technologies are 'baked' in the ovens of history, and when they emerge, political systems jump on the bandwagon and adjust to their power, pumping new energy to the lower social classes, curbing some of the privileges of the higher ones, and finally we recognize in our thinking what has happened and replace some

ideological illusions (which served the former power elites) with new ones (which serve the new power elites). What makes them different is that Lenin believed he had a blueprint for a perfect political organization (party–state dictatorship), while most representatives of the theories of network societies and organizations consider organizational forms to be evolutionary outcomes of attempts to adapt complex, co-ordinated activities to changing technological, social, political, cultural, and other environments.

16 This paradox may, of course, also be expressed in the less egalitarian metaphor of an expensive slave. A highly trained Air Force mechanic, although a private in the military hierarchy of ranks, cannot be randomly bossed around by an officer, who is meticulously instructed to ensure that his mechanics are not only physically fit but also psychologically balanced before carrying out maintenance on extremely expensive fighter jets (so that an element of coaching and assessment of psychological well-being drives up the quality of the working life of this mechanic, even though the military bureaucracy is one of the paragons of hierarchical organizations).

17 Boisot also thinks that technological optimism should be tempered, and adds: 'Our earlier discussion of convergence cautions against viewing network capitalism as an "attractor", a stable institutional order towards which both industrialized Western firms and Chinese family firms will be propelled by the imperatives of information technology'. As we saw in the previous chapter, it is at best one transactional option among others in modern capitalism's ever-evolving institutional repertoire.

18 Almost as an afterthought, in the last paragraph of the last chapter of his book, Holden writes of practitioners and knowledge officers, and introduces the concept of a 'domain specialist', someone 'whose real worth lies not just in interpreting (knowledge), but in making it convertible; that means appreciating its utility and relevance to users' existing knowledge domains. It seems logical that, as companies become more knowledge-based, they will increasingly need domain specialists. There is little doubt that when it comes to the cross-cultural transfer of knowledge, the issue of convertibility is paramount. This is where real value gets added to knowledge, where knowledge gets its competitive edge, where cross-cultural management can come into its own' (Holden, 2002, 309). One wonders what a 'domain specialist' would do if confronted with the possibility of establishing a Napster-like project in an average business company. Clearly, the convertibility of MP3 technology into a mass 'free lunch' for young, cash-starved audiences would be dealt with in a way that probably could not be classified as the restrained and patient stimulation of further learning processes.

19 'In an emergency situation, we use as much as possible a RFQ process. In the RFQ the response times are indicated. Suppliers know that they have to respond quickly. Sometimes the first faxes are returned within two hours. But in a rush, they just pick a supplier we know or one that has the items readily available' (Verduijn, 2004, 196).

20 'Besides the uncertainty related to the occurrence of disasters, there is a very high level of uncertainty because of limited and incomplete information on the actual situations and the needs. Information on the needs for specific relief items may change during the course of the operations. This is due to the quality and speed of the assessment process or (changes in) decisions made by local and national authorities. Other uncertainties are related to the unavailability of relief items. For some items, like tents, there are only a limited number of suppliers with limited stocks and capacity. In the preparation for the Iraq crisis, the UNCHR

bought the total production capacity of tents in Pakistan, which is the main supplier of tents in the world. The IFRC&RC was forced to find another solution and finally obtained tents from the stocks of the Iranian Red Crescent' (Verduijn, 2004, 199).

21 Pfeffer goes further than most representatives of managerial studies, because he does not shy away from mentioning the political and historical environment: 'The study of power was particularly vigorous in the early 1970s – a time at which both strategic contingencies (Hickson *et al.*, 1971) and resource dependence (Pfeffer and Salancik, 1978) perspectives developed. The 1970s was a particularly political period, comprising both the end of the Vietnam War and the associated political protests and the resignation of Richard Nixon as a consequence of the Watergate scandal. The 1980s and 1990s have been much more politically quiescent; this fact, coupled with a sometimes difficult job market, may also have made power and influence less likely to be subjects of as much research attention' (Pfeffer, 1977, 155).

22 Cf. my book *Class Struggle in Classless Poland*, which I published under the pseudonym Stanislaw Starski in Boston in January 1982, just a month after martial law was introduced in Poland in an unsuccessful attempt to prolong the communists' hold on power: 'The element which matters most in this world of nation-states and power blocks is the patient and bloodless reconstruction of political systems. . . . All liberation tactics of the present period – be it cultural revolution of the students and the young, be it a women's liberation movement or a leftist political struggle against the establishment's vested interests – all these appear within *Solidarity* and all of them rightly recognized the state owned by the ruling class as the major enemy of social development and the increase of social justice, political freedom and economic democracy. . . . This was the spirit of the Polish workers, students, peasants, of all strata of the Polish society which understood that they form a class of state employees exploited by the class of state owners' (Starski, 1982, 242).

23 This astonishing lack of symmetry between the de-Nazification of Germany and the long overdue de-communization of Russia enables representatives of the former Soviet secret services, for instance the current president, Putin, to deny genocide altogether. He closed investigations into the Katyn massacre of 22,000 Polish officers and prisoners of war, and declared that killing them on Stalin's orders was not an act of genocide. He said this to the visiting Polish president Kwasniewski in late September 2004. Denying genocide allows Putin to continue it, though this time under the ideological cover of a war on terrorism – for instance in Chechnya. By doing so, Putin is demonstrating the serious consequences of the relative neglect of power issues. His management of a post-Yeltsin Russian turn-around from market-oriented to autocratic state-centred society, recently illustrated with the destruction of the economic oligarchs, definitely deserves investigation as a case study in the accumulation of power.

24 For a fascinating discussion of the reasons for this asymmetry between the condemnation of Nazism and absence of moral condemnation of Soviet genocide and geopolitics, see a book written by Martin Amis about his father, Kingsley Amis. The older Amis had flirted with communism and even belonged to the Communist Party in spite of his knowledge of the Soviet genocide (6–8 million Ukrainian victims of artificial famine in the 1930s remain unacknowledged, while 22,000 Polish prisoners of war shot in 1940 have been recognized as victims of a mass murder ordered by Stalin, though Putin openly refuses to acknowledge this massacre as an act of genocide). Martin Amis's book about the

Soviet Union as a giant prison system is entitled *Koba the Dread. Laughter and the Twenty Million*, Koba being the Party pseudonym of Dzugashvilli before he became Joseph Stalin, and the 20 million referring to the victims of the Soviet terror after 1917 (cf. Amis, 2004). Three generations of naïve Western intellectual supporters of the cause of this criminal state are presented: first, the generation of those who went to the Soviet Union in the 1920s and 1930s, claiming that they 'have seen the future and it works' (H. G. Wells, G. B. Shaw); second, those who did so in the 1940s (Martin's father, Kingsley); and third, those of Martin Amis' own generation, like the former Trotskyist and the present columnist of *The Atlantic*, Christopher Hitchens.

25   The quotation has been taken from Sheldon Wolin's essay 'Fugitive Democracy', published in the volume edited by Seyla Benhabib and entitled *Democracy and Difference* (cf. after Keenan, 2003, 144). Wolin makes another remark that is essential for understanding the organizing and managing processes in a democratic society: 'Individuals who concert their powers for . . . a thousand other common concerns of ordinary lives are experiencing a democratic moment and contributing to the discovery, care and tending of commonality of shared concerns. Without necessarily intending it, they are renewing the political by contesting the forms of unequal power that democratic liberty and equality have made possible and that democracy can eliminate only by betraying its own values. . . . what is truly at stake politically: heterogeneity, diversity, and multiple selves are no match for modern forms of power' (Wolin, 1996, 44).

26   Transco is the fictitious name given by Casper Hoedemaekers to a public transport company, according to an agreement he had reached with it before conducting his research and interviewed the controllers employed through a temp agency for the purpose of this single project of manned entrance controls.

27   Interestingly enough, the intuitive understanding of TV's social significance by Marshall McLuhan is echoed by contemporary theoreticians of the virtual organization, who make use of ethnographic and discourse-analytic studies of organizational life. They note that with contemporary information and communication technologies, a much more precise record of 'who said what' at company meetings becomes available, which in turn modifies corporate communications, for instance, verbal behaviour at meetings: 'Recollections of past events by participants are treated as accounts, which are structured in accord with the speaker's current interests and objectives. Groupware thoroughly impacts upon the ability of participants to generate accounts in this way. The potential to provide a more complete record of the meeting, for example, makes it increasingly difficult for participants to provide alternative interpretations of what actually happened (or, at least, interpretations that can be presented and accepted as a valid account of what happened). It would seem that participants cannot refer, in general terms, to "the main thrust of the argument" presented in a meeting, or the "underlying tone of the discussion" (and thereby make the meeting's decisions more fluid and amenable to their own ends), when anyone can call up the full record of what was "said" and reinterpret it themselves' (Lilley, Lightfoot, Amaral, 2004, 123–4).

28   Czarniawska writes: 'New interpretations tend to be called misunderstandings. In time, some of these interpretations may win over others and acquire legitimacy; a new order is established and the information becomes predictable. Temporarily, however, meaning and information are opposed to each other. It is ambiguity that makes the world go on; perfect information is redundant. George Steiner takes this reasoning to the extreme, claiming that mistranslation is the cause of human creativity. The Tower of Babel is a frustrating situation but, he

says, perhaps the right way of managing such a situation is pidgin rather than Pentecost (Steiner, 1975/1992, 495).

29 In a call for papers for the Critical Organization Theory track of the 15th annual SCMOI or Standing Conference for Management and Organization Inquiry (Philadelphia, 7–9 April 2005), David Boje announced the Bachtin on-line dictionary of critical dialogism and quotes the Russian literary scholar approvingly: 'Individual consciousness is not the architect of the ideological superstructure, but only a tenant lodging in the social edifice of ideological signs' (cf. www.peaceware.com/scmoi/CriticalOrgTheoryTrack.htm).

30 Alvesson distinguishes between culture and discourse by defining more narrowly the role of language in producing culture and claiming that organizational reality cannot be reduced to the sheer act of linguistic utterance, since 'discourse can often be seen as expressing/revealing "deeper" meanings that have been developed over time and have "been there" prior to a particular linguistic act' (Alvesson, 2004, 331). Discourse is defined by Alvesson as 'specific use of language structuring a chunk of the world in a particular way. Discourse frames and constitutes identity and elements in subjectivity through specific communicative acts and thus expresses micro power' (ibid.). Alvesson uses the concept of 'micro' power (interactive at the individual level) as opposed to a macro or a structural power (constraints imposed by class differences and organizational hierarchies), derived from Foucault.

31 Tietze *et al.* quote Jackson and Carter (Jackson, Carter, 2000) to support their point about discourse analysis: 'Jackson and Carter's analysis elucidates our point that knowledge must not be thought of as natural or objective. Instead, it is mediated through different discourses, reflecting the interests and values of particular groups and institutions. However, such is the pervasiveness of these discourses that they appear to be "true" ' (Tietze, Cohen, Musson, 2003, 83).

32 Anecdotal evidence suggests that the description of a given national culture as 'Southern European' expresses the feeling of the superiority of 'the North'. While Germans may condescendingly regard the Austrians as being close cultural cousins of Italians or Greeks, Austrians themselves do not shy away from this term. Inhabitants of 'better' quarters of Vienna apply the same condescending term to the poorer, 'southern' housing areas, known for a high concentration of working class and immigrant population. Though not all of these areas are technically 'southern', the well-to-do Viennese used to say that south of the Danube one already steps into the Balkans.

33 Kainzbauer proffers the suggestion (backed by her comparative studies of the German and British educational systems) that the attitudes of German and British management trainees have been shaped by their respective national educational systems. Her suggestion accords with the concept of national business recipes and the comparative analysis of national clusters of high-tech companies, public authorities and top research universities by Richard Whitley (cf. Whitley, 2000; Morgan, Whitley, Moen, 2005). Kainzbauer sees differences between national educational systems as the sources of both German problem-orientation ('how come that things are this way') and British behaviour-orientation ('what to do in order to achieve this'). She quotes Schroll-Machl: 'Universities in Germany put a lot of emphasis on teaching theoretical knowledge. For the exams, the students often have to learn from long lists of specialist literature. The British system, on the other hand, stresses the practical approach to imparting knowledge. During the semester groups of students have to solve a number of case studies, and their grades usually combine exam results, presentations and case studies' (Kainzbauer, 2002).

4 Creative communication: the multimedia connection

1 In a personal communication (an outline of a public lecture entitled 'Every Picture Tells a Story – Losing the Plot in the Era of the Image'), Yannis Gabriel expressed his concern about some of the consequences of a shift towards visual information, iconic messages and new multimedia in the following way: 'The attempt to read a story in every image or indeed any meaningful text is symptomatic of an era which has lost its ability to tell and listen to stories. This is what I shall describe as narrative deskilling. Narrative deskilling involves the inability to develop individualized characters and plots, and the equation of every sensory image, stimulus or text with a story' (Gabriel, 2004, 1). It is clear that Gabriel directs his criticism towards the entire 'era' and not to any particular group of professionals who are linked to the media. However, the deskilling in question would have to be detected primarily in those groups who structure the 'sound-bites' and 'image-bites' for general media consumption. One is tempted to interpret the emergence of the New Journalism in the early 1970s in the US as a manifestation of such deskilling, which might also be interpreted as reskilling and gearing to the new, much more visually intensive media (as, for instance, with Tom Wolfe and Hunter S. Thompson).

2 In a chapter entitled 'Joyce, Light and the Road to Digiculture', a contemporary critic (and a former collaborator) of McLuhan, Donald F. Theall, develops the thesis that the present digiculture had already been prepared for by the avant-garde art and literature of the late 19th and the first half of the 20th century. While his reflections are interesting in their own right, they are too detailed for the present discussion of the influence the new alliance of culture and technology has exerted through the new media on prevailing organizational forms. However, a reader interested in following Theall's analysis would do well to consider the following passage: 'The experiments of artistic avant-garde movements such as the Dadaists, the Bauhaus, and the Constructivists, among others, and of individuals such as Duchamp, Klee, Eisenstein, or Louis Buñuel generated exploration of the semiotics and technical effects of multidimensional spaces and times and multi-sensory involvements. . . . The road to MIT's Media Lab and to cyberculture begins with this poetic and artistic experimentation in the late nineteenth and early twentieth century' (Theall, 2001, 176–7).

3 This strange mix of the emotional and cultural ideology of romanticism and the cult of modern information and communication technology has rightly been observed and critically traced in Western cultural traditions by Richard Coyne, who writes: 'For romanticism, the yearning is for unity with nature, the whole, freedom and creativity. For a technoromantic, it is for such a degree of absorption into technology that not only the body but technology is transcended. The electronic matrix is something greater than the contingencies of individual components, their physicality and their failings. We become one with each other and with our machines' (Coyne, 1999, 67).

4 Manovich characterizes the Sapir–Whorf hypothesis of different 'spectacles' offered by natural languages as the idea of a 'non-transparency of the code', by which he means that a native speaker of a natural language cannot perceive the difference between his or her word matrix and the matrix of a speaker of a foreign language without going 'out' of the original 'mental cage' of the native speaker's own language. Interestingly enough, Manovich mentions McLuhan's theory of the media as an example of a cultural theory that relies on the 'non-transparency of the code'. The issue is interesting, but far too complex for our purposes (as is Manovich's comparison of the Sapir–Whorf hypothesis with Derrida's logo-

centrism or Lakoff's cognitivism). Therefore let us limit ourselves to some brief remarks on McLuhan. Manovich refers to McLuhan's famous declaration that 'the medium is the me(a)ssage' (spelled in the 1970s with a pun on 'massage'), which suggested that the real 'message' of the new media (McLuhan thought mainly of radio and TV) is not what they say but how they change us and the societies in which they emerge. This is how he interprets the emergence of computer-aided communications in the light of 'the medium is the message' principle: 'The [human–computer] interface shapes how the computer user conceives of the computer itself. It also determines how users think of any media object accessed via computer. Stripping different media of their original distinction, the interface imposes its own logic on them. Finally, by organizing computer data in particular ways, the interface provides distinct models of the world. For instance, a hierarchical file system assumes that the world can be organized in a logical multilevel hierarchy. In contrast, a hypertext model of the World Wide Web arranges the world as a non-hierarchical system ruled by metonymy. In short, far from being a transparent window into the data inside a computer, the interface brings with it strong messages of its own' (Manovich, 2001, 65).

5 Metaphors of mirrors, windows and frames, given different twists of theoretical meaning in contemporary art theory (for instance in John Szarkowski's famous distinction between artistic photographs as either mirrors or windows reflecting the objective world or windows opening unique creative insights of artists to a mass audience), are quite common. In film theory all three have been used by Vivian Sobchack. (cf. Sobchack, 1992)

6 The reference to 'barely tamed wild and dangerous impulses which surface in moments of crisis' has been repeated a number of times, but the explanation of this sudden psychoanalytical twist among international students of management in Rotterdam is actually quite simple. The question explicitly referred to the ideological–political and biological–psychological interpretation of the film: 'What do you think the title *Underground* stands for? Is it a basic metaphor for non-democratic systems, for the skilful manipulation of war memories by the ruling class, or for barely tamed wild and dangerous human impulses, which surface in moments of crisis?'

7 Some of the critics noticed that the film is highly 'biased' and unrealistic. The extremist views and extreme intolerance displayed by some members of the jury in both versions of the film would have eliminated them in the process of selection. Moreover, it would have been very unlikely, even in the 1950s, to find a jury, especially in the case of a Latino youth, that would have been all white and all male. Others point out that the juror who finally changes the minds of all the others is actually replacing the defence attorney, and uses demagogic tricks (for instance purchasing a knife very similar to the one with which the victim had been murdered, or staging a 're-enactment' of some of the presumed events on the scene in order to prove that an old man could not have walked from his bed to the door in time as short as declared by him at the witness stand). Nevertheless, the dynamic action and dramatic clash of characters and their prejudices makes most of the viewers forget these critical concerns and reservations.

8 Interestingly enough, when the film appeared, it was not a commercial success. However, it was a modest *succes d'estime*, since it was nominated for three Academy Awards (Best Picture, Best Director, Best Adapted Screenplay), without winning any of them (all were collected by David Lean's *Bridge on the River Kwai*, which tends to be largely of historical interest today).

9 European philosophers and sociologists, of whom Jürgen Habermas is one of the best-known representatives, often interpret contemporary changes in social,

economic and political relations as a continuation of a grand project for the re-engineering of society that had emerged in the European Enlightenment. The industrial revolution in Great Britain, the French and American political revolutions (liberty, equality and fraternity), and the explosive growth of modern science – all these developments are deemed to belong to the consequences of the Enlightenment project that introduced the ideology of 'liberty, equality and fraternity' for all citizens. At the time the script of *Twelve Angry Men* was being written, both the Soviet communists and US capitalists claimed to be the legitimate heirs to the Enlightenment legacy, with the Soviets stressing economic equality and the Americans – political liberty.

10 The role of the Cold War in shaping the ideological, methodological and sociological aspects of contemporary academic institutions is only slowly being reconstructed in historical studies of the 1945–89 period of relative geopolitical stability. The reconstruction of the hidden injuries of the Cold War in contemporary science can also be found in the other areas of culture, for instance, in the arts. Historical studies of the performing arts and of the role of McCarthyism in policing Hollywood are slow in coming, but they point to a similar process of conservative engineering of 'political correctness', which makes the leftist liberal political correctness of the 1980s or 1990s pale by comparison. *Twelve Angry Men* can be interpreted today as a shot in the battle for cultural supremacy in the Cold War period, because it demonstrates the supreme wisdom of randomly chosen ordinary men, who, if the institutions they function in are democratic, can make truth prevail, even if it involves considerable effort and humiliation on their part.

11 Buchanan quotes a definition of social capital provided by Fukuyama in his study of trust: 'a capability that arises from prevalence of trust in a society or in certain parts of it. It can be embodied in the smallest and most basic social group, the family, as well as the largest of all groups, the nation, and in all other groups in between. Social capital differs from other forms of human capital in so far as it is usually created and transmitted through cultural mechanisms like religion, tradition or historical habit' (Fukuyama, 1995, 26).

Conclusion: managing cross-cultural competence

1 Latour is quite clear that he does not accept the 'chains' in which the disciplines of science are kept because of their false beliefs in heavily biased philosophies of science. He thinks that the academic community of practice has to liberate itself from these chains: 'The word "collective" itself at last finds its meaning; it is that, which *collects us all* in the cosmopolitics envisaged by Isabelle Stengers. Instead of two powers, one hidden and indisputable (nature), and the other disputable and despised (politics), *we will have two different tasks in the same collective.* The first task will be to answer the question; How many humans and nonhumans are to be taken into account? The second will be to answer the most difficult of all questions; Are you ready, and at the price of what sacrifice, to live the good life together? That this highest of political and moral questions could have been raised, for so many centuries, by so many bright minds, for *humans only* without nonhumans that make them up, will soon appear, I have no doubt, as extravagant as when the Founding Fathers denied slaves and women the vote' (Latour, 1999, 297).

2 Tyler Cowen argues in his treatise on the cultural blessings of globalization that local cultures do not become 'dumbed down' to the lowest denominator by audiovisual 'Americanization', but that they become reinvigorated because of

frequent cross-cultural hybridization. He opens his book with a quote from the chairman of the Australian Film Commission, who said that 'A country that makes a film like *Star Wars* deserves to rule the world' (cf. Cowen, 2002). This would suggest a recognition of the dominant position of the American culture in modern media. On the other hand, Cowen closes his study with a cosmopolitan, supranational credo: 'Cosmopolitanism is a secret account of our numerous and impressive cultural successes, but an account that dare not see the complete light of the day' (op. cit., 152). This might suggest that media-dominated contemporary cultures are much less national and much more cosmopolitan than their members are willing to admit.

3 'Culture wars', writes David Caute, 'unlike games of football and chess, do not yield undisputed winners and losers; they tend more towards the judgemental system prevailing in gymnastics, diving and ice-dancing, with jurors as much on trial as the performers' (Caute, 2003, 612).

4 One should not jump to the premature conclusions that the traditional ideology of managerialism is dead. It is not, as the new case of Wal-Mart amply illustrates. While *Fortune* and *The Economist* praise the company for its financial success in the retail market, critical journalists, trade union activists, scientists, and judges stress the burden it imposes on taxpayers by forcing the government to extend welfare benefits to underpaid employees, apart from discriminating against women and illegally suppressing unionization: 'Since 1995 the US government has issued sixty complaints against Wal-Mart at the National Labor Relations Board, citing the illegal firing of pro-union employees, as well as unlawful surveillance and intimidation of employees' (Head, 2004, 89).

5 Arjo Klamer, my colleague at the Erasmus University in Rotterdam, noted as an economist what sociologists studied already a century ago, namely that although a commercial transaction implies a contract, most daily transactions in the interactive life of a socialized individual are not like commercial transactions and more often than not require an adherence to the principle of reciprocity (he quotes examples of friendship or faith). Although the name of Marcel Mauss as the author of the famous sociological study of *The Gift* is not mentioned in the index of his book on the value of culture, which is devoted to the relationships between economics and arts, he – an economist by training – nevertheless observes that: 'Because of their built-in element of complicated mutual obligations, these exchanges make it difficult to walk away from the relationship, finish the deal and end the story. Reciprocity is the basis of each relationship as long as the values to be exchanged are left open to interpretation. Measurement is enforced only when relationships break up. Just think of divorce proceedings. Accordingly, measurement cannot only devalue the goods measured, but also a relationship' (Klamer, 1996, 24).

It is telling that Klamer, who is a university professor and a distinguished member of international research networks, does not feel comfortable in the institutional framework of a professional bureaucracy (even if it is represented by a relatively mild institution, a university), feels a need to mobilize inter-disciplinary networks of researchers by creating alternative semi-institutional platforms. He has been a *spiritus movens* behind the 'Academia Vitae', which should allow for a less-bureaucratic legitimization of interdisciplinary knowledge production and dissemination.

6 In Charles Hampden-Turner's and Fons Trompenaars' book entitled *Building Cross-Cultural Competence* and subtitled 'How to Create Wealth from Conflicting Values' (Hampden-Turner, Trompenaars, 2000) the authors propose a 'dilemma theory' for the idealized enlightened manager of the future. They

claim in the Preface that 'foreign' cultures differ from one another in a very regular and systematic way: namely by being each other's mirror images – mirroring values, reversing their hierarchies, structuring socialization of new members in different ways, but being basically constructed of a finite number of the same or comparable elements. It is hard to see why there should not be common elements that do occur in some, but not in all cultures, or why cultures should differ only in their distribution of cultural genes, not in the composition of this cultural–genetic pool. The assumption of universal symmetry allows them to construct an idealized vision of the main symmetries in cultural values and recommend their toolkit as an aid to reconciliation, in order to avoid the drama of culture clash and mutual or one-sided destruction. The toolkit is justified with arguments from Greek tragedy, Freud, Festinger, Bateson, Levi-Strauss, Maslow, Varela, Maturana, Porter, Mintzberg, Lipset, Sennett, Thurow, Kuhn, Schutz, Koestler, Piaget, Kohlberg, Buckminster Fuller, Ilya Prigogine 'and many others'. In a summary of their dilemma theory, by means of which managers can avoid conflict and produce more wealth for their organizations, they claim that 'values must achieve harmony if protagonists are not to clash tragically' (op. cit., 348) and postulate that 'combinations of values may grow synergistically and humanistically' (ibid.). Both these statements clearly deny the inevitable incommensurability of values and avoid the question about legitimacy of power struggles, authorized violence and war as the ultimate means of rejecting radically incommensurable values. However, in spite of the premature assumption of symmetry, of commensurability and of a finite pool of sequences of values, both authors note the significance of 'creativity' and 'moral development', though they fail to see that autonomous moral development may and sometimes should result in war against evil empires. A bowdlerized theory of culture leads to a sanitized cross-cultural toolkit for managers.

References

Abrahamson, Eric, *Change Without Pain. How Managers Can Overcome Initiative Overload, Organizational Chaos, and Employee Burnout*, Harvard Business School Press, Boston, 2004.

Adler, Peter, 'The Transitional Experience: An Alternative View of Culture Shock', *Journal of Humanistic Psychology*, 15, no. 4, Fall 1975.

Alvesson, Mats; Willmott, Hugh, *Making Sense of Management. A Critical Introduction*, Sage, London, 1996.

Alvesson, Mats, *Understanding Organizational Culture*, Sage, London, 2002.

Alvesson, Mats, 'Organizational Culture and Discourse', in: Grant, David; Hardy, Cynthia; Oswick, Cliff; Putnam, Linda, eds, *The Sage Handbook of Organizational Discourse*, Sage, London, 2004.

Amadae, S. M., *Rationalizing Capitalist Democracy. The Cold War Origins of Rational Choice Liberalism*, The University of Chicago Press, Chicago, 2003.

Amis, Martin, *Koba the Dread. Laughter and the Twenty Million*, Vintage, London, 2003.

Anderson, Benedict, *Imagined Communities*, Verso, London, 1983.

Appadurai, Arjun, ed., *Globalization*, Duke University Press, Durham and London, 2001.

Archer, Margaret; Tritter, Jonathan, eds, *Rational Choice Theory. Resisting Colonization*, Routledge, London, 2000.

Austin, J. L., *How To Do Things With Words*, Oxford University Press, Oxford, 1962.

Avery, Gayle C., *Understanding Leadership. Paradigms and Cases*, Sage, London, 2004.

Axelrod, Robert, *The Evolution of Cooperation*, Basic Books, New York, 1984.

Axelrod, Robert, *The Complexity of Cooperation*, Princeton University Press, Princeton, 1997.

Axelrod, Robert; Cohen, Michael D., *Harnessing Complexity. Organizational Implications of a Scientific Frontier*, Free Press, New York, 1999.

Bahra, Nicholas, *Competitive Knowledge Management*, Palgrave, Basingstoke, 2001.

Berry, J. W., 'Acculturation and Adaptation: A General Framework', in: *Mental Health of Immigrants and Refugees*, University of Texas Press, Austin, 1990.

Bijlsma-Frankema, Katinka, 'On Managing Cultural Integration and Cultural Change Processes in Mergers and Acquisitions' (unpublished typescript, University of Amsterdam, 1998).

Boisot, Max, *Information Space. A Framework for Learning in Organizations, Institutions and Culture*, Routledge, London, 1995.

Boisot, Max, *Knowledge Assets. Securing Competitive Advantage in the Information Economy*, Oxford University Press, Oxford, 1998.

Boje, David M., *Narrative Methods for Organizational and Communication Research*, Sage, London/Thousand Oaks, 2002.

Bollinger, D.; Hofstede, G., *Les differences culturelles dans le management*, Les Editions Organisation, Paris, 1987.

Borradori, Giovanna, ed., *Philosophy in Times of Terror. Dialogues With Jürgen Habermas and Jacques Derrida*, The University of Chicago Press, Chicago, 2003.

Boski, Pawel, 'On Being a Pole Abroad and on Changes of Cultural National Identity Abroad', in: Boski, Pawel; Jarymowicz, Maria; Malwska-Peyre, Hanna, eds, *Identity and Cultural Difference*, Institute of Psychology, Polish Academy of Sciences, Warsaw, 1992.

Boski, Pawel, 'The Double Trap of Uncertainty Non-Avoidance. Bureaucratic Over-regulation and Organizational Improvisation', paper presented at the ERIM research seminar 'Organizing for Performance', 5 Dec. 2003, Erasmus University Rotterdam.

Brown, John Seely; Duguid, Paul, *The Social Life of Information*, Harvard Business School Press, Boston, 2000.

Buchanan, Mark, *Nexus. Small Worlds and the Groundbreaking Science of Networks*, Norton, New York, 2002.

Byrne, Richard W.; Whiten, Andrew, *Machiavellian Intelligence: Social Expertise and the Evolution of Intellect in Monkeys, Apes, and Humans*, Oxford University Press, Oxford, 1990.

Cairncross, F., *The Death of Distance; How the Communications Revolution will Change our Lives*, Orion Business Books, London, 1998.

Cameron, Kim; Quinn, Robert, *Diagnosing and Changing Organizational Culture. Based on the Competing Values Framework*, Addison Wesley, Reading, Mass., 1999.

Catan, Cristina; Death, Adam; Flores, Berenice, Assignment about *Merry Christmas, Mr Lawrence*, submitted in the course 'Cross-Cultural Management', Erasmus University Rotterdam, October 2004.

Chomsky, Noam; Herman, Edward, *Manufacturing Consent. The Political Economy of the Mass Media*, Vantage, New York, 1988.

Ciborra, Claudio, *The Labyrinths of Information. Challenging the Wisdom of Systems*, Oxford University Press, 2002.

Clegg, Stuart; Kornberger, Martin; Pitsis, Tyrone, *Managing and Organizations. An Introduction to Theory and Practice*, Sage, Thousand Oaks, 2004.

Collins, Randall, *Interaction Ritual Chains*, Princeton University Press, Princeton, 2004.

Cowen, Tyler, *Creative Destruction. How Globalization is Changing the World's Cultures*, Princeton University Press, Princeton, 2002.

Coyne, Richard, *Technoromanticism. Digital Narrative, Holism and the Romance of the Real*, The MIT Press, Cambridge, Mass., 1999.

Czarniawska, Barbara, *A Narrative Approach to Organizational Studies*, Sage, London, 1998.

Davenport, Thomas; Prusak, Laurence, *Working Knowledge. How Organizations Manage What They Know*, Harvard Business School Press, 1998.

Deal, Terrence; Kennedy, Allen, *Corporate Cultures. The Rites and Rituals of Corporate Life*, Addison-Wesley, Reading, Mass., 1982.

D'Iribarne, *La logique de l'honneur: gestion des enterprises et traditions nationales*, Seuil, Paris, 1989.

Dogra, A.; Haandrikman, F.; Li, Y.; Lian, W. H.; Mubarik, F., Assignment on *Merry Christmas, Mr Lawrence*, submitted in the course 'Cross-Cultural Management', Erasmus University Rotterdam, October 2004.

Earley, Christopher; Ang, Soon, *Cultural Intelligence. Individual Interactions Across Cultures*, Stanford University Press, Stanford, 2003.

Eichhorn, Peter, 'Globalization and Regional Responsibility. Challenges for Leaders', in: Ricciardelli, Marina; Urban, Sabine; Nanopoulos, Kostas, eds, *Globalization and Multicultural Societies. Some Views from Europe*, University of Notre Dame Press, Notre Dame, Indiana, 2003.

Eisele, J., 'Die helfte geht chief', *Absatzwirtschaft*, 5/96, 1996, 86–96.

Etounga-Manguelle, Daniel, 'Does Africa Need a Cultural Adjustment Program?', in: Harfrison, Huntington, ed., *Culture Matters. How Values Shape Human Progress*, Basic Books, New York, 2000.

Europublic (anon.), 'Cultural Due Diligence', in: www.europublic.com/articles/05-CulturalDueDiligence.php.

Fairclough, Norman; Jessop, Bob; Sayer, Andrew, 'Critical Realism and Semiosis', in: *Journal of Critical Realism*, 5(1), 2002, 2–10.

Ferrara, Maria; Roberson, Lorian, *Reconceptualizing Individualism – Collectivism and Analyzing its Relationship with Entrepreneurship and Cooperation*, paper at the IACCM Conference, Universita Parthenope, Naples, Italy, 21–2 May 2004.

Field, Alexander J., *Altruistically Inclined? The Behavioural Sciences, Evolutionary Theory and the Origins of Reciprocity*, The University of Michigan Press, Ann Arbor, 2004.

Franck, Georg, *Ökonomie der Aufmerksamkeit. Ein Entwurf*, Hanser, München/Wien, 1998.

Fukuyama, Francis, *Trust*, Free Press, New York, 1995.

Fuller, Steve, *Knowledge Management Foundations*, Butterworth/Heinemann, Boston, 2002.

Gabriel, Yannis, with Hirschhorn, Larry; McCollom Hampton, Marion; Schwartz, Howard S.; Swogger, Glenn, Jr, *Organizations in Depth. The Psychoanalysis of Organizations*, Sage, London/Thousand Oaks, 1999.

Gabriel, Yannis, 'Every Picture Tells a Story – Losing the Plot in the Era of the Image', outline of a public lecture presented at the Erasmus Research Institute in Management, Erasmus University Rotterdam, 17 January 2005.

Gabriel, Yannis, *Myths, Stories and Organizations*, Oxford University Press, Oxford, 2004.

Geertz, Clifford, *Available Light. Anthropological Reflections on Philosophical Topics*, Princeton University Press, Princeton, 2000.

Gitlin, Todd, *The Whole World Is Watching. Mass Media in the Making and Unmaking of the New Left*, University of California Press, Berkeley, 2003.

Gooderham, Paul; Noordhaug, Odd, 'Are Cultural Differences in Europe on the Decline?', *European Business Forum*, Winter 2001/2002.

Grant, David; Hardy, Cynthia; Oswick, Cliff; Putnam, Linda, eds, *The Sage Handbook of Organizational Discourse*, Sage, London, 2004.

Grzymała Moszczyńska, H., 'Poles from Kazakhstan: A Strategy for Coping with Acculturation "Back Home"', in: *From Homogeneity to Multiculturalism: Minorities Old and New in Poland*, School of Slavonic and East European Studies, Warsaw, 2000.

Hampden-Turner, Charles; Trompenaars, Fons, *Building Cross-Cultural Competence. How to Create Wealth from Conflicting Values*, Yale University Press, New Haven, 2000.

Han, L. G. L., Een weg naar de lerende organisatie?, unpublished MA thesis, Rotterdam School of Management, Erasmus University Rotterdam, 2003.

Harris, Martin; Wegg-Prosser, Victoria, 'The BBC and Producer Choice. A Study of Public Service Broadcasting and Managerial Change', in: Zimmerman, Patricia; Bradley, Ruth, eds, 'A Festschrift in Honour of Erik Barnauw', *Wide Angle. A Quarterly Journal of Film History, Theory, Criticism and Practive*, vol. 20, no. 2, 1998, pp. 150–63.

Harris, Robert; Moran, Philip, *Managing Cultural Differences. Leadership Strategies for a new World of Business*, Gulf Publishing, Houston, 1996.

Harrison, Lawrence; Huntington, Samuel, eds, *Culture Matters. How Values Shape Human Progress*, Basic Books, New York, 2000.

Head, Simon, 'Inside the Leviathan', *The New York Review of Books*, vol. LI, no. 20, 16 Dec. 2004.

Hines, Colin, 'Time to Replace Globalization with Localization', in: Michie, Jonathan, ed., *The Handbook of Globalization*, Edward Elgar, Cheltenham, 2003.

Hoedemaekers, Casper, 'I Don't Think I'm the Kind of Person Who Neglects His Task: Panoptic Control in a Dutch Public Transport Company', unpublished typescript, Erasmus University Rotterdam, 2004.

Hofstede, Geert, *Cultures and Organizations. Software of the Mind. Intercultural Cooperation and Its Importance for Survival*, McGraw-Hill, London, 1991 (second, enlarged edition 2003).

Hofstede, Geert, 'Dimensions Do Not Exist – A Reply to Brendan McSweeney', in: *Human Relations*, no. 56(2), 2002.

Holden, Nigel, *Cross-Cultural Management. A Knowledge Management Perspective*, Prentice-Hall, Harlow, 2002.

Honneth, Axel, *The Struggle for Recognition. The Moral Grammar of Social Conflicts*, MIT Press, Cambridge, Mass., 1996.

Hooker, John, *Working Across Cultures*, Stanford University Press, Stanford, 2003.

House, Robert J.; Hanges, Paul; Mansour, Javidan; Dorfman, Peter; Gupta, Vipin, *Culture, Leadership and Organizations: The Globe Study of 62 Societies*, Sage, Thousand Oaks, 2004.

Huntington, Samuel P., *The Clash of Civilizations and the Remaking of World Order*, Touchstone, London, 1998.

Ibarra, Herminia, *Working Identity. Unconventional Strategies for Reinventing Your Career*, Harvard Business School Press, Boston, 2004.

Inglis, Fred, *Culture*, Polity Press, Cambridge, 2004.

Jacobs, Gabrielle; Keegan, Anne; Christe-Zeyse, Jochen; Sedeberg, Ilka; Runde, Bernd, 'The Fatal Smirk. Insider Accounts of Organizational Change Processes in a Police Organization', unpublished typescript, Erasmus University Rotterdam, 2004.

Jacobs, Jane, *Dark Age Ahead*, Random House, New York, 2004.

Jackson, Norman; Carter, Pippa, *Rethinking Organizational Behaviour*, Pearson Educational, Harlow, 2000.

Johansen, Robert; Swigart, Rob, *Upsizing Individuals in the Downsized Organization. Managing in the Wake of Reengineering, Globalization, and Overwhelming Technological Change*, Addison-Wesley, Reading, Mass., 1994.

Joinson, Adam, *Understanding the Psychology of Internet Behaviour. Virtual Worlds, Real Lives*, Palgrave, London, 2003.

Kainzbauer, Astrid, *Kultur im Interkulturellen Training. Der Einfluss von Kulturunterschieden in Lehr- und Lernprozessen an der Beispiel Deutschland und Grossbritanien*, IKO Verlag, Frankfurt am Main, 2002.

Kanter, Rosabeth Moss, *Evolve! Succeeding in the Digital Culture of Tomorrow*, Harvard Business School Press, Boston, 2001.

Keenan, Alan, *Democracy in Question. Democratic Openness in a Time of Political Closure*, Stanford University Press, Stanford, 2003.

Keohane, Robert O., 'Global Governance and Democratic Accountability', in: Held, David; Koenig-Archibugi, Mathias, eds, *Taming Globalization. Frontiers of Governance, Polity*, Cambridge, 2003.

Kivisto, Peter, ed., *Illuminating Social Life. Classical and Contemporary Theory Revisited*, Pine Forge Press, Thousand Oaks, 2001.

Klamer, Arjo, *The Value of Culture. On the Relationship Between Economics and the Arts*, Amsterdam University Press, Amsterdam, 1996.

Lamont, Michele, *Money, Morals and Manners. The Culture of the French and American Upper-Middle Class*, The University of Chicago Press, Chicago, 1992.

Lamont, Michele; Thevenot, Laurent, eds, *Rethinking Comparative Sociology. Repertoires of Evaluation in France and the United States*, Cambridge University Press, Cambridge, 2000.

Lane, Robert, *The Loss of Happiness in Market Democracies*, Yale University Press, New Haven, 2000.

Latour, Bruno, *Pandora's Hope. Essays on the Reality of Science Studies*, Harvard University Press, Cambridge, Mass., 1999.

Lawrence, Paul R.; Nohria, N., *Driven. How Human Nature Shapes Our Choices*, Jossey-Bass, San Francisco, 2002.

Leinberger, Paul; Tucker, Bruce, *The New Individualists. The Generation After the Organization Man*, Harper Collins, New York, 1991.

Lemert, Charles, 'Multiculturalism', in: Ritzer, George; Smart, Barry, eds, *Handbook of Social Theory*, Sage, London/Thousand Oaks, 2003.

Lesser, Eric; Fontaine, Michael; Slusher, Jason, *Knowledge and Communities*, Butterworth/Heinemann, 2000.

Lewis, Richard, *The Cultural Imperative. Global Trends in the 21st Century*, Intercultural Press, Yarmouth, Maine, 2003.

Leyer, L.; Fourne, S.; Maak, T.; Helterich, A.; Hamer, R.; Heusbergen, L., assignment on *Underground* for the course Cross-Cultural Management, IBA program, Erasmus University Rotterdam, November 2004.

Lilley, Simon; Lightfoot, Geoffrey; Amaral, Paulo M. N., *Representing Organization. Knowledge, Management, and the Information Age*, Oxford University Press, Oxford, 2004.

Magala, Sławomir, 'Cold Wars and Hot Issues: Management of Responsibilities', *Human Resources Development International*, vol. 5, no. 4, December 2002, pp. 493–505.

Magala, Sławomir, 'Honing and Framing Ourselves (Extreme Subjectivity and Organizing)', *ERIM Report Series Research in Management*, ERS-2004-076-ORG, Erasmus University Rotterdam, August, 2004, Also available online: http://hdl.handle.net/1765/1583

Magala, Sławomir, 'Political Economy of Senses. Frames, Mirrors and Windows of Organizing', paper for the track 'Space + Time in Organizations' of the 4th Critical Management Studies Conference, Cambridge, July 2005.

Mamdani, Mahmood, *Citizen and Subject. Contemporary Africa and the Legacy of Late Colonialism*, Fountain Publishers/Princeton University Press, Kampala/Princeton, 1996.

Manovich, Lev, *The Language of the New Media*, MIT Press, Cambridge, Massachusetts, 2001.

McGarthy, Craig; Yzerbyt, Vincent; Spears, Russell, eds, *Stereotypes As Explanations. The Formation of Meaningful Beliefs about Social Groups*, Cambridge University Press, Cambridge, 2002.

McLuhan, Marshall; Powers, Bruce, *The Global Village: Transformations in World Life and Media in the 21st Century*, Oxford University Press, Oxford, 1989.

McSweeney, Brendan, 'Hofstede's Model of National Cultural Differences and Their Consequences: a Triumph of Faith – a Failure of Analysis', *Human Relations*, no. 55(1), 2002.

Mignolo, Walter D., 'The Many Faces of Cosmo-polis: Border Thinking and Critical Cosmopolitanism', in: Breckenridge, C.; Pollock, S.; Bhabha, H.; Chakrabarty, D., eds, *Cosmopolitanism*, Duke University Press, Durham and London, 2002.

Mirowski, Philip; Sent, Esther-Mirjam, eds, *Science Bought and Sold. Essays in the Economics of Science*, The University of Chicago Press, Chicago, 2002.

Mirowski, Philip, 'The Scientific Dimensions of Social Knowledge and Their Distant Echoes in the 20th Century American Philosophy of Science', unpublished typescript, third draft, November 2003.

Morgan, Glen; Whitley, Richard; Moen, Eli, *Changing Capitalism?* Oxford University Press, Oxford, 2005.

Mouzelis, Nicos, *Sociological Theory: What Went Wrong? Diagnosis and Remedies*, Routledge, London, 1995.

Nickels, William; McHugh, James; McHugh, Susan, *Understanding Business*, McGraw-Hill, Boston, 2002.

Nolan, Peter, *China's Rise, Russia's Fall. Politics, Economics and Planning in the Transition from Stalinism*, Macmillan, London, 1995.

Nonaka, Ikujiro; Takeuchi, Hirotaka, *The Knowledge Creating Company. How Japanese Companies Create the Dynamics of Innovation*, Oxford University Press, Oxford, 1995.

Nonaka, Ikujiro; Nishiguchi, Toshihiro, eds, *Knowledge Emergence. Social, Technical, and Evolutionary Dimensions of Knowledge Creation*, Oxford University Press, Oxford, 2001.

Odlyzko, A., 'Content is Not King', *First Monday*, issue 6 on-line. Available at http://firstmonday.org/issues/issue6_2/odlyzko

Osland, Joyce; Bird, Allan, 'Beyond Sophisticated Stereotyping: Cultural Sense-making in Context', in: *Academy of Management Executive*, 2000, vol. 14, no. 1.

Palma, Gabriel, 'National Inequality in the Era of Globalization', in: Michie, Jonathan, ed., *The Handbook of Globalization*, Edgar, Cheltenham, 2003.

Parker, John, *Structuration*, Open University Press, Buckingham, 2000.

Pfeffer, Jeffrey, *New Directions for Organization Theory. Problems and Perspectives*, Oxford University Press, Oxford, 1997.

Pianta, Mario, 'Democracy vs Globalization. The Growth of Parallel Summits and Global Movements', in: Archibugi, Daniele, ed., *Debating Cosmopolitics*, Verso, London, 2003.

Reed, Mike, 'Getting Real About Organizational Discourse', in: Grant, David; Hardy, Cynthia; Oswick, Cliff; Putnam, Linda, eds, *The Sage Handbook of Organizational Discourse*, Sage, London, 2004.

Rejmer, Zuzanna, 'Cultural National Identity of Immigrants from Kazakhstan and their Psychological Well-being', unpublished MA thesis, Institute of the Psychology of Intercultural Relations, Department of Psychology, Warsaw School of Social Psychology, Warsaw, 2004.

Ritzer, George, *The Globalization of Nothing*, Pine Forge Press, Thousand Oaks, 2004.

Ritzer, George, *Explorations in Social Theory. From Metatheorizing to Rationalization*, Sage, London, 2001.

Ritzer, George, *The McDonaldization Thesis. Explorations and Extensions*, Sage, London, 1999.

Roberts, K. H.; Boyacigiller, N. A., 'Cross-National Organizational Research: The Grasp of the Blinded Men', in: *Research in Organizational Behaviour*, 6, 1984.

Robertson, Roland, 'Globalization Theory 2000+; Major Problematics', in: Ritzer, George; Smart, Barry, eds, *Handbook of Social Theory*, Sage, London/Thousand Oaks, 2003.

Ross, Norbert, *Culture and Cognition. Implications for Theory and Method*, Sage, Thousand Oaks, 2004.

Russell, Bertrand, *Unpopular Essays*, Simon and Schuster, New York, 1950.

Said, Edward, *Humanism and Democratic Criticism*, Columbia University Press, New York, 2004.

Sanbonmatsu, John, *The Postmodern Prince. Critical Theory, Left Strategy, and the Making of a New Political Subject*, Monthly Review Press, New York, 2004.

Schein, Edgar, *Organizational Culture and Leadership*, Jossey Bass, San Francisco, 1989.

Schneider, Susan; Barsoux, Jean-Louis, *Managing Across Cultures*, Prentice-Hall, Harlow, 1997.

Schinkel, Willem, 'The Autopoiesis of the Artworld After the End of Art'. Unpublished paper prepared for the workshop 'Collapsing Cultural Canon: Elite Culture, Popular Culture, and Politics in Late Modernity', Ecole des Hautes Etudes en Sciences Sociales, Marseille, 28–9 October 2004.

Seale Clive, ed., *Researching Society and Culture*, Sage, London, 2004.

Sen, Amartya, 'East and West: the Reach of Reason', *The New York Review of Books*, 20 July 2000.

Sennett, Richard, *Respect in a World of Inequality*, Norton, New York, 2003.

Shweder, Richard A., *Why Do Men Barbecue? Recipes for Cultural Psychology*, Harvard University Press, Cambridge, 2003.

Smith, Marc; Kollock, Peter, eds, *Communities in Cyberspace*, Routledge, London, 1999.

Sobchack, Vivian, *The Address of the Eye: A Phenomenology of Film Experience*, Princeton University Press, Princeton, 1992.

Søderberg, Anne-Marie; Björkman, Ingmar, 'From Words to Action? Socio-cultural Integration Initiatives in a Cross-Border Merger', in: Søderberg, Anne-Marie; Vaara, Eero, eds, *Merging Across Borders. People, Cultures and Politics*, Copenhagen Business School Press, Copenhagen, 2003.

Starski, Stanislaw, *Class Struggle in Classless Poland*, South End Press, Boston, 1982.

Steiner, *After Babel. Aspects of Language and Translation*, Oxford University Press, Oxford, 1975/1992.

Swaan, A. de, *Words of the World. The Global Language System*, Cambridge, 2001.

Tayeb, Monir, 'Hofstede', in: Warner, Malcolm, ed., *International Encyclopaedia of Business and Management*, Thompson Press, London, 1996.

Tayeb, Monir, *The Management of a Multicultural Workforce*, John Wiley, Chichester, 1996.

Taylor, Charles, *Modern Social Imaginaries*, Duke University Press, Durham and London, 2004.

Theall, Donald F., *The Virtual Marshall McLuhan*, McGill-Queen's University Press, Montreal, 2001.

Therborn, Göran, *European Modernity and Beyond. The Trajectory of European Societies 1945–2000*, Sage, London, 1995.

Tietze, Susanne; Cohen, Laurie; Musson, Gill, *Understanding Organizations Through Language*, Sage, London, 2003.

Turner, Stephen, *Brains/Practices/Relativism. Social Theory After Cognitive Science*, The University of Chicago Press, Chicago, 2002.

Umar, Ebru, *Burka & Blahniks. Manifest van een dertiger*, Archipel, Amsterdam/Antwerpen, 2004.

Wallerstein, Immanuel, *The End of the World as We Know It. Social Science for the Twenty-First Century*, University of Minnesota Press, Minneapolis, 1999.

Wallerstein, Immanuel, *The Essential Wallerstein*, New Press, New York, 2000.

Wallerstein, Immanuel, *The Uncertainties of Knowledge*, Temple University Press, Philadelphia, 2004.

Walsh, Peter, 'The Web, the Expert, and the Information Hegemony', in: Jenkins, Henry; Thorburn, David, eds, *Democracy and New Media*, MIT Press, Cambridge, Mass., 2003.

Ward, Colleen; Bochner, Stephen; Furnham, Adrian, *The Psychology of Culture Shock*, Routledge, Hove, 2001.

Weick, Karl, *Making Sense of the Organization*, Blackwell, Oxford, 2001.

Westwood, Richard; Linstead, Steve, eds, *The Language of Organization*, Sage, London, 2001.

Whiten, Andrew; Byrne, Richard W., *Machiavellian Intelligence II: Extensions and Evaluations*, Cambridge University Press, Cambridge, 1997.

Whitley, Richard, *Divergent Capitalisms. The Social Structure and Change of Business Systems*, Oxford University Press, Oxford, 2000.

Wierzbicka, Anna, *Understanding Cultures Through Their Key-Words: English, Russian, Polish, German, Japanese*, Oxford University Press, New York, 1997.

Wolin, Sheldon, 'Fugitive Democracy', in: Benhabib, Seyla, ed., *Democracy and Difference. Contesting the Boundaries of the Political*, Princeton University Press, Princeton, 1996.

Woolgar, Steve, ed., *Virtual Society? Technology, Cyberbole, Reality*, Oxford University Press, Oxford, 2002.

Yudice, George, *The Expediency of Culture. Uses of Culture in the Global Era*, Duke University Press, Durham, 2003.

Žižek, Slavoj, *Did Somebody Say Totalitarianism? Five Interventions in the (Mis)Use of a Notion*, Verso, London, 2002.

Žižek, Slavoj, 'Underground or Ethnic Cleansing as a Continuation of Poetry by Other Means', 2004, in: http://www.ntticc.or.jp/pub/ic_mag/ic018/intercity/zizek_E.html

Index

For Product Safety Concerns and Information please contact our EU
representative GPSR@taylorandfrancis.com Taylor & Francis Verlag GmbH,
Kaufingerstraße 24, 80331 München, Germany

Printed and bound by CPI Group (UK) Ltd, Croydon, CR0 4YY
08/05/2025
01864366-0013